Robert Penn Warren after *Audubon*

SOUTHERN LITERARY STUDIES

Fred Hobson, *Series Editor*

Robert Penn Warren after *Audubon*

The Work of Aging and the Quest for Transcendence in His Later Poetry

Joseph R. Millichap

LOUISIANA STATE UNIVERSITY PRESS BATON ROUGE

Published by Louisiana State University Press

Manufactured in the United States of America
First printing

Designer: Laura Roubique Gleason
Typefaces: Minion text, Tribute display
Printer and binder: Thomson-Shore, Inc.

Library of Congress Cataloging-in-Publication Data
Millichap, Joseph R.
Robert Penn Warren after Audubon : the work of aging and the quest for transcendence in his later poetry / Joseph R. Millichap.
p. cm. — (Southern literary studies)
Includes bibliographical references and index.
ISBN 978-0-8071-3456-6 (cloth : alk. paper) 1. Warren, Robert Penn, 1905–1989—Poetic works. 2. Aging in literature. 3. Transcendence (Philosophy) in literature. I. Title.
PS3545.A748Z785 2010
813'.52—dc22

2009009893

The paper in this book meets the guidelines for permanence and durability of the Committee on Production Guidelines for Book Longevity of the Council on Library Resources. ♾

For Pat, as always

Tell me a story.

In this century, and moment, of mania,
Tell me a story.

Make it a story of great distances, and starlight.

The name of the story will be Time,
But you must not pronounce its name.

Tell me a story of deep delight.

ROBERT PENN WARREN (1905–89)
Audubon: A Vision (1969)

Contents

Preface

The present study evolved during the most recent phase in my long-term critical dialogue with the literary legacies of Robert Penn Warren. When I was a college freshman, my English textbook was *Understanding Literature,* and I first read *All the King's Men* as a new graduate student. In turn, I taught Warren's critical and creative works in several academic settings, including in Finland as a Fulbright professor. My professional publications on him did not begin until 1984, when I moved to Warren country as English department head at Western Kentucky University, at which I later helped to found the Center for Robert Penn Warren Studies in 1989. My initial Warren studies were concerned with his novels, and my first Warren book was *Robert Penn Warren: A Study of the Short Fiction* (1992). Chapters on his fiction and poetry also became parts of my two most recent books, *Dixie Limited: Railroads, Culture, and the Southern Renaissance* (2002) and *A Backward Glance: The Southern Renascence, the Autobiographical Epic, and the Classical Legacy.* Although I retired from Western Kentucky in 2004, I continued to publish on Warren, especially in regard to his centennial in 2005. Recent Warren work of mine is more concerned with his poetry than with his fiction, however, particularly with his later poems. Writing new essays on Warren's poetic forebears such as Robert Frost and on poetic heirs like Dave Smith has led me to a reading of Warren's later poetry as the conclusion of his self-epic in the work of aging—poems about age and death that attempt an autobiographical life review, contemplate psychological transcendence, and aspire to the literary sublime.

My extended reading of Warren's later poems from the perspectives in this study opens with a "Prologue" defining my theoretical approaches by way of developmental psychology, gerontology, and end-of-life studies.

The rest of the Prologue presents necessary information on Warren's developing literary career, emphasizing the beginnings of an autobiographical self-epic in the poetry during his early and middle periods, initially through *Brother to Dragons* (1953) and then again through *Audubon* (1969). In chronological order, each of my next six chapters then considers one of Warren's half-dozen later volumes in terms of its reordering of new, published, or even previously collected poems. Each new collection thus becomes a discrete poetic text within the Warren canon, all of them unified by work of aging: time and memory, age and death. These interpretations are supported by a close reading of each volume's selections and sequences, especially those which Warren includes in his final *Selected Poems* of 1985, though each chapter considers other developments in the writer's life and work as well. The "Epilogue" traces Warren's reputation through his death in 1989 and his centennial in 2005 up to the present.

To the extent that my study achieves its purposes, recognition must be extended to those who provided encouragement and assistance during its lengthy but steady evolution over the past several years. Most important, of course, is the primary inspiration and example of Robert Penn Warren himself in terms of both his life and literature, especially his poetry and criticism. Next in significance is the work of those developmental psychologists who provide my theoretical foundation in this study, particularly the enduring legacies of Carl Jung and Erik Erikson. Those Warren scholars and critics who influence my general and specific formulations about his later poetry are acknowledged formally below, though I should single out my special debt to Joseph Blotner for his authorized biography and to John Burt for his definitive edition of the collected poems. Of course, many others afforded less formal though still substantial influences on my training as a student and reader and on my career as a teacher and scholar. I could list, for example, most members of the national Robert Penn Warren Circle, with whom I have shared many scholarly and social exchanges at our annual meetings. Closer to home, my students, colleagues, and administrators at Western Kentucky University provided me with sympathetic attention, useful suggestions, and professional support for my teaching of and writing about Warren. My wife, Patricia Bradley, also a colleague in the scholarship of southern studies, shared and sharpened my insights here. The study also owes much to the persistent encouragement of Executive Editor John Easterly and his several colleagues working with the Louisiana State University Press—in particular, the anonymous initial reader of my study for the press; Fred Hobson, the editor of the Southern Literary Studies Series; and Jo Ann Kiser, my copy editor.

Robert Penn Warren after *Audubon*

Prologue

Autobiography, Aging, and Warren's Poetry through *Audubon*

> For everything there is a season.
>
> But there is the dream
> Of a season past all seasons.
>
> —*Audubon: A Vision*

1

In 2005, the centennial of poet and fictionist, critic and editor Robert Penn Warren provided an ideal perspective not just for further reflection on his career spanning more than half of the twentieth century but also for contemplation of his canon's continuing significance for the twenty-first. Literary criticism traditionally identified Warren as the "Renaissance Man" of modern American letters, though recent scholarship has focused most positively on his poems, in particular the extraordinary poetic accomplishments of his late years. Despite nearly universal critical appreciation for the many achievements of Warren's later poetry, critical differences persist about its sources, its themes, and its meanings. Although Warren's critics now generally agree on the division of his poetry into early, middle, and late periods, they disagree on a starting point for its final stage. In my view, it begins in the years directly after *Audubon* first appears in 1969.

Harold Bloom, the critic most often cited in these matters, uses his "Foreword" in John Burt's definitive edition of the *Collected Poems* (1998) to proclaim that Warren "enjoyed a poetic renascence fully comparable to the great final phases of Thomas Hardy, William Butler Yeats, and Wallace Stevens"; he then attributes this rebirth to the poet's "agonistic spirit that . . . internalized drama, in a great contest with time, with cultural and family history, and above all, with himself" and dates it to Warren's collection *Incarnations* published in 1968 (xxiii). In *A History of Modern Poetry* (1987), David Perkins finds greatness as early as the breakthrough collection *Promises* in 1957, when Warren created "a more relaxed and natural way of speaking, [and] he retained undiminished his narrative and constructive power, his psychological alertness and reflective tenacity" (360). Calvin Bedient, one of the earliest critics to affirm Warren's later greatness, traces its start to *Audubon* in 1969 and to its author's fresh "determination to concentrate on poetry as the extreme resource of language-knowledge" (3). The closest reader of the later poetry, Randolph Paul Runyon, locates the beginning of Warren's best efforts in *Now and Then* in 1978, where his poetic sequences become both "extraordinarily accessible [and] remarkably interrelated" (*Braided Dream* 6). I believe, however, that Warren's great final phase opens with *Or Else* in 1974 as it becomes his first work of aging, or his quest for poetic sublimity and personal transcendence by way of an autobiographical life review that persisted almost until his death in 1989.

My trope of aging begins with the basic denotation of any work done in age, or simply "age-work," as suggested by the useful German critical term *Alterswerk*. In my formulation of age-work, however, I also wish to suggest work not just completed in age but specifically concerned with the concluding stages of life. All Warren's literary efforts completed after an arbitrary date such as 1970, when he reached the traditional retirement age of sixty-five, could be considered as his late work, but the later writing in which the poet makes his peace with the passage of time, the inevitability of age, and the imminence of death through a poetic review of his life provides us with his most authentic work of aging.

Theoretical sources for these richer connotations of age-work might be located in neo-Freudian developmental psychology, particularly in the seminal work of Carl Jung. The diverse grouping of psychosocial thinkers now denominated as neo-Freudians are united by the foundation of their works in Freud's psychological theory and psychoanalytic practice, but they are differentiated by their many variations on this common heritage. Important neo-Freudians include figures as markedly dissimilar as Carl Jung, Alfred Adler, Karen Horney, and Erich Fromm; in turn, later psychoanalytic theorists and practitioners including Erik and Joan M. Erikson, Robert N. Butler, and Lars Tornstam then might be designated as neo-Jungians. All of these later psychoanalysts theorized a more widely focused and dynamic concept of ego development, especially in terms of cultural and social influences. If Freud emphasized the initial developments of selfhood in early "psychosexual" phases, Jung posited in "Stages of Life" (1930) a more extended development of the self in three grand life phases—youth, midlife, and age—and also suggested in this same essay the several psychological tasks essential for the "individuation" or full human realization of the self.

Although Warren's earlier canon, both creative and critical, has been regarded generally as Freudian, I would suggest that his later poetry and criticism become ever more Jungian. *Democracy and Poetry* (1975), the published revision of his 1974 Jefferson lectures, provides some textual evidence in its twofold analysis of America entering its third century of independence. In the two parts of his volume, "America and the Diminished Self" and "Poetry and Selfhood," Warren posits the "diagnostic" and "therapeutic" functions of poetry for democracy (*Democracy* 3, 42). For Warren, a democratic society requires "individuation" of the self within the determinations of mass culture, and his formulation of this balance between individual and society recalls not just Whitman but Jung (*Democracy* xii). Warren twice cites Jung's *The Undiscovered Self* (1957), one of the two works by Jung in his personal library, along with *Modern Man in Search of a Soul* (1933), in his discussion of the therapeutic role of poetry in preserving American selfhood (*Democracy* 65, 69).

Building on Jung's formulations, Erik Erikson considered the life process through seven successive psychosocial stages that extended active individual development from birth through life, a process concluded only in debilitation and death. Erikson and his colleagues also distinguished the differing phases of identity development through acquisition of appropriate personal qualities in response to the psychosocial crises inevitably accompanying each life passage. For Erikson, old age balances the quest for integrity against the threat of despair during life's final stage. Eriksonian integrity becomes the ultimate fusion of the personality through an arduous individual introspection devoid of selfish ego defenses, something like Jungian individuation of the self by fulfilling the tasks of aging but within a more social context. In Erikson's view, old age is not just a time of physical devolution but also one of psychological evolution and the only stage of life in which either integrity or despair may be fully realized. As he frames it late in his own life, "Only in old age can true wisdom develop in those so 'gifted'" (*Dialogue* 54). Erikson describes this hard-won knowledge in terms of a "kind of informed and detached concern with life itself, in the face of death itself" (Cole 275). Although an undeveloped individual may be lost to despair, the integrated personality continues to develop even in the shadow of death, "To be, through having been to face not being" in Erikson's neat formulation (*Identity* 178).

The many contributions of developmental psychologists to changing ideas of age and death were an important part of the overall intellectual milieu that forms the background for Warren's later life and work, one that would have interested him for many reasons. For example, the development of end-of-life studies and hospice care in the theory and practice of Cicely Saunders, Elisabeth Kubler-Ross, and others was fostered at Yale University; its Medical Center opened the nation's first in-patient hospice in 1974, the year after Warren retired from its English Department ("Hospice" NHPCO). As early as *Who Speaks for the Negro?* in 1965, Warren cites Erik Erikson's foundational essay "Identity and the Life Cycle" (1959) to support his belief that slavery had robbed African blacks of both their individual and cultural identity. Later, Warren uses Erikson's *Dimensions of a New Identity* (1974) in *Democracy and Poetry* (1975) to buttress his diagnosis of and remedy for the malaise of America in the post-Watergate era (*Democracy* 14, 44–45, 99). In fact, Erikson had delivered his own Jefferson lecture in 1973, and his then-contested exercise in what he calls "psychohistory" may have influenced Warren's organization and tone in his 1974 lecture on poetry and democracy as diagnostic therapy (*Dimensions* 12). Despite these meaningful connections between Warren and the new interest in aging and death during this period, however, my study is not based on determinations of direct "influence" but rather on a more generally inclusive "intertextuality."

Such is certainly the case with the neo-Freudians' more recent successors in both the theory and practice of individual and social psychology. Erikson's theoretical consideration of old age as a significant final phase of the life cycle encouraged psychoanalytic practitioners such as geriatrician Robert N. Butler to transform the psychological treatment of the elderly. Although Butler is best known for his coinage of "ageism" in his formulation of contemporary culture's institutionalized prejudice against the aged, under the influence of Eriksonian theory he also introduced the important gerontological concepts of "productive aging" and "life review." Before Butler's pioneering efforts, old age too often was considered essentially unproductive, while reminiscence in the elderly was viewed as "dysfunction" at best and "pathology" at worst ("Life Review" 65). In an article from 1963, Butler affirmed that "the life-review [is] a naturally occurring universal mental process characterized by the progressive return to consciousness of past experiences . . . particularly the resurgence of unresolved conflicts" ("Life Review" 66). Butler also observes that the life review may take many narrative formats ranging from internal dialogue, to informal conversation, to written memoir or autobiography. In both his early and later works, Butler often illustrates his theoretical formulations with literary examples drawn from a wide range of poems, plays, novels, and films. Butler posits this late self-scrutiny as a "process by which a person evaluates his or her life as it nears its end," producing as its goal "serenity, philosophical acceptance of what has occurred in the past, and wisdom," or something like the transcendence Warren essays in his later poetry (Butler, "Age, Death, and Life-Review").

This increasing emphasis on the special integrity and wisdom of the aged on the part of Erikson and Butler generated considerable interest, both theoretical and experimental, in what psychologists of aging have come to call gerotranscendence. The term arose as an alternative to the traditional theory of old age as simply personal disengagement after the social engagement of earlier life stages (Tornstam 31–33). Qualitative and quantitative studies in the 1970s and after weakened this previously accepted theoretical paradigm and eventually replaced it with a more positive vision of even the end-of-life stage. Taking their directions from the work of both Jung and Erikson, gerontologists redefined a rather negative disengagement as a more positive "transcendence." One pioneering practitioner of this change is Joan M. Erikson, Erik Erikson's colleague and life mate, who extended a possible eighth stage, transcendence in the preparation for death as an addition to her husband's earlier model (123–29). This formulation is associated most closely, however, with the work of Swedish gerontologist Lars Tornstam in his definitive study *Gerotranscendence: A Developmental Theory of Positive Aging* (2005).

Although Tornstam's terminology proves useful enough for social gerontology, my literary study of Warren's later poetry will use the more familiar form of transcendence. Like both Joan Erikson and Tornstam, I am using the word "transcendence" in its more general, or psychological, sense and not in a specifically religious or even spiritual manner (Erikson 124–25, Tornstam 46–47). She seconds Tornstam's synthesis of earlier quantitative studies that found no correlation between the transcendent "state of mind and the existence of a religious belief or religious practice in the patients [of nursing homes]" (Erikson 124). Warren was always more stoic than pious in his personal belief, a position which he characterized himself as that of a "non-believer," but of a "yearner," one with a "religious temperament, you see, with a scientific background" (*Talking* 213). Warren affirmed these same lifelong beliefs in discussions with his palliative physician, Thomas N. Byrne, even as he neared death (Blotner 497).

Another critical concept that should be defined at the outset is the "sublime." By it, I intend here more or less what that magisterial critic Harold Bloom suggests in his use of the term in the "Foreword" to Warren's *Collected Poems* and throughout his voluminous criticism of Warren and other heirs of the Romantics. Like Bloom, I believe that although Warren achieves poetic sublimity occasionally in his earlier works—certainly in *Brother to Dragons, Promises, Tale of Time,* and *Audubon*—it is not until the volumes after *Audubon* that the sublime is achieved with consistency. My supposition that Warren does not maintain consistent sublimity until his later poetry suggests that here we may be dealing with what Barbara Hernnstein Smith, Eve Kosofsky Sedgwick, and others have called the "senile sublime," that art that achieves a sublime simplicity in the confrontation with dissolution and death. Like Tornstam's "gerotranscendence," however, Smith and Sedgwick's "senile sublime" seems too awkward a formulation to be used comfortably in an extended discussion of a major body of work such as Warren's later poetry, and I will use instead the simpler and more traditional terms "transcendence" and "sublime."

In fact, Warren himself often employs diction and definitions similar to those of the developmental psychologists, not just in his later poems but in his own prose commentary concerning the poetry. At age seventy-five, Warren states in his prose "Afterthought" to his collection *Being Here: Poetry 1977–1980* that his volume is not ordered by a simple chronology despite its subtitle, as "certain poems composed during the general period are not included" (441).[1] Warren then goes on to say that his structure is ordered "thematically, but with echoes, repetitions, and variations in feeling and tonality," as "concerned with the reviewing of life from the standpoint of age," in a thematic intertextuality that suggests to me Erikson's sense of the most important sort of age-work (441). Warren also observes that one of the poems collected in *Being Here,* "Ballad of Your Puzzlement," prefaces the concluding section by means of its parenthetical subtitle, "(*How not to recognize yourself as what you think you are, when old and reviewing your life before death comes*)," which sounds like a literary variation on Butler's autobiographical life review (423).

Against this burden of matter and theme, Warren projects another order, that of "a shadowy narrative, a shadowy autobiography, if you will. But this is an autobiography which represents the fusion of fiction and fact in varying degrees and perspectives" (441). Warren's "Afterthought" to *Being Here* then concludes with a statement that recalls Erikson's formulations as well as those of Wallace Stevens: "Indeed, it may be said that our lives are our own supreme fiction"—or a recreation representing a final human effort to transform a brief and random existence within time into the unchanging order of timeless art (441). In the midst of his late renascence, Warren thus adumbrates the themes of age-work and autobiography, of transcendence and sublimity in relation to the continuity of the self—as we will see them develop through the six collections of his later poetry.

2

The myriad details of Warren's life and work can be traced across the arc of a developing self-epic from the initial explorations of his early years, through the many complications of his midcareer, to the grand resolutions of his later phases.[2] In *A Backward Glance: The Southern Renascence, the Autobiographical Epic, and the Classical Legacy,* I connect Warren's images of poetry as "shadowy autobiography" and "supreme fiction" with the trope of the "autobiographical epic"—also referred to as "personal epic," "psychological epic," and "epic of the self" in contemporary criticism. No matter how denominated, work of this sort recreates the life of the author in a narrative structure ordered at least to some extent by the influence of or intertextuality with the ancient epos and mythos. Although I consider some of his later poetry in the Warren chapter of *A Backward Glance,* my emphasis there is on the writer's overall career and canon in terms of his southern and classical legacies, so I will not repeat those formulations here. However, I recall that trope now to suggest Warren's long-term engagement with both life review and autobiography in the early and middle stages of his poetry.

Warren was engaged initially by his legacies as person and writer, by his literal and his literary genealogies as it were. As to the former, he was the first of three children born in Guthrie, Kentucky, to Robert Franklin Warren and Anna Ruth Penn, both descended from agrarian families from the Black Patch, the dark-fired tobacco country in western Kentucky and Tennessee. As evidenced by both his creative and critical works, Warren would remain a lifelong southerner despite his later northern exile, especially in terms of the racial complications inherent in his regional heritage. Warren's literary legacy proves a great deal less parochial than his personal one, however. He excelled at local schools and later at Vanderbilt University in Nashville, the so-called Athens of the South, matriculating in 1921.

Although the burgeoning Southern Renascence had its other outposts, the Nashville Fugitives were already active when Warren arrived at Vanderbilt. No other venue in the South would prove as amenable to the shock of modernity, and the poetry in their literary journal, *The Fugitive,* often considered southern subjects by way of Modernist forms. In particular, the most important poetic precursor for Warren's work was T. S. Eliot's *The Waste Land,* as evidenced by Warren's not only reading but memorizing this Modernist masterpiece on its publication in 1922, that *annus mirabilis* of Modernism that also saw the publication of James Joyce's *Ulysses* (Blotner 35). Encouraged by his teachers such as John Crowe Ransom and by students such as Allen Tate, Warren would publish personal poetry about his regional background while an undergraduate.

Following his graduation from Vanderbilt in 1925, Warren enrolled as a graduate student at the University of California in Berkeley. Despite a romance with his future wife Emma "Cinina" Brescia, the daughter of an emigrant Italian musician and professor, Warren decided to pursue a doctorate at Yale after earning his master's degree at Berkeley in 1927. During his first year in New Haven, however, he was awarded a prestigious Rhodes scholarship to New College at Oxford. The young writer revisited America in 1929, seemingly to demonstrate his maturation by secretly marrying Cinina in California and by publishing his first book, an ironic biography entitled *John Brown: The Making of a Martyr,* a work which languished following the Wall Street crash. Taking his bachelor of literature from Oxford in 1930, Warren declined a graduate fellowship to finish a doctoral dissertation at Yale; instead, he returned home to seek an academic position, declaring to all who would listen, "I'm going to be a writer" (Blotner 107).

In 1931, Warren became an acting assistant professor at Vanderbilt and published a pair of intertextual prose works that began his lifelong dialogue with his cultural and personal past—his controversial defense of segregation in "The Briar Patch" and his first published fiction in "Prime Leaf," a novella that chronicled the earlier Tobacco Wars of his patria in all of their darker complications of race and class (*Talking* 33). His best poems of this early period also recall his Fugitive roots, combining his private and his public legacies to explore family and home through Modernist themes and images. Perhaps the most notable example is found in "The Return: An Elegy" (1934), an autobiographical reflection of his overly protective mother's untimely death in 1931. Warren insisted that he originally wrote this ironical confession of an Eliotian poetic persona well before Ruth Warren's fatal illness was diagnosed, but he later admitted that the poem proved a sort of psychological catharsis for him (Blotner 117–18). Warren's relations with ambiguous and/or abstracted father figures were presented more symbolically in the poem "History" (1935), where biblical, national, and personal patriarchs are conflated in nightmare scenes. Several decades later, Warren would still be coming to a final acceptance of his mother's and father's deaths in the poetry that would form a portion of his own age-work and life review at the time of life when he had lived beyond the years his parents had achieved in theirs.

In 1934, Warren's Vanderbilt friend Cleanth Brooks helped him secure a more permanent academic appointment as an assistant professor at Louisiana State University. Warren's residence in Baton Rouge would prove a turning point in his literary career in many ways. First of all, one of his new duties was coediting *The Southern Review,* which was launched in 1935 and which soon became a literary quarterly with national stature. Brooks and Warren coedited a series of groundbreaking textbooks that literally changed the academic study of English, beginning with *An Approach to Literature* in 1936. That same year, Warren published his first collection of poetry, *Thirty-Six Poems,* which included other autobiographical examples such as "Letter of a Mother" and "Genealogy."

Most important of all for his later literary success, however, Warren was living in Louisiana during the last days of Huey Long, whose daughter Rose was one of his students (Blotner 224). During an Italian sabbatical in 1938, Warren began work on a poetic drama based on Long's tragic fall that evolved into *All the King's Men,* published in 1946 to immediate critical and popular success. In the interim, Warren became a full professor at the University of Minnesota in 1942. Exempted from military service during the war years because of the vision problems created by a boyhood accident that had cost him an eye, Warren's only official wartime service was as consultant in poetry to the Library of Congress during 1944. All of these prominent positions were well deserved as Warren's publications continued to appear with increasing regularity and to growing acclaim. His first published novel, *Night Rider* (1939), developed from the treatment of the Tobacco Wars in his earlier novella "Prime Leaf," and, like it, proved a focused piece of fiction also well received by the critics. Both fictions recreated the life experiences of his maternal grandfather, Gabriel Thomas Penn, an important boyhood mentor who appears as a character in both works but who would reappear as himself in Warren's later poetry of age-work and life review.

A second novel, *At Heaven's Gate,* was published in 1943; based on Tennessee history during the 1920s, the book provided a preview of Warren's subsequent treatment of Louisiana politics during the 1930s in *All the King's Men.* Warren's second poetry collection, *Eleven Poems on the Same Theme* (1942) also demonstrated a new level of poetic power in several ironic poems about love, as well as an inclination toward narrative poetry that would come to fruition in "The Ballad of Billie Potts" (1944), an extended literary ballad based on a legend of the Kentucky frontier. It was collected along with new poems and most of the two earlier collections in *Selected Poems: 1923–1943* (1944), the first of Warren's four self-selected volumes. Other books from these years included two more of the groundbreaking texts edited with Cleanth Brooks, *Understanding Poetry* in 1938 and *Understanding Fiction* in 1943.

By 1946, Warren was an academic writer with wide publication but modest recognition; then the blockbuster success of *All the King's Men* changed his professional and personal life in ways that even he could not have imagined (Blotner 227). Warren became a best-selling author receiving offers from book clubs and movie studios.[3] Awards came more immediately when *All the King's Men* won the Pulitzer Prize for Fiction in 1947, and Warren was awarded a Guggenheim Fellowship for that same year. Nineteen-forty-seven also saw the quick publication of Warren's single collection of short fiction, *The Circus in the Attic and Other Stories,* which included some of his finest fictional efforts, such as the title novella, "Prime Leaf," and his most frequently anthologized story, "Blackberry Winter." Warren then spent his Guggenheim year in Italy working on a new novel that was published in 1949 as *World Enough and Time,* his fictive version of the "Kentucky Tragedy," a historical account of love and jealousy, murder and suicide that had inspired several nineteenth-century American writers. As in many of Warren's works, the protagonist's search for a father surrogate preoccupies his central character, but this novel is a demanding text—long, complex, and thick with ideas and images. Its prose often strains to be poetry, so that its style is suggestive of Warren's three long narrative poems that would follow over succeeding decades.

All of these changes in Warren's professional career influenced his personal life as well. In particular, his relationship with his wife, which had been problematic even from its earliest days, was affected. Certainly, children were never a possibility over the more than two decades they remained married. The new pressures of Warren's phenomenal success with *All the King's Men* soon affected the marriage, especially in terms of various real and imaginary physical problems. Both Warrens were drinking heavily during the late 1940s, and Cinina had to be institutionalized several times (Blotner 253, 260). Finally, the strain on their relationship became too severe, so they separated and were divorced in 1951. After the divorce, they both went on successfully in their separate lives but never saw each other again, though they always lived in close proximity. Warren paid Cinina substantial alimony until her death in 1969, but several poems that form his later life review indicate a lingering guilt still in need of resolution.

Several professional changes accompanied Warren's personal ones. He resigned from the University of Minnesota in 1949, hoping that a new setting might help his failing marriage. In 1951, he accepted a visiting professorship at Yale, where his old friend Cleanth Brooks was now employed (Blotner 267). At almost the same moment, Warren was elected to the esteemed American Academy of Arts and Sciences and was granted his final divorce papers from Cinina, ironically enough. Soon his personal life achieved the stability of his professional career, however, in terms of his evolving relationship with Eleanor Clark, an attractive younger woman and a talented writer herself who had been an acquaintance for several years. After Warren's divorce, their friendship blossomed as romance, so that they were living together in her New York apartment by the spring of 1952. Warren and Clark were married in December of that year, and the children Warren had always wanted soon followed—their daughter Rosanna in 1953 and their son Gabriel in 1955. During these years, the Warrens settled into an old farmhouse and barn that they restored themselves in Fairfield, Connecticut, convenient both to New Haven and New York City.

3

Warren's new personal commitments then enriched his professional work as well. For almost a decade Warren had been unable to complete any lyric poetry, preoccupied as he was with his personal crises, his fiction, and his criticism. His long lyric drought ended with the publication of *Brother to Dragons: A Tale in Verse and Voices* in 1953. This poem of epic length told the terrible tale of how Thomas Jefferson's nephews, the two sons of his sister Lucy Jefferson Lewis, savagely murdered a slave on the Kentucky frontier in 1811; though the founding father lived for another fifteen years, Warren discovered that he evidently never acknowledged his kinsmen's brutal crime (Blotner 284). For Warren, this omission in Jefferson's personal history would become a fitting symbol for the moral amnesia that often enough accompanied the development of the American republic, particularly in terms of displacing Native Americans, enslaving African Americans, and exploiting poor white Americans. Warren's recreation of Jefferson in relation to his own search for a moral, intellectual, and literary father figure allows the writer to introduce his literal father. When R.P.W., as Warren names his poetic persona, prepares to climb Rocky Hill to explore the ruins of the Lewis mansion, his father, "pushing eighty," remains behind drowsing in the car. "For he had climbed his mountain long ago, / And met what face—ah, who can tell? / He will not" (*Brother to Dragons* 28). The puzzle of Robert Franklin Warren's own age-work and life review would continue to intrigue Warren even in his last book published in his lifetime, *Portrait of a Father* (1988).

Warren's new family developments affected his poetry even more directly in a flourish of new lyrics inspired by a sabbatical in Italy during 1954. Although Warren always had considered himself primarily a poet, in midcareer he was best known and best regarded as a novelist, especially in response to *All the King's Men.* Critical, if not popular, opinion began to change in 1957 with the opening of Warren's poetic middle phase in *Promises: Poems 1954–1956.* This collection not only marked the end of Warren's midlife lyric drought but earned his second Pulitzer Prize in 1958; a half century later, Warren still remains the only writer to have won Pulitzers in both fiction and poetry. *Promises* also marked his maturing beyond the anxieties and influences of his Fugitive years, in particular those of his most important poetic forebear, T. S. Eliot.

Perhaps because of Warren's New England residency, Robert Frost became an ever more important influence. Although Warren's most direct critical reaction to the New England poet in his provocative essay "The Themes of Robert Frost" (1947) roughly marks the beginning of his decade-long lyric silence, his most obvious poetic reaction to Frost forms one section of his return to lyric poetry in *Promises.* Warren's title for the autobiographical Subsection XVII is "Boy's Will, Joyful Labor without Pay, and Harvest Home (1918)." Clearly, Warren is recalling the title of Frost's first collection a poetic generation earlier and a continent away. The poem becomes both Warren's personal life review and his poetic response to Frost poems such as "Mowing" and "After Apple-Picking" in its dream like contemplation of youthful labor. For all the transcendent possibilities implied in Warren's dedicating *Promises* to the infant children of his new marriage and pictured in several of its poems, the dark reminiscences of his own childhood in Sections I through VII reveal the disappointment, failure, and guilt of everyman at midlife that prefigure those of his later age-work and life review.

Although new collections of lyric poetry would follow *Promises* with regularity, Warren would remain as active in prose, both in terms of fiction and of nonfiction. His fifth novel, *Band of Angels,* was published in 1955 to somewhat mixed reviews but sufficient popular success to allow Warren to retire from Yale for the first time in the same year. The racial issues in Warren's new novel were more thoughtfully considered by his parallel work of nonfiction, *Segregation: The Inner Conflict of the South,* published in 1956. This book of personal reportage began as an article commissioned by the popular publication *Life,* for which Warren traveled through four states interviewing dozens of white and black southerners on every side of the controversial and complex issue. Rather than writing a summary conclusion, Warren finished his study with a self-interview in which he finally came to terms with his conflicted racial heritage; in the quarter century since his contribution to *I'll Take My Stand,* Warren had evolved from a benevolent segregationist into an apologetic integrationist.

In the late 1950s, Warren embarked on major works of fiction, drama, and poetry that came to simultaneous fruition. *Selected Essays* in 1958 showed the range of Warren's criticism, both theoretical as in "Pure and Impure Poetry" and practical as in introductions to his personal favorites such as Frost and Faulkner. His sixth novel, *The Cave,* was published in 1959, to somewhat mixed reviews but with initial sales better than any of his earlier novels (Blotner 326). Although *The Cave* was not optioned by the movies, its royalties still afforded the Warrens the opportunity in 1959 to purchase a country retreat in rural Vermont. As Warren was retired from teaching, at least temporarily, he was able to spend more time at this rural setting that more and more reminded him of his boyhood Kentucky. During this period, Warren worked at playwriting as well, trying to achieve success in the one genre that had eluded him. In one major project, he dramatized *All the King's Men,* taking the story back to its dramatic roots. His play had a brief New York run in 1959, to indifferent reviews, and his script was published as *All the King's Men: A Play* in 1960 to mediocre sales.

A more successful work of that year was his new collection of poetry, *You, Emperors, and Others: Poems 1957–1960.* The most significant of the collection's several sequences is the third, "Mortmain," an autobiographical reaction in five parts to the death of Robert Franklin Warren in poetry influenced by the father's early interest in the classics. The Latin roots of

"Mortmain" literally mean "dead hand," but the word survives in English through its French transformation as the legal term defining the perpetual entailment of property in a last will and testament. The opening poem's symbolic gesture is neatly summarized if not analyzed by the journalistic title Warren often affected in midcareer: "After Night Flight Son Reaches Bedside of Already Unconscious Father, Whose Right Hand Lifts in a Spasmodic Gesture, as Though Trying to Make Contact: 1955." This ambiguous gesticulation certainly portends more than the universal realization of the son's future fate in the death of the father; rather, Warren demonstrates how his own self-narrative results not just from his genealogy but from his linguistic, legal, and literary patrimony—the very materials that will shape his own age-work and life review as he lives on toward the completion of his father's term of years.

The year 1961 was marked by the excitement of the Civil War centennial, both nationally and personally, as Warren's lifelong interest in the topic inspired his literary responses in several genres. The first completed that year was *The Legacy of the Civil War: Meditations on the Centennial,* which was excerpted in *Life* magazine and then presented as a slim volume. Within the same year, Warren published his seventh novel, *Wilderness: A Tale of the Civil War,* in which he attempted to realize these same themes in fiction. Although the nonfiction study of the Civil War by Warren had won nearly universal praise, save for a few New York reviewers who thought him a southern sympathizer, his novel was not as well received. Warren would admit to an interviewer that its central observer, the German idealist, was involved "*only* intellectually"; the truth was that the same might have been said for the creative consciousness behind him (*Talking* 161). The same problem would become more or less evident in Warren's next pair of novels, *Flood* (1964) and *Meet Me in the Green Glen* (1971).

Another, less direct result of Warren's Civil War interests was his return to Yale in 1962, where he now would teach only every other term. Certainly, he was able to pursue his own work in addition to his light teaching schedule. In 1965, Warren published another very successful nonfiction work on troubled American race relations, *Who Speaks for the Negro?* In this new complex of dialogues, Warren's southern journey in *Segregation* a decade earlier is extended to the nation as a whole in the present, both in an excerpt in *Look* magazine and in his new book. Extensive interviews with black leaders and thinkers in both the South and the North range from Martin Luther King Jr. to Malcolm X. As might be anticipated, Warren's greatest interest is in the creative response to the crisis of integration, and two chapters are spent on long interviews with Ralph Ellison, an old friend, and the more antagonistic James Baldwin.

Warren turned his creative efforts more toward poetry than to prose in the second half of the 1960s, however, perhaps in response to social and cultural developments in contemporary America and possibly as the beginning of his age-work, life review, and search for sublimity and transcendence. His second volume of *Selected Poems* was published in 1966; it included a gathering of previously uncollected work under the title *Tale of Time.* Another new collection, *Incarnations,* followed in 1968, and a second try at an epic poem, *Audubon: A Vision,* closed the decade in 1969. All of Warren's new poetry in these books proved to be mature, powerful work, particularly inasmuch as it is informed by his own autobiography. In Warren's 1966 *Selected Poems,* his subtitle, *New and Old 1923–1966,* enabled him to retain the best of his earlier work and to juxtapose it with his more recent efforts. Warren continued the practice of his 1944 *Selected Poems* by presenting his poetry in what he later called "anti-chronological order" (Burt 724). The structure of Warren's book thus becomes a backward glance over some four decades of his poetry in a poetic life review as he enters his seventh decade. Admitting his revision of poems published earlier, Warren remarks in the collection's prefatory note: "But in revising old poems, I have tried not to tamper with meanings, only to sharpen old meanings—for poems are, in one perspective at least, always a life record, and live their life by that fact" (Burt 689).

Warren's title, *Tale of Time,* points his reader toward the emerging elements of autobiography, as he opens with a sequence of ten poems under the significant title "Notes on a Life to Be Lived." Later, seven of these ten poems would be recycled in the construction of Warren's 1974 collection *Or Else,* the actual beginning of his later poetry as I will demonstrate in my next chapter. Since these poems are rewritten for the later volume, I will follow Warren's example and postpone my discussion of them, contending, however, that the excision of these seven poems from *Tale of Time* along with their revision for *Or Else* is one of the most important indications of Warren's life review in all of his later poetry. His three volumes from the late 1960s—*Tale of Time, Incarnations,* and *Audubon*—all present some sense of age-work and life review, as well as of transcendence and sublimity, but the volume still is composed for the most part of poems that do not fit within the formulations at work in my study, leaving *Or Else* as the key transitional work for Warren's later career.

For a good example, the three poems from the "Notes on a Life to Be Lived" sequence that are not recycled in *Or Else*—"Patriotic Tour and Postulate of Joy," "Dragon-Tree," and "Ways of Day"—prove to be at once too topical and too abstracted to operate as age-work or life review. Likewise, the long sequence "Homage to Emerson, On Night Flight to New York" is as much or more concerned with the ideas of its title figure as with the emotions of its persona. In a similar manner, "The Day Dr. Knox Did It," an autobiographical sequence drawn from Warren's own youth, is more interested in the motivations of its subject, a suicidal local physician, than in those of the persona as a bewildered boy and as a man who finally comprehends the dead doctor's life of quiet desperation in Guthrie, Kentucky. Even the autumnal imagery of "Fall Comes in Back-Country Vermont," a scene from Warren's present dedicated to his fellow poet William Meredith, remains more focused on the symbolic figure of a newly dead New Englander than on the deracinated persona who perceives this other as one of the many memento mori in which he can trace the course of his own life journey.

Only in the autobiographical poems concerned with the loss of his mother in the powerful "Tale of Time" is Warren engaged in age-work and life review. Warren begins with his confusion of feelings after the death of his mother, as in the much earlier "The Return: An Elegy": here his persona cries, "Grief? You pray / To God that this be grief, for / You want to grieve" (185). In the second section, by means of his memories years later the poet walks the streets of Guthrie, trying imagine the faces of its inhabitants whom his mother saw in her young womanhood. He can recall only the town's old, mad druggist who had promised to omit the name of nice "Miss Ruth" from the list of townsfolk he intended to poison for the improvement of the community. Section III, only four lines long, turns on the idea of the death wish, asking in conclusion "*Whose wish*?" (187). Warren then remembers the evening after his mother's funeral when his family visited their black nursemaid, who was by then too old and ill to attend the earlier services. Like his father's in "Mortmain," her dying hand "rises like revelation" (188). When she touches Warren's cheek, her recognition forgives him, even while his father leaves her a twenty-dollar bill as a guilt offering. Warren finds a startling solution to death's dilemma revealed in a symbolic dream: "You / Must eat the dead" (190). Consumed as a sacrament, if only in imagination, the dead are part of the living, so that in the transcendent terms of the final line, "Immortality is not impossible, / Even joy" (190).

Warren's succeeding collection, *Incarnations*, is subtitled *Poems 1966–1968*, and it prefigures his major age-work and life review in several poems, especially in "The True Nature of Time," which also would reappear in *Or Else*. However, *Incarnations* is not focused fully by these aspects of aging. It seems as if Warren purposely turns his attention toward living his life in the present, chronicling his visits to a Mediterranean isle, to a southern prison, to Manhattan streets—and finally to Alpine ski slopes that anticipate the mountain imagery of *Altitudes and Extensions*. Although age is an issue in *Incarnations*, it is often presented through the aging of a symbolic other, for example an "old hunchback in bikini" in "Myth on Mediterranean Beach: Aphrodite as Logos," a "grizzled" southern prisoner stuck "in the pen" for the last forty years in "Keep That Morphine Moving, Cap," and an "old . . . Poor" black woman struck down by a Cadillac on a Manhattan street in "The Event" (228, 236, 242).

Warren's second attempt at a poetic epic on American themes, *Audubon: A Vision*, ended the decade in 1969, and it also anticipated what would become his own age-work, life review, and transcendence beyond time in a creative review of the life and work of another artist. In this disjunctive text, Warren deftly traces the painter's evolution from ambiguous origin to wilderness peril to artistic maturity to final self-acceptance realized at the moment of death. In the pivotal Section IV,

> His life, at the end, seemed—even the anguish—simple.
> Simple, at least, in that it had to be,
> Simply what it was, as he was,
> In the end, himself and not what
> He had known he ought to be. (261)

Thus, Warren parallels his own vision with Audubon's, especially in terms of visual imagery and symbolism that result in such "blessedness" (261).

> To wake in some dawn and see
> As though down a rifle barrel, lined up,
> Like sights, the self that was, the self that is, and there
> Far off but in range, completing the alignment, your fate. (261)

Then, after assessing of his nineteenth-century forebear's life and work, the poet recognizes himself as a part of a timeless continuity into the present that concludes in the final Section VII, "Tell Me A Story." This last narrative begins,

> Long ago, in Kentucky, I, a boy, stood
> By a dirt road, in first dark, and heard
> The great geese hoot northward. (266)

Although Warren's personal history moves on through "this century, and moment, of mania," it also includes suggestions of transcendence in this story of "great distances, and starlight" because "The name of the story is Time" (267). The poet's "*Vision,*" like Audubon's, becomes as "a story of deep delight," or in other words a "shadowy" epic of the self or "supreme fiction" drawn ultimately from his own life and work (267). In the years after *Audubon*—to recall the title of my study—Warren's age-work and life review would create a narrative of poetic sublimity and personal transcendence in his pivotal volume *Or Else* and in the five collections of his poetry that would follow it.

1

Predication and Interjection

Or Else: Poem/Poems 1968–1974

> But let us note, too, how glory, like gasoline spilled
> On the cement in a garage, may flare, of a sudden, up,
>
> In a blinding blaze, from the filth of the world's floor.
>
> —*Interjection #7: Remarks of Soul to Body*

1

The subtitle of *Or Else: Poem/Poems 1968–1974* suggests not only the volume's twofold poetic structure but its dual vision of time past as subject matter: not just the half-dozen years spanning its composition but also the poet's recreated life from 1905 forward, his "shadowy autobiography" as it were. Indeed, the half decade or so after *Audubon* did become a transitional period of considerable importance in terms of Warren's life and work. Although he retired from teaching permanently in 1973, Warren's professional energies were undiminished, as evidenced by his publication of several prose works over these years in addition to *Or Else.* The most important was his penultimate novel, *Meet Me in the Green Glen* in 1971, another "romance" of contemporary Tennessee much like *The Cave* and *Flood.* Like them also, this new novel demonstrates the difficulty of reconciling its more romantic and realistic elements, so that the result seems like an uneasy union of Thomas Hardy and Theodore Dreiser. *Meet Me in the Green Glen* received a lukewarm critical reception, unlike Warren's nonfiction works of the same period, which were generally well received. They included editions of Herman Melville's and John Greenleaf Whittier's poetry, a study of Dreiser's prose, as well as an American literature anthology edited with Cleanth Brooks and R. W. B. Lewis.[1] The several positive responses to these critical texts complemented the other rewards of Warren's distinguished career that continued to accumulate during this six-year period, including the National Medal for Literature in 1970, the

Jefferson Lectureship in the Humanities in 1974, and the first of many honorary degrees and visiting professorships.

In terms of his personal life, however, Warren must have felt the burden of time in several respects. Despite a healthy life style that centered on a regimen of swimming, weight lifting, and hiking, Warren endured a series of medical problems during this period, including a life-threatening liver infection in 1972. Although Eleanor Clark was eight years his junior, her health began to deteriorate as she approached her sixties; the most disturbing difficulty for his wife was an untreatable eye condition that threatened her sight. Their children Rosanna and Gabriel also seem to have suffered more than the normal illnesses and accidents of youth, so as older parents the Warrens worried over them all the more. The rapid transformation of their offspring into young adults during high school and college must have underscored the swift passage of the years for their aging mother and father. All of these life changes surely pulled Warren the poet back into his personal past—in nostalgia that would blossom in his later poetry.

Warren used *Essay Toward the Human Understanding* as a working title for his new collection that became *Or Else,* and his variation on John Locke's earlier title implies a model of human development rooted in the psychology of experience (Blotner 414). In his somewhat ambiguous and disquieting final title, *Or Else,* Warren also suggests an existential unease resulting from just such an evolution from birth through life toward death. The addition of *Poem/Poems 1968–1974* as his subtitle then raises questions of subject matter and of poetic form. As Warren further explained this formal tension in his untitled prefatory note to *Or Else,* "This book is conceived as a single long poem composed of a number of shorter poems as sections or chapters" (Burt 709). The form of this collection proves more complicated in its dual sequencing of predications and interjections differentiated by Roman and Arabic numerals than sequencing is in any of Warren's earlier collections and thus more significant to its overall success.[2] In my view, the binaries of form and matter implied in Warren's subtitle, *Poem/Poems 1968–1974,* provides a key to the centrality of the poet's age-work, life review, and hope for transcendence in this pivotal collection.

Warren's major themes of time, age, death, and memory provide unity to the individual poems and sections of *Or Else* as Eriksonian age-work. Warren imbues his individual poems and his carefully organized gathering of them with a concern for time, in terms not just of the collection's narrative progression but of the philosophical abstraction often noted as "Time." Aging becomes an element of almost all the work's collected pieces, as Warren's poetic persona approaches most of his subjects from the transforming perspectives of advancing years. Death is dramatized, imaged, or referenced in at least a dozen poems gathered in the volume, while it is implied in a dozen more. *Or Else* is structured by just the sort of reminiscence and autobiography that Butler formulated as life review. The book's complex sequences, especially its final triptych of late-life revelations, also reveal a progression toward possible transcendence in age of the sort formulated by Tornstam by means of Bloom's poetic sublimity.

Most critics of *Or Else* begin their discussions by agreeing or disagreeing with Warren's formulation of his twofold structure as "*Poem/Poems,*" generally in terms of how successful they find the collection as a whole. Reviewers in popular publications were often puzzled by the format, but most later critics and scholars are more positive. James Justus in his foundational study, *The Achievement of Robert Penn Warren* (1980), decides that "it is something of both," though he believes that many of the individual pieces fit awkwardly into the whole (97). Dave Smith, an important southern poet and critic himself, concludes that Warren "has caused his 32 poems to operate as something like panels which form a loose sequential movement . . . through the juxtaposition and oblique continuities of remarkably varied poems" (Smith 40, 46). Randolph Paul Runyon's recent close reading of the volume concludes that the continuities between "the poems taken two by two betray a strange tendency to become the same poem" (*Ghostly* 173).[3] In these judgments, however, Warren's critics often neglect the rest of his untitled headnote to the collection, where he reveals that despite its chronological limits of 1968 to 1974, "a few short pieces come from a period some ten years before when I was working toward a similar long poem" (Burt 709). As mentioned earlier in my prologue, eight of the thirty-two poems comprising *Or Else* had been collected already. After identifying the sources of these interpolations, Warren reveals that he decided that these pieces "have a place in the thematic structure of this poem"—that is of *Or Else* as a unified "poem" (Burt 709).

2

Warren's juxtaposition of these revised poems with his entire published output between 1968 and 1974 reinforces my view of *Or Else* as the beginning of his later poetry because of his increasing interest in age-work and life review. As Warren went on to explain in his introductory note to the new collection, seven of the eight recycled poems were drawn from an abortive "long poem" of ten pieces under the general title "Notes on a Life to Be Lived," first collected for *Tale of Time,* the new gathering of poetry that prefaced the 1965 *Selected Poems* (709). Warren's title for that earlier attempt at a longer sequence as a cohesive "poem" composed of ten parts certainly suggests an autobiographical impulse. In *Or Else* he gathers seven of the original ten pieces into his evocation of his past while omitting three more topical and less personal ones. Although themes of aging permeate all seven of these recycled pieces, they are made paramount in Warren's eighth republished addition, XIII, "The True Nature of Time," first collected in his preceding volume, *Incarnations.*

As is the case with many pairings of poems in Warren's later canon, "The True Nature of Time" becomes something of a diptych, consisting of physical imagery in part 1, "The Faring," and psychological consideration in part 2, "The Enclave," here unified as an intertextual sequence probing the human perception of time. The archaic diction and syntax of the first part suggest a nostalgic recreation of a personally significant crossing of the English Channel, a spatial image of the geographical and psychological distances that separate even lovers. The more speculative presentation of "Time" in the second part extends the imagery of a literal voyage in the first to the more symbolic journey of life. According to Warren's biographer, "The True Nature of Time" has an autobiographical basis in his European sojourn with Eleanor Clark in 1952, a decade and a half before he wrote these paired poems (Blotner 378). In "The Faring" Warren contrasts a gray seascape with flashes of sunlight illuminating the reunion of the lovers at harborside, particularly as reflected in the woman's golden hair, and their later lovemaking in what appears to be a seaside grotto, especially as lit by the reflections of yellow roses touched by fading sunbeams. In the parallel part 2, "The Enclave," the persona recovers the bright image of his beloved in the golden grotto within his dreaming memory during the darkness of a night much later in life. The very prosody of Warren's stanzas underscores his puzzlement at the persistence of experience. In perfectly balanced lines, he finally asks how

> May I know the true nature of Time, if
> Deep now in darkness that glittering enclave
> I dream, hangs (301)

All seven of the poems added to *Or Else* from the earlier "Notes on a Life to Be Lived" sequence are revised for republication here in similar terms of personal and philosophical relations to time, aging, death, and memory. Four of the seven pieces concern various aspects of Warren's family relations with his wife and children as seen from the perspective of his advancing age. For example, the next poem after "The True Nature of Time" in the new order of *Or Else,* XIV, "Vision Under the October Mountain: A Love Poem," announces its theme in the subtitle. The poem then opens with bright, sunlit, and painterly images recalling the European scenes of harbor and grotto: "Golding from green, gorgeous the mountain / high hangs in gold air," as if arrayed by nature before an aging couple as an image "of authority, of reality" (301). The poetic persona next creates a philosophical dialectic typical of Warren's poetry, "—or, is it—?"(301). Warren goes on to muse upon whether this archetypal image somehow persists as a psychological "dream" from a Platonic prenatal darkness through the "miracle" of love and procreation within "the human scheme of values," extending it forward to the mature love of the aging couple (301–2).

A corresponding vision also resonates in Poem XVIII, "Composition in Gold and Red-Gold," the imagistic recreation of another landscape, probably in the mountains of Vermont, where the Warrens established a rural retreat during their child-rearing years. This autumnal scene also suggests several sorts of human "falls" in images rich with traditional symbolism. The poetic persona perceives that "Between the event and the word, golden / The sunlight falls . . . in pitiless plenitude, and every leaf / On the ruined apple tree is gold, and the apples all / Gold, too, especially those // On the ground" (307). So too, the hair of Warren's "little girl is as brown-gold as / Brook water braiding in sunlight"; yet she still learns of death when her gold-eyed cat kills a chipmunk, "Golden in gold light," spilling its blood in "a faint smear of flame-gold at the base / Of the skull" (308). Again almost painterly, "This effect / Completes the composition" (308).

In the poem directly preceding this one, XVII, "Little Boy and Lost Shoe," again recycled from the "Notes on a Life to Be Lived" sequence, autumnal landscape creates a golden aura around the poetic persona's little son, as "Sunlight touched the goldenrod, and yellowed his hair," and he too discovers a world of human loss (307). Like Shakespeare's golden lads, or A. E. Housman's Shropshire boys closer in time, or Robert Frost's lost youths even closer to home, Warren's children both live within a fallen world where he is powerless despite his father's love to protect them from time, loss, and death. Children, perhaps autobiographical, also appear in the other pieces from his earlier attempt at a long poem. Poems VIII, "Small White House," and XV, "Stargazing," again remind the poetic persona of all the years that separate him from the days of his own youth. The child who cries within that small white house that centers a July landscape brown with heat may not be his own progeny, but it becomes a person symbolic of his own ambiguous place among generations—parents now dead and children just starting to live. The spontaneous girl who recalls the persona to his own childhood nights of stargazing with his parents may or may not be his own daughter, yet she recalls "all I have lived / In the years I looked at stars" (302).

Even more demonstrative of Warren's age-work are the other two poems derived from *Tale of Time*—IV, "Blow, West Wind," and VII, "Chain Saw at Dawn in Vermont in Time of Drouth"—because these poems demonstrate the deaths of father and brother figures as prefigurations of the poetic persona's fate. Both titles also recall works from earlier literature in English; the first proves intertextual with the anonymous lyric "Western Wind," and the second uses the archaic form of "Drouth" to emphasize the psychological aridity discovered in the contemporary decline of the older order in rural New England. In "Blow, West Wind," a triad of remembered images ranges from the present into the distant past—a kestrel suspended in a western sky, his father's cold sweat on his death's bed, and his own boyish hand dripping bright creek water—and all three remind Warren of his own mortality. The material images cause his persona to insist that "I know, I know," yet he at last concludes, "But you believe nothing, with the evidence lost" (273). This "evidence" remains obscure, perhaps so because of the harsh reality of age that lurks behind the images recovered from memories accreted during the passage of his lifetime. In any case, it seems that Warren's persona must balance both the inevitability and the finality of his own death (273).

Such also seems the case in Poem VII, "Chain Saw at Dawn in Vermont in Time of Drouth," another diptych where Warren's autobiographical persona acquaints himself with death through the imagined age-work of a dying neighbor. As in Poem XIII, "The True Nature of Time," Warren contrasts himself with a symbolic other in this two-part poem, though here he reverses the order of presentation. In the untitled part 1, the chain saw screech that wakes him at dawn from a dream of the past, that "is // The self," insists on the harsh reality of the present moment in a "steel-snarl and lyric" that "Sings: *now*! Sings: / *Now, now, now*" (285). When the chain saw at last ceases its uproar, Warren's persona hears a crow call, as if echoing from his rural boyhood "with the crystalline beauty / Of the outraged heart" (286). Beyond present and past, Warren contemplates the future in his concluding question: "Have I learned how to live?" (286).

Part 2 then shifts to Warren's mirror self, as "On the other side of the woods, in the village, a man / Is dying" (286). This symbolic double also wakes to the chain saw's clamor, but having been a sawyer in his working life he hears its "scream of castration" as an echo from his past that prefigures his imminent death (286).[4] Although he had "a good wife . . . his boy turned out bad" (286). "He himself never managed to pay off the mortgage. . . . So now thinks: / *I have not learned how to die*" (286). "Mortgage" is a perfect word for a life review, as a legal bond that once could be ended only by death. In another wonderful image, the saw's sound becomes a "glee of steel," with the archaic sense of a song for three or more voices as well as its popular meaning of a wild joyfulness that here echoes in its "whirl-tooth hysteria / Of *now, now, now!*" (286). Warren then combines the poem's two parts in a more philosophical conclusion as he rises to face another day of drought, desiccation, and despair in the decline of rural New England and its literary traditions, both of which he has come to appreciate during his residence in Vermont: "I must endeavor to learn what / I must learn before I must learn / The other thing. If / I learn even a little, I may, / By evening, be able / To tell the man something" (287). Then, in a stanza of a single line that Warren often employs to conclude his later poems, "Or he himself may have learned by then" (287). That "other thing" is how to die, of course, but to achieve that difficult knowledge Warren's poetic persona first must learn how to live and perform the tasks of age.

3

In contrast to the poems collected earlier and later added to *Or Else,* Warren also includes two new ones, previously unpublished. Interestingly enough, these brand-new pieces become the first and the last of the eight poetic "Interjections" that Warren counterpoints by means of Arabic numerals to the main sequence of twenty-four poetic predications ordered by Roman numerals, including all eight additions from the earlier collections. Between these two major strands of *Or Else,* Warren maintains a quizzical dialectic, contrasting his thematic statements in the longer narrative and philosophical pieces and his poetic questioning of them in these tighter, more lyrical interjections. In I, "The Nature of a Mirror," for example, Warren combines harsh images drawn from both nature and culture in his poetic persona's present and past to conclude "Time // Is the mirror into which you stare" (271). It is followed by the italicized title of one previously unpublished piece, "*Interjection #1: The Need for Re-evaluation,*" which answers its own question, "*Is this really me*? Of course not, for Time / Is only the mirror in a fun-house" (271). Warren's thematic ironies are emphasized even more when this persistent counterpointing is read in terms of age-work. We know ourselves only in the unreeling of time, of course, but the reflection of an aging visage in a mirror is often a startling visual revelation of deterioration to the person reflected. In this regard, Butler twice lists mirror images among the visual aspects of late life review ("Life Review" 68, 74). Like the distorting mirror of a sideshow, Warren's poetic interjection reveals an altered vision of our place in the human narrative. Warren abruptly concludes his three-line interjection, insisting "You must re-evaluate the whole question" (271).

The thematic variations and narrative deviations in Warren's eight "Interjections" demonstrate that he does not see himself as the wise old man of traditional age poetry like Wordsworth, Longfellow, or even Frost.[5] For example, "*Interjection #2*" entitled "*Caveat,*" is dedicated to John Crowe Ransom, who stopped writing poetry from fear of repeating himself ("Notes"

327). The very shape of Warren's lines then reveal that life may appear to be continuous,

> But only, oh, on-
> ly, in discontinuity, do we
> know that we exist. (274)

Later, the quest for the ultimate reality in *"Interjection #3: I Know a Place Where All Is Real"* is interposed between the "original dream" of Poem V, "I Am Dreaming of a White Christmas: The Natural History of a Vision," and the imagined nightmare of VI, "Ballad of Mister Dutcher and the Last Lynching in Gupton." Vietnam appears in *"Interjection #4: Bad Year, Bad War: A New Year's Card, 1969,"* where the harsh reality of America's fallen present in contrast to our wishfully innocent past is wedged between two images of childhood innocence observed by Warren's personae in VIII, "Small White House," and IX, "Forever O'Clock," the title of the last becoming another childlike allusion to the puzzling riddle of time.

After three long narratives concerning self-concerned writers—Warren himself, Theodore Dreiser, and Gustave Flaubert—*"Interjection #5: Solipsism and Theology"* presents a questioning take on the problematic relation of creative ego and "the dark pit of self" (299). It is followed by three shorter lyrics concerned with familial love—XIII, "The True Nature of Time"; XIV, "Vision Under the October Mountain: A Love Poem"; and XV, "Stargazing"—in which poetic references to God lead in turn to *"Interjection #6: What You Sometimes Feel on Your Face at Night,"* where a dreamed caress in sleep is "God's . . . who . . . wants only to love you, perhaps" (302). In *"Interjection #7: Remarks of Soul to Body,"* Warren uses a convention of early English poetry to capture the "baroque ironies of Time" occasioned by a birthday party in late age (309). The second previously unpublished poem collected in *Or Else* is *"Interjection #8: Or, Sometimes, Night,"* which provides a philosophical transition between three poems concerned with dead parents and friends of the past—XIX, "There's a Grandfather's Clock in the Hall"; XX, "Reading Late at Night, Thermometer Falling"; and XXI, "Folly on Royal Street before the Raw Face of God"—and the volume's three final poems essaying transcendence—XXII, "Sunset Walk in Thaw-Time in Vermont"; XXIII, "Birth of Love"; and XXIV, "A Problem in Spatial Composition." Thus, Warren's lyric "interjections" function like their grammatical counterparts in the logic of the long predication of aging and death that is the narrative sequence of *Or Else* as "*Poem*." These interjections not only counterpoint the thematic structure of that overall predication but punctuate the groupings of "*Poems*" into subsections within it. Perhaps because of their functional nature, Warren omitted all of them from the last self-edited *Selected Poems* he would publish in 1985.

4

The 1985 *Selected Poems* includes twelve of the twenty-four remaining poems, however, and my analyses here will mirror Warren's in its emphases. Reprinted without their Roman numerals and counterpointed interjections, they lose some of their rich context as part of Warren's unifying structure in *Or Else.* For example, the first interjection follows Poem I, "The Nature of Time," but it precedes II, "Natural History"; III, "Time as Hypnosis"; and IV, "Blow, West Wind," which are then completed by a second interjection as an initial gathering of lyrics concerned with the poet's maturation. The title of Poem II, "Natural History," recalls that of I, "The Nature of Time," of course, and both poems project rather unnatural pictures of parental archetypes, somewhat like the distorted images of funhouse mirrors suggested by the first interjection. As Randolph Paul Runyon has shown, the mother figures in both of these poems "are mad, but in different ways" (*Ghostly* 144). The several father figures include a young "F.D.R." who has yet to "run for office even" in the first poem, and in the second a "naked old father" who dances in the rain when he should be quiet in his grave (271). The dead father returns briefly in IV, "Blow, West Wind," as the persona regresses into childhood, but the son appears once more as a more realistic figure of boyhood in III, "Time as Hypnosis."

In this puzzling title, Warren seems to use the word "hypnosis" more in the sense of meditation than of sideshow mesmerism. On a wintry night, his poetic persona recalls a "dream" of "whiteness," when he regresses back into his boyish identity as if in a trance, an image Warren often uses in regard to artistic vision achieved through the subconscious (272).[6] Nature is transformed to a Lockean blank tablet by one of the rare snows in his region during the years of his boyhood—save for a red drop of mouse blood marking the spot where a swooping owl intersected the path of tiny footprints etched in the snow. Looking back, the persona can see how his "own tracks march at me"; stretching ahead, "Was the blankness of white" (273). Like Frost's symbolic snowscapes, Warren's "landscape that had been / Brown fields and black woods" becomes "White emptiness and arches," while "The white light / Filled all the vertiginous sky" that seems to represent the cold comfort of nonbeing—first for the field mouse, then for the boyish persona, and last now the aging poet (272). At the conclusion, the boy returns home to sit by the fire and to dream of snow, "the glittering metaphor / For which I could find no referent," at least at that point of his life, though he implies that he discovered its reference point by finally facing death (273).

"*Interjection #2*" provides a "*Caveat*" to drawing any line of easy continuity between child and adult, however, and this skepticism must apply also to the gathering of poems that follows in the much longer sequence V, "I Am Dreaming of a White Christmas: The Natural History of a Vision." Even as the subtitle creates diverse continuities with several other poems in the volume, "White Christmas" ironically evokes sentimental holiday songs or Christmas card verses. Yet the logic of the tripartite narrative involves the subconscious imagery of dreams, as its settings triangulate a dreary December in western Kentucky of the poet's youth, a smoggy summer in the New York City of his present, and his timeless future as implied by the first snowfall of the year on the western mountains. As Warren tells us in the concluding section: "All items listed above belong in the world / In which all things are continuous, / And are parts of the original dream which / I am now trying to discover the logic of" (281). The poem evolves into a redeeming vision through the process of finding consequential continuities among past, present, and future, despite the preceding "*Caveat*" against attempting exactly that sort of easy reconciliation.

In fact, the first eight of the twelve sections of "White Christmas" seem to be a sort of nightmare image from an appalling family album revealing the past in all its irrevocable finality. Although the poet recalls his parents as if in a Christmas morning pose, they appear as if in a ghastly "daguerreotype" of a scene from the past in the chronological present, decades after their literal deaths (275). No wonder the opening line insists by both typography and punctuation: "*No, not that door—never!*" (275). Naturalistic details prove especially jarring in their mundanity, whether his father's

Roman nose "bold-jutting yet but with / Nostril-flanges gone tattered in Time," or his mother's sweet smile, though "There are now no / Lips to kiss with" (276, 277). Most striking in terms of visual imagery are their now darkened eye sockets—"His Eyes / Had been blue. // Hers brown"—corresponding to the cold hearth with its gray ashes (276). In this grim, fairy-tale world, three small chairs await the three Warren children, and under the desiccated Christmas tree sit "three packages. / Identical in size and shape" (278). Without opening his, the persona realizes that his parents' most significant legacy to him is their very mortality.

The ninth and tenth sections significantly are set in the present of the early evening "smog-glitter" of late summer in New York City's "Times Square," where "the eye is inimical" (279). The air is haunted with "ectoplasmic" shapes of aircraft and the "big sluice" of Broadway traffic, so that the aging poet seems to rediscover images of his dead parents in the sound of a madwoman's cries from the mental ward at Bellevue Hospital and the sight of "Old men come out from the hard-core movies" (279, 280). The penultimate section (11) opens: "In any case, / I stand here and think of snow falling" (281). The "Brown-lacquered" photographic scene of the Kentucky past and the hazy skies, "yellow as acid," of New York City's present pollution are altered by the descending whiteness, much as in III, "Time as Hypnosis" (276, 279).

> The first flakes,
> Large, soft, sparse, come straight down
> And with enormous deliberation, white
> Out of unbreathing blackness. (281)

This snow scene is a vision of the Nez Perce Pass between Idaho and Montana, one of the settings for Warren's final poetic epic, *Chief Joseph of the Nez Perce,* which would appear in 1982. Snowfall becomes an important image in Warren's later poetry, perhaps because of his long residence in New England, as well as his personal and professional relationships with Yankee poets past and present, though Warren's recreated snows sometimes recall rare occurrences in his southern home place or his later sojourns in the mountain West. Warren often invests his snowfalls, especially those of yesteryear, with an ambivalent burden of obliteration and transformation. In particular, these implications prove true in "White

Christmas," where Warren uses falling flakes to punctuate the poem's crucial question; "Will I never know / What present there was in that package for me, / Under the Christmas tree? (281). In his sublime final lines, Warren unravels the logic of his dream as his rich legacy of the past, real agency of the present, and possible transcendence of the future: "This / Is the process whereby pain of the past in its pastness / May be converted into the future tense // Of joy" (281).

5

"*Interjection #3: I Know a Place Where All Is Real*" then separates this longest of Warren's narratives from another substantial one, VI, "Ballad of Mister Dutcher and the Last Lynching in Gupton," which in turn forms a gathering with VII, "Chain Saw at Dawn in Vermont In Time of Drouth," and VIII, "Small White House," both discussed earlier. "*Interjection #3*" extends the questing in the western mountains in the previous poem. This place of the "real" is not easily accessed; even when it is achieved, some "find that they cannot stand the altitude," a situation that prefigures Warren's final collection, *Altitudes and Extensions.* The poem's dedication to Austin Warren, a literary theorist and friend though no relation to the poet, seems to indicate that reality exists at some higher level of abstraction than the literal dreamscape of the preceding poem or the imagined naturalism of the one that follows in the literary ballad about Mister Dutcher and his unsuspected talent as an executioner. Although Warren's ironic poem suggests a persona not much older than the boy who experienced the revelations of the snowfall of III, "Time as Hypnosis," the actual lynching in Guthrie on which the poem is based took place when Warren had achieved manhood and had left his home place for California (Watkins 71). Warren imagines the harsh details of this brutal southern ritual, but he distances himself from the action that he did not experience directly by means of the ballad's ironic stance. The long narrative poem also portends the civil-rights-era racial violence of Poem XVI, "News Photo," in which a white minister is murdered, ostensibly for "*Working Up the Niggers*" (303).

In his analysis of *Or Else,* James H. Justus connects "News Photo" with "*Interjection #4: Bad Year, Bad War: A New Year's Card, 1969*" as "the worst in the volume" in their uneasy blending of "topical comment" and "abstract inquiry" (97). Yet "*Interjection #4*" might serve as well as a New Year's card for the present. Similar pictures of a discontinuous present are used to reveal the continuing puzzlement of the poetic personae in the Times Square sequences of V, "I Am Dreaming of a White Christmas: The Natural History of a Vision," the nightmarish Middle America glimpsed in the "Vital Statistics" (2) sequence of XI, "Homage to Theodore Dreiser," and even in the initial sequence of IX, "Forever O'Clock," with its imagery of a western execution and universal adultery. In fact, the tripartite structure of "Forever O'Clock" serves as a sort of introduction to the three longer narratives that follow it—portraits of the literary artists Warren, Dreiser, and Flaubert. In "Forever O'Clock," Warren's persona ranges from a disordered present in the West, to the past in a Dixie ridden by "drouth" during the Depression, to an ominous future in his elongated last line—"A clock somewhere is trying to make up its mind to strike forever o'clock" (289–90).

Poem X, "Rattlesnake Country," dedicated to Warren's colleague in southern poetry James Dickey, then combines the several themes developed in IX, "Forever O'Clock." In this longer narrative sequence, Warren's poetic persona ranges between his past and his present in South and West, while exploring human betrayal and guilt in relation to time, age, and death in both personal and philosophical terms. Warren's title here resonates with that of an earlier narrative poem, "Dragon Country" from *Promises,* which revealed the darkness lurking in the poet's home place in the Black Patch of western Kentucky; "Rattlesnake Country" develops similar revelations in the high country of the far West through imagery of another scaly monster. Warren's poetic persona seems to be visiting a dude ranch of some sort, where a Native American hired hand, ironically nicknamed Laughing Boy, kills rattlesnakes on the lawn by setting them aflame with gasoline as they slither toward their holes, a striking image in a poem rife with destructive sexuality. Warren had experienced a similar setting himself when he established a Nevada residence before his divorce from his first wife in 1951 (Blotner 268–69). Although he would have many later sojourns in the West, this one is suggested by the time elapsed since the persona's visit, time measured in age and death as his "host's twin baby daughters . . . are, // Long since, dead" (292–93). The immediate occasion of the poem may have been his ex-wife Cinina's untimely death in 1969 just a few years before the poem was written. Warren's concluding section becomes a grim catalog of the girls lost to death, their father to despair over their mother's serial infidelities, and Laughing Boy to prison for a drunken murder. Yet Warren's persona still ponders the high price paid in life for the wisdom that Erikson discovers in age: "What was *is* is now *was.* But / Is *was* but a word for wisdom, its price?" (293). This psychological conundrum will become the epigraph for Warren's next gathering of his poetry, *Can I See Arcturus From Where I Stand? Poems 1975,* which accompanies the 1975 edition of the *Selected Poems.* It could make as good an epigraph for the two following selections of *Or Else*—XI, "Homage to Theodore Dreiser," a poem that first appeared in Warren's critical volume of the same title in 1971, and XII, "Flaubert in Egypt," a narrative of another writer's nineteenth-century sojourn into the Orient of imagination. Although both are interesting works, neither of these poetic biographies is directly concerned with age-work in the manner of "Rattlesnake Country," and they need not concern us here.[7]

6

"Interjection #5: Solipsism and Theology" ends this gathering of three long narratives concerned with flawed writers and effects a transition to another grouping concerned with Warren's familial memories, several of which were considered above—XIII, "The True Nature of Time"; XIV, "Vision Under the October Mountain: A Love Poem"; and XV, "Stargazing." In turn, *"Interjection #6: What You Sometimes Feel on Your Face at Night"* marks another transition to a yoking of the topical "News Photo" (XVI) with two other poems about family addressed above: XVII, "Little Boy and Lost Shoe," and XVIII, "Composition in Gold and Red-Gold." Next, *"Interjection #7: Remarks of Soul to Body,"* in this case an aging one, introduces three poems concerned with dead parents and friends—XIX, "There's a Grandfather's Clock in the Hall"; XX, "Reading Late at Night, Thermometer Falling"; and XXI, "Folly on Royal Street before the Raw Face of God." The last of these three concerns Warren's days in New Orleans during the 1930s, carousing with his young friends "C. and M.," both now lost to him, the first to death and the other to the depression of age (Blotner 548, n. 19).

The other pair of texts, however, forms an even more significantly personal intertextuality; "There's a Grandfather's Clock in the Hall" is concerned with Warren's memories of his dead mother and "Reading Late at Night, Thermometer Falling" with those of his dead father. The grandfather's clock in the initial title announces another variation on the theme of time closely linked to imagery of age and death.

This patriarchal timepiece represents the regular, inevitable progression of the years, of course, but it also suggests timeless continuities across time in the passage of the generations. So in the interstices of "no-Time" between the convulsive movements of the old clock's minute hand, the persona relives his life from childhood to maturity to decline, though stated here in the second person as is so often the case in the later poems (309). First "you are a child again," then boy, man, and elder (309). From age, you are transported to your mother's wedding, an event you could have attended only if she were not the virgin you claim her to be. Most of this poem, however, is concerned with your mother's deathbed scene, again projected in second person—"she is asking if it is a / new suit that you are wearing" (310). We know from his biography that these were his mother's last words to Warren, and additional details in the poem also appear in other accounts of Ruth Warren's demise (Blotner 120–22). Her dentures rest in a glass on the bedside table, as "With gum-flabby lips" she asks "that question [that] makes your heart hurt" with its "murderous triviality" at the same time you wonder if you "will ever have to wear false teeth" (310). In recognition of the existential ironies inherent in these details that once seemed inconsequential, Warren ends his poem with a striking philosophical formulation, "Time thrusts through the time of no-Time" (310).

The ultimate truth of Warren's balancing of time with "no-Time" is demonstrated again in the following selection, Poem XX, "Reading Late at Night, Thermometer Falling." His son images Robert Franklin Warren at about the age he himself now has achieved. The father's later life was made lonely by his wife's early death in 1931, however, and further diminished by his personal bankruptcy during the Depression. Warren guiltily pictures him, living on as he did to age eighty-five in a dreary "old folks" home, "blanket / Over knees, woolly gray bathrobe over shoulders, handkerchief / On great bald skull spread, glasses / Low on big nose, sits" (310). Under a "bare hundred-watt bulb that glares / Like truth," the father reads at a book propped in his lap (310). Although the persona is unable to discern its title, he cites a list of possibilities that suggest both his father's and his own historical, classical, psychological, and legal patrimonies.

> Hume's *History of England,* Roosevelt's
> *Winning of the West,* a Greek reader,
> Now Greek to him and held in his hands like a prayer, or
> Some college text book, or Freud on dreams, abandoned
> By one of the children. Or, even,
> Coke or Blackstone, books forbidding and blackbound . . . (311)

As in the earlier "Mortmain" sequence from *You, Emperors, and Others* (1960) that pictured his father's deathbed scene, the old man's stoic endurance of age and illness is recalled and admired; perhaps it is portrayed more realistically here as the poet approaches the ills and pains of later life himself: "A prostate big as a horse-apple. Cancer, of course" (314). Ironically enough, it would be the same type of cancer that would also test Warren's heritage of stoicism in the days before his own death two decades later.

The Freudian reading of dreams in this poem recalls Poem V, "I Am Dreaming of a White Christmas: The Natural History of a Vision," and the present poem also conflates past, present, and future through its dreamlike imagery. The ominous books of law evoke a memory from his personal past when Warren remembers finding "an old photograph" (311), dated "1890" (312), of his father as a law student, posed with a hand on his textbooks, "eyes / Lifted into space. // And into the future" (311). That future never was to be, and his father tore up the rediscovered portrait to cast it "Into the fire" (312). The father's poetic ambitions came to a similar fate: "Later, I found the poems. Not good," in the view of a more accomplished poet (312). Yet the writer reminds us in his own poem's philosophical conclusion that "Man lives by images" (312). His father's future is recast in the present image of another old man's winter night, recalling Frost's poem of that title, or into that of his "Drouth-night of August and the horned insect booming / At the window-screen," in the son's memory of the past (312).

The most significant burden of all these accreted images is discovered in both the father's and the son's life reviews. Warren recalls his father saying "I've failed in a lot of things," but from the vantage of his "own ignorance and failures" the persona tells the old man's shade that he has "forgiven you all your virtues" (313). Rather than end with this puzzling thematic summary, however, Warren concludes his homage to his father with a strikingly heroic metaphor. Time past is like a glacier that moves "so imperceptibly" that we are startled when it reveals in its "ice-screen" a great creature of "preternatural height" and of "magisterial gaze" (315). Although Warren's sublime imagery could suggest literary fathers such as John Crowe Ransom, T. S. Eliot, or Robert Frost, it invokes most directly his literal father, and Warren thus seems to echo Erikson's observation that the transcendence of age "means a different love of one's parents, free of the wish that they should have been different, and an acceptance of the fact that one's life is one's own responsibility" (*Identity* 104).

7

After the melancholy memories of untroubled youth and young friends lost to time, age, and death in XXI, "Folly on Royal Street before the Raw Face of God," *"Interjection #8: Or, Sometimes, Night,"* introduces the final gathering of three poems essaying the possibilities of Tornstam's psychological transcendence—XXII, "Sunset Walk in Thaw-Time in Vermont"; XXIII, "Birth of Love"; and XXIV, "A Problem in Spatial Composition." This final interjection reacts to the preceding gathering with a countering assertion of "The unsleeping principle of delight" discovered even in age in "the apple's rondure," "A girl's thigh," "The flushed dawn cumulus," "the breaker's crest," or "The lone snow-flake dance" at "unlikely moments . . . by day or, sometimes, night" (317). The four numbered parts of "Sunset Walk in Thaw-Time in Vermont" then illustrate this principle in a number of natural images gathered on an afternoon's forest walk near Warren's rural retreat in the spring of 1973 (Blotner 548, n. 19).

As happens so often in Frost's poems, such as "Dust of Snow" (1916), Warren's persona is apprehended by meaning at a moment of transition—here tripled in impact by the time of day, of year, and of life. Although it is the beginning of spring, a "great partridge cock" shakes down "the snow from / Black spruce boughs," its shadow "black against flame-red" of sunset (317). Once again, Warren's persona enters the "dark cave of / No-Time" to inquire "Where / Have the years gone?" (318). His central symbol for the flow of time is a neighboring stream—"thaw-flooding" now "In the deep certainty of its joy"—remembered and then projected again in both memory and prospect of summer's "Shadow-shimmered and deep-glinting liquidity" in the third part of the poem (318). After considering the symbolism of this New England stream both in winter and in summer, Warren compares it to his own past and present so that he finally is inspired to ask what he has learned in the seasonal currents of his own life.

> To be made worthy of my human failures and folly, and
> Worthy of my human ignorance and anguish, and of
> What soul-stillness may be achieved as I
> Stand here with the cold exhalation of snow
> Coiling high as my knees. (318)

This "folly" recalls the title of Warren's earlier poem set in the warmer spring on Royal Street as well as other poems listing his human failures in his relations with friends and family, or with parents and children. The peace that Warren does achieve here is possessed by a deathly stillness, as if the last breath of the expiring snow curls about him like a spirit. Even as he contemplates his "ignorance and anguish" Warren's persona realizes at some level of consciousness that on the eastern slopes of these mountains "darkness coagulates," sublimely, in the "massive geometry" of ice (319).

Between the first and the fourth parts of his poem, Warren has shifted the balance of image and idea, so that the final part becomes a sort of riddle of time. Thus Warren imagines his own son a half century hence "in thaw-season, at dusk, standing / At woodside and staring / Red-westward, with the sound of moving water / In his ears," and wonders "what / Blessing should I ask for him?" (319). The answer is complicated enough to compel several rereadings, but Warren's ultimate benediction seems to be that his son would bless his own boy on into the future much as the father figure does here. Warren's concluding stanza returns to the sublime themes of time and mortality, with a very carefully parsed trust in transcendence: "For what blessing may a man hope for but / An immortality in / The loving vigilance of death?" (319). Once again, Warren finds sublime diction for his poetic purposes in "vigilance," with its dual suggestions of the night watch over the dead as a religious rite and of the philosophical preoccupation with death poised in its universal equilibrium against life.

Poem XXIII, "Birth of Love," proves the most straightforward of the several love poems presented in *Or Else* and, therefore, the most satisfying of them. This is not to deny the poem's intellectual complexity, as at several points its cerebral twists threaten its very real emotions. Even Warren's title proves a complicated pun. Although at first it seems to refer just to the renascence of the persona's love for his wife after a twilight swim, he also connects it to the births of the couple's children, while his delight in seeing "The first star pulse into being" in the summer dark also suggests the title of Botticelli's masterpiece "The Birth of Venus" (319). This brief narrative seems located at the swimming pond behind the Warren family's rural home in Vermont. As the opening line indicates, "Season late, day late, sun just down," their immersion must be the last swim of the day and perhaps of the summer, so the prospects of evening and autumn raise all the themes of age-work—time, age, death, and memory (319). From the darkening pool, she "Rises," so that "Against / The new-curdling night" her "nakedness / Glimmers" (319). Yet "Motionless in the gunmetal water," he perceives "all / History dissolving from him" as he "Sees // The body that is marked by his use, and Time's" (319). Despite the changes wrought by age, "This moment is non-sequential and absolute," so that it "Subsumes all other, and sequential, moments" (320). If in emotional terms, this rebirth of love seems timeless and unending; then intellectually Warren's persona, still "Suspended in his darkling medium," wishes, "if only / He had such strength," to guard her from the rising of the years—from time and age, as well as from death. Left alone with the newborn evening star, the poet cannot say with certainty "what promise it makes to him," though it may be one of transcendence beyond time (320).

The closing poem of Warren's collection, XXIV, "A Problem in Spatial Composition," proves an apt choice in several senses. Most obvious are the reiterations of place and time, of image and theme from the poems that have preceded it, particularly the first two in this last gathering of three. Warren's sublime poem presents a tripartite vision framed by his Vermont study's window on a late summer evening. In the first part, we learn that "Over the green interstices and shambling glory, yet bright, of forest, / Distance flees westward, the sun low" (321). Warren then suggests the meaning of such departures: "What we know, we know," that "pure, pure and forever, the sky / Upward is" (320). Incremental repetition reinforces theme, as the window "by interruption, // Confirms what the heart knows: *beyond* is *forever*" (321). In other words, the beauty of nature, if ever changing in its particulars, is ever infinite in its totality, reminding its aging observer that he is not, especially now in the evening of his days. Then in the second part, Warren turns this image from nature into a work of art, one at once visual and verbal; in its revelation of nature, the window both frames a picture and fixes it as a scene. Like a nineteenth-century landscapist, the poet foregrounds "the stub / Of a great tree, gaunt-blasted and black," from which "A single / Arm jags upward, higher goes," from the artist's "perspective" even higher than the mountain (321). In Warren's vision, this arm "Stabs," pointed like some physical or perhaps metaphysical extension of his selfhood, "at the infinite saffron of sky" (321). At this moment of artistic transcendence, the composition framed by the window is completed by one of Warren's symbolic hawks. The bird "glides, / In the pellucid ease of thought" to perch atop "The bough's sharp black and skinny jag skyward" (321–22). The concluding third part becomes a coda consisting of one simple sentence in a single tetrameter line, "The hawk, in an eye blink, is gone," as if into the eternity of the sublime (322).

Warren's choice of "A Problem in Spatial Composition" proves appropriate for his concluding selection in a structural sense as well, as the poetic form of *Or Else* as *Poem/Poems 1968–1974* is really the product of an extended spatial composition. In his subtitle, Warren affirms that his twenty-four poems completed over this six-year span may be read together as a single unified poem within his new ordering. However, Warren's addition of eight selections from his two previous collections demonstrates that this union is accomplished by his emphasis on the pervasive themes of time, age, death, and memory. These themes and these structures also are perceived in Warren's use of eight poetic interjections, including two written specifically for this volume, to counterpoint his thematic groupings of lyric and narrative poems. Unlike most other critics of his poetry, I believe that Robert Penn Warren's greatest period of poetry begins with the initial age-work and life review of *Or Else* in 1974 and that this concluding phase is transformed by his quest for personal and artistic integrity, wisdom, and sublimity in this and the succeeding collections that culminate in 1985 with his final, self-edited *Selected Poems* and its new section significantly titled *Altitudes and Extensions.* However, Warren's gradual movement through age-work and life review toward transcendence also can be discerned in the question asked in the title of his next gathering of poetry, this one for his *Selected Poems* in 1975—*Can I See Arcturus From Where I Stand?*

2

Lyric and Logic

Can I See Arcturus From Where I Stand? Poems 1975

> . . . will you be with me when
> I arrive and leave my own cart of junk
> Unfended from the storm of starlight and
> The howl, like wind, of the world's monstrous blessedness,
> To enter, by a bare field, a shack unlit?
>
> —"Old Nigger on One-Mule Cart Encountered Late at Night When Driving Home From Party in the Back Country"

1

In 1976, the third of the four editions of Warren's *Selected Poems* opens with a gathering of his most recent work, the ten *Poems 1975* of his subtitle; his overall title for this grouping is the question posed by the last line of the book's final poem, *Can I See Arcturus From Where I Stand?* As Warren's personal and professional life during his early seventies might suggest, this new poetry is as much focused by age-work and life review as was *Or Else,* and like his preceding collection this one considers the possibilities of psychological transcendence in several of its sublime selections. In 1974, Warren's early mentor John Crowe Ransom died at the age of eighty-six, and Warren attended his memorial that fall along with other surviving Fugitive/Agrarians. Later that year, Warren not only excused himself from the gathering of the aging Vanderbilt group for Allen Tate's seventy-fifth birthday celebration, but he even found himself unable to summon up a celebratory poem for an old friend who was expiring slowly from emphysema (Blotner 420). As he himself turned seventy in 1975, Warren suffered a recurrence of earlier health problems, especially physical and psychological difficulties concerning sight. With his wife's vision worsening each year, the couple came to fear that blindness would overtake them both (Blotner 424–25).[1]

Complementing the important poetry written in his early seventies, Warren also published major works in prose, in particular an elaboration of his earlier Jefferson lectures from 1974 as *Democracy and Poetry* in 1975 and his tenth and final novel, *A Place to Come To,* in 1977. By their very nature, both books also prove redolent of age-work, life review, and transcendence, thus providing significant parallels with Warren's poetry from the same period. His naming as the annual Jefferson Lecturer by the National Endowment for the Humanities in 1976 provided Warren an occasion for a public discourse on the American experience during the national Bicentennial year. The first section of *Democracy and Poetry,* "America and the Diminished Self," traces the "diagnostic" function of American "poetry," which Warren discusses as literary "art in general," in revealing the decline of an individuated American "self," defined as "the felt principle of significant unity" (*Democracy* 3, 4). In "Poetry and Selfhood," the second section of *Democracy and Poetry,* Warren comments on the "therapeutic" role of poetry to cure the "decay" of American selfhood diagnosed in the first part (*Democracy* 42). Warren's imagery of diagnosis and therapy proves decidedly more psychological than historical, however, and its theoretical basis seems neo-Freudian in general and Jungian in particular (*Democracy* 65, 69). Warren accomplishes his purposes in *Democracy and Poetry* in a life review of the national psyche as revealed through American literature in his first section; then in his second section Warren rejects post-Watergate despair and asserts American selfhood in terms of individual and national transcendence.[2]

Although it is perhaps Warren's most autobiographical fiction, his last novel, *A Place to Come To,* is not an effort in the style of Thomas Wolfe's long books. Warren's final effort in the genre seems more in the mode of Theodore Dreiser's novels wherein the protagonists all project some deeply held element of their creator's personal psychology rather than the biographical details of its actual incarnation within the social world. Warren's conclusion about Dreiser in his 1971 study of the naturalistic novelist, that "in the deepest sense, Dreiser's only story was always to be that of himself," might be made about Warren's own works as well (*Homage* 19–20). Warren's choice of Dreiser as a critical subject at the later stages of his career indicates not just his widening literary tastes, but his evolving fascination with the creative possibilities of biography and autobiography in terms of his fiction and poetry as well as of his criticism. Indeed, Warren's critical engagement with Dreiser while writing his own final novel helps make it the best of his later fictions in terms of the book's realistic treatment of its characters' romantic visions of themselves.

Warren's first-person point of view in *A Place to Come To* also becomes another source of the novel's strength in comparison to the several that had directly preceded it. His protagonist, Jediah Tewksbury, narrates the progress of his personal development over a half century from his youth in a small Alabama textile town during the Depression, through his education in Chicago, a wartime sojourn in Italy, a postwar teaching stint in Nashville, and a distinguished professorship in Chicago once more. Like Jack Burden in *All the King's Men,* however, Jed Tewksbury is another lost soul seeking meaning and order in the modern wasteland through the search for a true father figure, the surrogates for whom most often turn out to be self-destructive frauds. Again like several others of Warren's fictive protagonists, Jed must become his own father. This quest culminates in his early sixties when he is reunited with his estranged son from his failed second marriage and with his widowed stepfather from his mother's second marriage. In other words, the narrative proves to be Jed's life review at the outset of his age-work, an *Altersroman* or novel of age.[3]

Although Warren's protagonist in *A Place to Come To* becomes a distinguished Dante scholar in professional terms, it is Dante's mentor Virgil who provides him with a personal model of heroic selfhood in the character of Aeneas, who sought a new order for his life accompanied by his son, Ascanius, and bearing the burden of his father, Anchises. Lacking a true father, Jed appropriates literary figures who provide narratives of acceptance, again much as Warren himself discovered through his classicism. Traveling to his first academic job at the opening of book 2, Jed imagines himself in distinctly Virgilian terms: "Well, when I came to Nashville, my cloud was a ramshackle bar car, and if my progress was presided over by a Goddess of Love, she was embodied in the poor, drunken, courageous female with the clanging charm bracelet and the bum gam" (*Place* 125). Jed's Nashville experiences will turn out to be frustrating and inconclusive, much like Aeneas's sojourn in Carthage, Warren's return to teach at Vanderbilt during the 1930s, or Dreiser's early career in Chicago, imaged by Warren in his earlier poem "Homage to Theodore Dreiser" through similar classical references. Warren, like Dreiser, uses the heroic patterns of the ancient epic to imagine for his protagonist, and perhaps for himself, a life story that will replicate the classical "Matter of Troy" in a recreation of the modern wasteland that Jed names the "Matter of Nashville."

2

As its title implies, *Can I See Arcturus From Where I Stand? Poems 1975* also is involved with such classical and heroic matters, especially personal integrity and transcendence as aspects of age-work and life review. Arcturus is the ancient name for the fourth brightest star in the heavens; the word itself combines the Greek roots *arktos* and *ouros,* or bear and guard, from the star's position beside the constellation known from classical times as Ursa Major. This reference combines Warren's interests in the classics and in astronomy, and both quite often become sources of ideas and images for his poetry. Classical references often enhance his poems, and stars often enrich his imagery, as we have seen in several poems collected in *Or Else.* In citing his star by its classical name, however, Warren unites both interests in a manner unique to his poetic canon (Brooks, "Episode," 557). Again, Warren's title is also the last line of his final selection, thus doubling the import of Arcturus as both image and symbol.

Other readers have discovered possible literary sources for Warren's use of Arcturus and thus have advanced related interpretations of the star as symbol. Warren's friend and colleague Cleanth Brooks, for example, suggests that the poet might have recalled the star's name from the Bible. This always formidable critic points out that Arcturus is referenced twice in the *Book of Job* (9:9, 38:32), though he notes considerable disagreement among biblical scholars about the exactness of these references ("Episode" 558–59). In any case, Brooks concludes that Warren echoes Job, in trying "to discover some human meaning in a universe that is at once beautiful, terrifying, almost infinitely remote, and awesomely majestic" ("Episode" 559). Randolph Paul Runyon has proposed a possible classical source in Sophocles' *Oedipus* (line 1137), where the appearance of the star as a marker of time is recalled during the revelation of the hero's true parentage (*Ghostly* 186). Runyon also uses this reference to support his Oedipal reading of the poet's career and canon: "Could this be what Warren means—

that one can see Arcturus when one is about to discover the truth about what one has done to one's parents?" (*Ghostly* 186).

Given the breadth of Warren's reading and the depth of his learning, both of these sources for Arcturus are plausible, and, as we have seen, the poet at this stage of life and work is probing his personal relation to the universe, past and present. However, I will propose a differing source for Warren's reference, David Lindsay's *Voyage to Arcturus* (1920), a work that projects themes of age-work, life review, and possible transcendence and thus informs Warren's gathering of recent poems including its final selection. Although Lindsay's book is described most often as a science-fiction novel, one that has stayed in print since its initial appearance thanks to its cult status, it is better regarded as an allegorical fantasy that employs some generic conventions of science fiction to question the nature and meaning of the universe by means of an epic narrative tracing a heroic quest. The protagonist, Maskull, is an everyman transported by Krag, a mysterious trickster figure, to an imaginary planet of Arcturus named Tormance, where the questing hero must discover the secrets of the godlike Crystalman by stealing the sacred fire from the Muspel tower. The intricacies of Lindsay's action and of his allegory are difficult even to summarize, while their meanings are virtually impossible to interpret with any degree of certainty—at least in my view.

Yet the omnivorous reader and critic Harold Bloom describes *Voyage to Arcturus* as his "personal favorite among modern fantasies" because it is "the most sublime and spiritually terrifying death-march in all of fantastic literature, in some respects even overgoing sinister journeys from Dante on to Browning's *Childe Roland to the Dark Tower Came*" (*Agon* 200). Bloom was so taken with Lindsay's book, in fact, that it inspired his only work of fiction, a narrative "sequel" entitled *The Flight to Lucifer* (1980); however, Bloom the critic has since expressed his dissatisfaction with his only creative effort. As one of Warren's friends and colleagues at Yale, Bloom also provides a connection between the poet and *Voyage to Arcturus.* After his own discovery of this underground classic, Bloom enthusiastically proclaimed Lindsay's genius to all who would listen. In answer to a query of mine, he replied, "I remember discussing the Lindsay novel with Red Warren, but can't recall whether he actually went on to read it" (Bloom, e-mail). Although Warren may not have read *Voyage to Arcturus,* he knew enough about the book from Bloom's discussion of it to associate the name of the star with the most ancient of human quests, that of understanding the individual human being's place within the universe.

This source for Warren's title also suggests the most significant aspects of age-work, life review, and transcendence. Although starlight illumines Warren's poetry from his first undergraduate efforts forward, it becomes ever brighter in his later poems. At age seventy, Warren, when he asks in the title of his new gathering of poems *Can I See Arcturus From Where I Stand?* really wonders if he has progressed far enough in the course of his own journey in time to glimpse something of its eternal consequence as represented by his spatial relation to that distant star. In particular, Warren often triangulates his own human position with those of the heavenly bodies and those of the physical presences of earthbound others who surround him. We have seen such triangulation in earlier poems such as "Stargazing" from *Or Else,* but it becomes an ever more prominent feature of Warren's later poetry, perhaps another aspect of his *Alterstil,* or late style. Such triangulation and other aspects of his later craft become most notable in the final poem of the *Arcturus* gathering, but they also illuminate the conclusion of Warren's lifelong questing as found in the nine preceding pieces

3

Compared to the complex structuring of *Or Else,* the organization of *Can I See Arcturus From Where I Stand? Poems 1975* appears rather straightforward, at least at first glance. The ten unnumbered selections seem to proceed directly toward their conclusion in its single long poem. This capstone piece, "Old Nigger on One-Mule Cart Encountered Late at Night When Driving Home From Party in the Back Country," is differentiated from the other poems in both its elongated title and its extensive text. The use of the epithet "Nigger" in both has made the poem something of a crux in the critical consideration of Warren and race. As important as this element of the poet's work proves for contemporary readers and critics, race is not my primary interest here, so I will postpone my discussion of it to the conclusion of this chapter. In my analysis, I will contend that Warren's poem combines age-work, autobiography, and transcendence as parts of

Warren's quest for universal human meaning. Warren's "One-Mule Cart" (to simplify its title and postpone racial discussion) rolls inexorably from his past to his present to his future—from the Deep South of his Louisiana years, to the New England of his retirement, and to a snow-filled forest symbolic of what he calls in his introduction to the volume "the unpredictable future" of death (Burt 724).

Careful reading of *Can I See Arcturus From Where I Stand?* also reveals that Warren's first nine selections all anticipate the predominant themes of his "One-Mule Cart," though not in any simple, progressive order. Other readers have discussed varied aspects of the intertextualities among these ten poems. In an article on Warren's late poetry, Valerie M. Morrison discusses a hieroglyphic pattern in which "the movement of Warren's poetry in *Arcturus* approaches a loop or a circle, not an interwoven thread" (132). As he does with all the collections, Randolph Runyon discovers "persistent sequential echoes" in the *Arcturus* gathering, though with "symmetrical echoes . . . linking the first poem with the last, the second with the next to last, and so forth" (*Ghostly* 176). Victor Strandberg astutely observes of the gathering, "the ten poems subserve that collective title in their recurring reach toward transcendence ('Arcturus') from a generally postlapsarian environment" ('Where I Stand')" ("Robert Penn Warren" 436).

All of these approaches are plausible, but I believe Warren provides the best image of his method in "One-Mule Cart":

> In the lyrical logic and nightmare astuteness that
> Is God's name, by what magnet, I demand,
> Are the iron and out-flung filings of our lives, on a sheet of paper,
> blind-blank as Time, snapped into a polarized pattern. (335)

The source of Warren's conceit is an act of recollection in itself, as it is derived from a traditional schoolroom experiment. Iron filings on a sheet of paper are polarized by a bar magnet beneath it to demonstrate the North/South polarity of the earth's magnetic field. The polar magnetism Warren suggests here seems more psychological than physical, however, perhaps somewhat akin to the hibernal trance in "Time as Hypnosis" from *Or Else*. Such a reading also fits the context of "One-Mule Cart" where on a wintry midnight Warren's persona has "risen / In darkness" to confront his past and his future, both imaged with "nightmare astuteness" (334, 335). Warren's metaphorical iron filings represent the psychic detritus of a long lifetime, the bits of disparate memories that cohere momentarily in his dreams and visions. Significantly, these black specks also reveal their "lyrical logic" on "A sheet of paper, blind-blank," suggesting both the Lockean *tabula rasa* of human consciousness and the empty page the poet must fill with the typographical symbols of his words and lines (335). "One-Mule Cart" becomes another poem about writing poetry, one in which Warren reveals his own evolution as person and as poet, which we will see in the analysis below.

On the opening page of *Can I See Arcturus From Where I Stand? Poems 1975*, Warren's overriding pattern of intertextuality is evident, not just in the title itself, but in its epigraph, "*Is* was *but a word for wisdom, its price?*" a question first asked in "Rattlesnake Country" from *Or Else* (323). Warren's allusion recalls not only the age-work of the preceding volume but the elements of his own life review concerning the failure of his first marriage that play against his dedication of *Selected Poems 1923–1975* to "Eleanor, Rosanna, and Gabriel," his second wife and their two children. Before asking the question reiterated in his epigraph to *Can I See Arcturus From Where I Stand?* Warren had declared "What was *is* is now *was*" in "Rattlesnake Country" (293). Thus Warren suggests, somewhat like Erikson, that "Only in old age can true wisdom develop in those so 'gifted,'" by way of their life experience (*Dialogue* 54). In his *Arcturus* sequence, especially in the sublime "One-Mule Cart," Warren continues his quest for the psychological integrity that Erikson suggests, through confrontation of his personal story that Butler's life review requires, in order to achieve the transcendence of age that Tornstam theorizes.

As often is the case with his gatherings of poems for book publication, in *Can I See Arcturus From Where I Stand?* Warren recreates poetic tensions between the universal and the personal, the logical and the emotional, as well as the lyrical and the narrative—though in less complicated patterns than he had essayed in *Or Else*. "One-Mule Cart" takes the concluding position in the grouping of ten as it proves the predominant piece in terms of both size and significance. Although most critics consider "One-Mule Cart" the heart of the gathering, Warren kept four of the initial nine pieces for his next and last *Selected Poems* a decade later. Interestingly enough, these four include two of the more obvious pairings from the 1975 gathering—"A Way to Love God" and "Evening Hawk," its first and second selections, as well as "Paradox" and "Midnight Outcry," its fifth and sixth poems. Both pairs demonstrate the tensions of the universal and the personal as well as of the logical and the emotional. Between these two pairs, the third poem, "Loss, of Perhaps Love, in Our World of Contingency," becomes another universalized statement of the human dilemmas that are then personalized in the fourth poem, "Answer to Prayer." The seventh and eighth selections, "Trying to Tell You Something" and "Brotherhood in Pain" both present lyrical exclamations that are echoed as narratives in the ninth and tenth pieces, "Season Opens on Wild Boar in Chianti" and "One-Mule Cart." Although "One-Mule Cart" will remain our major focus, we need to trace the notable achievements of the preceding nine pieces in order to fully comprehend its significance by fully exploring all of these varied thematic tensions.

4

The overarching opposition of Warren's new gathering, however, exists between the intellectual and rational matters associated with the word "logic" and the lyrical and emotional ones represented by the word "love." The opening selection announces one pole of this tension in its title, "A Way to Love God," and reiterates it in the concluding line, "That is a way to love God" (325). Between this beginning and ending, Warren seems to define this divine way to love in the harsh, intellectual terms of his Modernist poetry from the 1930s and 1940s—in hard lines such as "Boot heels, like history being born, on cobbles bang" (325). The line that follows in a stanza comprising a single sentence proves the pivot of the poem: "Everything seems an echo of something else" (325). This echoing resonates not only within the poem and this gathering, as Randolph Paul Runyon deftly demonstrates in a chapter on the *Arcturus* poems in his *Ghostly Parallels*, but, in my own view, between Warren's earlier and later poetry.

In the thirty-seven metrically attenuated lines of "A Way to Love God," Warren marshals a number of complex images to illustrate the Platonic thesis announced in the first of them: "Here is the shadow of truth, for only the shadow is true" (325). These shadows from Plato's cave of human consciousness include both the natural world—oceans and mountains, stars and moon, sheep and fish—as well as human history—a dying father, a cruel dictator, a decapitated queen. All of this imagery is distanced further by Warren's use of the second and third persons in addition to the first. For example, in a complex image close to age-work and life review, Warren tells us that " your father's death rattle / Provides all biographical data required for the *Who's Who* of the dead" (325). Warren was listed by *Who's Who in America,* of course, and its annual updating ritual must have reminded him that at some time in the ever-nearing future the parenthesis presenting his life span as (1905–) would be closed with the date of his death. Warren also compares the uncomprehending eyes of sheep he has seen huddling in the misty dark of the historically contested Saarland to those "of a scholar who has lost faith in his calling," perhaps like some of his lifelong colleagues in the decline of their age. In any case, the placid incomprehension of motionless sheep, fat fish, and despairing men provides at least "One Way to Love God," the earlier title used for the poem's initial publication in *Yale Review.*

The next poem in the new gathering, "Evening Hawk," pairs with "A Way to Love God" in several philosophical and personal contrasts as Warren evokes one of his signature hawks to present an alternate vision, and by implication another, better way to love the world—if not God. Although many scholars have remarked the persistence of Warren's hawk images, his Yale colleague Harold Bloom provides a definitive reading of them in "Sunset Hawk: Warren's Poetry and Tradition" (1984). Bloom correctly cites Warren's "Evening Hawk" as "surely one of his dozen or so lyric masterpieces, a culmination of forty years of his art" ("Sunset" 70). Most readers agree with this high praise; appropriately enough, "Evening Hawk" was read aloud by the Robert Penn Warren Circle at sunset in his birthplace in Guthrie, Kentucky, on his centennial birthday, April 24, 2005, and sequentially at dusk in other places significant to his life around the globe. Bloom also implies that the reason for its sublime accomplishment lies in Warren's fusion of High Modernist intellection and irony from his earlier poetry and Postmodern autobiography and emotion more typical of his later poems. When, after a five-line stanza of introduction, "The hawk comes," like a grim reaper;

> His wing
> Scythes down another day, his motion
> Is that of the honed steel edge, we hear
> The crashless fall of stalks of Time. (326)

Certainly, such is the stuff of age-work, as the hawk's cyclic motion sweeps off more than just another day or dollar. In the light of this recognition, "The head of each stalk is heavy with the gold of our error" (326). As a creature of nature, the hawk "knows neither Time nor error," so that his eyes—unlike those of sheep, fish, or scholars in "A Way to Love God"—are "unforgiving," finally, while "His wisdom / Is ancient, too, and immense" (326). Does this hawk's darkling descent derive from a remembered southern evening from the poet's youth? Warren does not tell us, and his image may spring from his northern experiences, his European sojourns, or even his western trips. Hawks persist as significant symbols in Warren's work beginning with his first published story, "Prime Leaf" (1930), his initial study of his own patria in the Black Patch. In Warren's later poetry of age-work and autobiography, his ongoing poetic reiteration of these creatures soaring above the earth is defined by their preternatural vision, a symbolism that surely rings with multiple tensions and ironies since as his physical eyesight declined, his psychological insight developed.

Warren balances the third selection within the *Arcturus* poems, "Loss, of Perhaps Love, in Our World of Contingency," with the fourth, "Answer to Prayer," in contrasts of the intellectual and the emotional, the universal and the personal, as well as the lyrical and the narrative. The first poem's opening lines project the most important of these tensions, referencing the love mentioned in his title by means of the pronoun "it" and then contrasting the primal emotion with intellectual thought. "Think! Think hard. Try to remember / When last you had it. There's always // A logic to everything, and you are a part / Of everything, and your heart bleeds far // Beyond the outermost pulsar" (326). The reference to the far distant pulsar, or pulsating neutron star discovered by radio astronomy only a few years earlier in 1968, suggests the contingencies of time as well as of space and recalls the bright star named in the title of Warren's new gathering. Love is easy enough to overlook in the naturalistic world implied not just by these universal infinities but in finite images that include a mirrored face unrecognizable in age, an old tramp shuffling along the pavement, and violets buried under dead leaves and snowdrifts. Even if one recalls "The earliest thing you remember, the dapple // Of sunlight on the bathroom floor while your mother / Bathed you," it is hard to know if love existed even for that moment (327). Interestingly, the last image is Warren's own first memory, though his poetic persona universalizes it here by means of the second person (Blotner 9). In any case, the poetic persona reminds the reader that "We must learn to live in the world," no matter what our complicated human contingencies may be (326).

"Answer to Prayer" is subtitled "A Short Story That Could Be Longer," implying its narrative component as well as its personal and emotional import. Much as in "Loss, of Perhaps Love, in Our World of Contingency," Warren tells a story about a loss of love, or something like it, in "Answer to Prayer," but in contrast Warren's narration now is focused by a single autobiographical incident, one that again recalls the epigraph he adopted for his grouping of new poems from "Rattlesnake Country" from *Or Else*: "*Is was but a word for wisdom, its price?*" (293). As demonstrated in my preceding chapter, the earlier poem's western setting was derived from Warren's period of required Nevada residence in the early 1950s before his divorce. The incident recalled in "Answer to Prayer" would have occurred a few years earlier during the dissolution of his marriage to Cinina while Warren was teaching at the University of Minnesota. Although Warren names neither time nor place, his biographer readily identifies them, and many details of the narrative support such a reading (Blotner 422). Briefly retold, an alienated couple are moving tensely through the dark and snow of a winter evening, eventually toward dinner and bed, all the while hoping that "sincerity could be bought by pain," when she rushes into what seems to be a Catholic church to say a prayer for his happiness (327). At the moment that her impulse occurred in time, Warren's poetic persona believes the woman's act to be "sentimental idiocy," but through his newly discovered perspective of "was" he now realizes that her prayer marked an ironically "savage peripeteia" in both their lives (327, 328).

> Her prayer, yes, was answered, for in spite of my meager desert,
> Of a sudden, life—it was bingo! was bells and all ringing like mad,
> Lights flashing, fruit spinning, the machine spurting dollars like
>   dirt—
> Nevada dollars, that is—but all just a metaphor for the luck I now
>   had. (328)

This gaudy imagery is drawn from the gaming casinos Warren had visited in Reno, of course, but the earlier evocation of the "peripeteia," the Aristotelian turning point in a Greek tragedy along the naturalistic suggestion of "the machine spurting dollars like dirt" raise uneasy feelings that question whether all his "luck" is really much more than mere contingency after all (328).

The fifth poem in the *Arcturus* gathering suggests another ancient philosopher, for the "Paradox" of its title is the best known of Zeno's paradoxical formulations and another indication of Warren's classical interests. However, "Paradox" and "Midnight Outcry," the short narrative paired with it as the sixth selection, also present dual aspects of Warren's second marriage that contrast in turn with the failure of his first as revealed in "Answer to Prayer." The learned trope that organizes the four intricately rhyming quintain stanzas of "Paradox" also makes the poem less personal if more positive in its conclusions than "Answer to Prayer." Somewhat simply stated, Warren's poetic paradox places himself in a relation to Eleanor Clark that recalls that of Achilles and the tortoise in Zeno's paradoxical demonstration of change as an illusion. The philosopher hypothesized that if it seems Achilles will always overtake the tortoise in a foot race, despite the head start the hero gives his opponent, this result is never logically possible because the slower creature's initial lead will always persist in their very motion—that is the paradox. In Warren's "more complex / Version," the poetic persona first chases a dazzling beauty down a beach, "far away and long ago," but this "race you won" then suggests to him now "whatever shore reflects / Our flickering passage through the years" (329). In a biographical sense, the older Warren now realizes that the age difference between himself and his younger mate will exist no matter how close their psychological relationship becomes, so that she finally will outlast him in the unchanging race of life.

Although distanced from autobiographical reference by its third-person viewpoint, "Midnight Outcry" comes to represent an earlier stage of the marital relations between Warren and his younger wife. When summarized, the brief poem seems somewhat like one of Nathanial Hawthorne's stories that Warren publicly admired in his literary criticism. The husband is awakened in midnight by an outcry from his sleeping wife, a wrenching "*Oh!*" that "is so / Much deeper and darker than any love may redeem" (329). In the bright dawn of the next day, "his heart leaps in joy" as he watches her nurse their baby, until recalling the midnight's "echo of fate beyond faith or luck" (329). The poetic persona then carefully studies his smiling mate for some sign, "some logic, some white / Spore of the human condition that carries, / In whiteness, the dark need that only at night / Finds voice" (329). After pondering the seeming paradox of his wife's midday countenance and her midnight outcry, he can discover only "the terrible distance in love, and the pain" (329). Warren's closing lines echo the poetic narratives of another New England forebear, Robert Frost, in this persona's ultimate self-evasion, as he sits, "Smiling back at the sunlit smile, even while shrinking / From recall of the nocturnal timbre, and the dark wonder" (329).

"Trying to Tell You Something," the seventh poem of the *Arcturus* gathering, pairs with Warren's eighth selection, "Brotherhood in Pain," in both matter and form, but it also connects with the ninth poem, "Season Opens on Wild Boar in Chianti," as one of the two in the gathering with personal dedications. The first is "To Tinkum Brooks," the wife of Warren's longtime friend and colleague Cleanth Brooks, who is called here by her family nickname, while the second is "To Guerino and Ginevra Roberti," a younger couple who were befriended by the Warrens in Italy. Just as the dedications of these two poems span Warren's personal history, they also connect his American home with his foreign sojourns. Although the second-person "you," addressed in "Trying to Tell You Something" should not be identified directly with Mrs. Brooks, she was an aging friend of Warren's who could share his concern with mortality. For the "something" that the steel cables anchoring an ancient oak "sing" in the cold wind of a dark December night certainly suggests human transience (330). Like the strings of the Aeolian harp so dear to the Romantics, "They sing / Of truth, and its beauty" (330). The great-rooted oak is "Immense, older than Jamestown or God," and "In its fullness of years," the iron hoops and rods that support it contract in "a slow throb like pain" (330). "Brotherhood in Pain" then picks up these motifs as the world's objects feel a universal ache "in the obscene moment of birth," as much as in the moment of death implied in these paired poems (331). Finally, the death of the totemic animal hunted to his death in "Season Opens on Wild Boar in Chianti" transforms it to a new condition of "was" following the moiling kill; now the dead boar is "lashed to a pole slung from shoulders," its feet "point starward. . . . While eyes blank in wisdom stare hard" (332). Perhaps the creature's dead gaze plays on the import of Warren's epigraph from "Rattlesnake Country," "*Is* was *but a word for wisdom, its price?*" as death seems like the ultimate extension of "*was*" (323).

5

The tensions of matter and form, theme and image discovered in the first nine selections of the *Arcturus* gathering reappear in "Old Nigger on One-Mule Cart Encountered Late at Night When Driving Home From Party in the Back Country." The recovered narrative that the poetic persona reluctantly recalls is summarized in its omnibus title—including a drunken revel, a barely escaped collision between car and cart, and a loveless sexual encounter that all mar a hot night in the bayou country.[4] These materials, ones that Warren could as well have used in *All the King's Men,* are presented here in wasteland imagery reminiscent of his early poetry. The most memorable of these dreamlike, cinematic passages is the freeze-framed image of the older black man's startled reaction to the near catastrophe: "In black face, in black night, and man-mouth / Wide open, The shape of an *O,* for the scream / That does not come" (334).

This minstrel show exaggeration then reappears in the poetic persona's drunken nightmare "Floating in darkness above the bed the / Black face, eyes white-bulging, mouth shaped like an *O*" (334). This stereotype of his psychic double then had occasioned a sonnet intertextual with Wordsworth in form and theme, from which Warren now repeats the concluding couplet.

> One of those who gather wire and junk to use
> For purposes that we cannot peruse. (334)[5]

Yet when the poetic persona recalls all of these matters half a life later in the wintry North, evidently first in dream and then in memory, he creates something more like a meditative ode by imagining how the black cart man arrives at his darkened shack to conclude his night. The poem's concluding apostrophe reveals that his double's return is part of an eternal cycle, as time has resurrected the black, poor, aged, and now dead "other" of the poet's youth to become his "Brother, Rebuker, my Philosopher past all / Casuistry" (335).

Most important, a Frostian epiphany glimpsed through the icy window of his Vermont cabin marks not just a transition between his southern past and northern present but one between his life in time and timeless infinity.

> Have you ever,
> At night, stared into the snow-filled forest and felt
> The impulse to flee there? Enter there? Be
> There and plunge naked
> Through snow, through drifts floundering, white
> Into whiteness, among
> Spectral great beech-boles, birch whiteness, black jag
> Of shadow, black spruce-bulks, snow-shouldered, floundering
> Upward and toward the glacial assertion that
> The mountain is? (334–35)

This primal urge is determined by the same human impulses that motivated the reckless drinking, driving, and coupling recreated in the long-ago Louisiana of the poem's opening lines. At this juncture, however, it provides a transition to a more developed personal resolution. As Warren had observed in a critical essay three decades earlier, the final lines of Frost's best-known poem, "Stopping by Woods on a Snowy Evening," offer another evolution from negative to positive fulfillment of these primal human needs: "There will be beauty and peace at the end of the journey, in the terms of fulfillment of the promises, but that will be an earned beauty stemming from action" ("Themes" 290).

Warren's own promise as a matured husband and poet thus includes a sober judgment not just of his own earlier life and work but of the cultural and the literary traditions into which he was initiated as a youth. Despite the nay-sayings of some revisionist critics who cannot move past the negative connotations of Warren's recontextualized "Nigger" in both title and text, "One-Mule Cart" is a better indication of Warren's later racial reconciliations than his volumes of reportage and of cultural criticism *Segregation: The Inner Conflict of the South* (1956) and *Who Speaks for the Negro?* (1965). It is so precisely because of its greater fidelity to his own life experience and to his own best purposes as a writer of reminiscent and meditative poetry in his age. It proves particularly interesting to compare the title and the conclusion of *Who Speaks for the Negro?* with those of "Old Nigger," to use a more racially charged abbreviation of the poem's omnibus title. Warren's concluding self-interview in the earlier book is still halting and defensive, if apologetic and honest, while the final vision of his poem achieves the sublimity of truth, resolution, and transcendence.[6]

In the poem's last long verse paragraph the persona reflexively recognizes that even this psychological and poetic achievement, like all of his achievements and honors, is just another sort of trash to be left behind upon entering into the dark abode of death (335). Passing into this ultimate night, both men, black and white, finally will possess but one thing, "a name— / Like a shell, a dry flower, a worn stone, a toy—merely / A hard-won something" (335). In Jungian or Eriksonian terms, the name represents an individuated or integrated identity as a developed self, in Warren's terms a "small, sober, and inestimable / Glow, trophy of truth" (335). In its symbolic function, this talisman proves much like the glimmering star whose name provides the complex classical allusion for the title of this gathering and is then reiterated as the final line of its last and best poem, "Can I see Arcturus from where I stand?" (335). Robert Penn Warren was seventy years old when his penultimate *Selected Poems* was published in 1975, but his age-work and life review were just beginning to evolve into a quest for transcendence, as I will demonstrate in the course of the chapters below, each considering one of his final four collections followed by a summary epilogue.

3

Nostalgia and Speculation

Now and Then: Poems 1976–1978

> And I pray that in some last dream or delusion,
>
> * * * * *
>
> I'll again see the first small silvery swirl
> Spin outward and downward from sky-height
> To bring me the truth in blood-marriage of earth and air. . . .
>
> —"Red-Tail Hawk and Pyre of Youth"

1

In his early seventies, Robert Penn Warren endured many of the common problems of later life, but he also enjoyed an uncommon portion of its varied compensations. In personal terms, Warren's mutually rewarding union with Eleanor Clark persisted despite their individual infirmities, while his relationships with his daughter and son matured as both Rosanna and Gabriel developed into promising young artists (Blotner 433–34). Writing and publishing into his eighth decade, with his new works in poetry and prose still garnering positive reviews and impressive sales, Warren also remained a maturing artist himself. Indeed, the aging writer seems a good example of what Erik Erikson theorized during this same period as the psychological evolution possible in age despite its inevitable physical devolution. As if in evidence of the artistic integrity Warren had achieved, he now received more recognition of his lifelong achievement. He was given a surprise seventieth-birthday present in the form of the 1975 Emerson-Thoreau Award from the American Academy of Arts and Sciences; it was accompanied by a check substantial enough for him to tell Allen Tate that "if Emerson can stand it, I can" (Blotner 422). In 1976, he accepted the Copernicus Award and a ten-thousand-dollar stipend presented by the Academy of American Poets for "overall achievement as well as the contribution to poetry as a cultural force," while his newest *Selected*

Poems also was recognized by the Harriet Monroe Poetry Award from the University of Chicago (Blotner 426). Most important, Warren earned his third Pulitzer Prize in 1979 for his new collection *Now and Then,* though this recognition undoubtedly represented the lifetime of poetry that preceded this volume subtitled *Poems 1976–1978.*

His third Pulitzer also indicated a more general recognition of the growing critical consensus that Warren would be remembered best for his later poetry, especially in terms of its age-work, life review, and transcendence. Most reviewers made at least some reference to these topics in their generally favorable responses to *Now and Then.* Although much of this response was occasioned simply by Warren's advancing age, the matter and form of his new collection also contributed to these initial reactions, ones that have been reiterated by later critics and scholars. Warren's title suggests a sense of present and past, while its contents are divided into two sections titled "Nostalgic" and "Speculative" that imply his continuing consideration of what was *Then* and what is *Now.*[1] The "Nostalgic" section opens with six reminiscent texts all seemingly based on Warren's Kentucky boyhood, pivots with "Red-Tail Hawk and Pyre of Youth," which edges into his young manhood, and ends with three pieces derived from his later years. By contrast, the poems comprising the "Speculative" section "are more tied to idea," in Warren's own words, than to particular times or places, though these works are grouped in several topical subsections (*Talking* 298).

In general, earlier criticism has posited many variations of Warren's own distinction between the book's two named sections, a reading that is reinforced by consideration of *Now and Then* as part of his ongoing life review. James Justus contrasts the dual parts of *Now and Then* with the structure of narrative statements and lyric interjections that characterizes *Or Else.* In Justus's view of *Now and Then,* "portraits and situations presented as 'Nostalgic'" are contrasted with "a series of speculative poems in which the speaker struggles to reconcile rational assessment of the past . . . with more tentative and subliminal assertions of meaning" (100). In his study of Warren's autobiographical sources, Floyd C. Watkins acknowledges similar distinctions by way of his own title, *Then & Now: The Personal Past in the Poetry of Robert Penn Warren* (1982). Victor Strandberg universalizes these contrasts by positing them in terms of Edenic memory and postlapsarian consciousness on the part of Warren's poetic personae, though he makes the accurate observation that the best poems in either of the two major sections combine both memory and analysis ("Poetic Vision" 18–19). Randolph Runyon also recognizes continuities of image and theme between the "Nostalgic" and "Speculative" sections, in particular the subconscious imagery that is interpreted by the cognitive self so that it exists simultaneously as both *Now and Then* (*Braided Dream* 186–87). Joseph Blotner likewise seconds such connections in his authorized biography by asserting that the poems in both parts of *Now and Then* are unified around Warren's persistent themes: "the nature of time, the problem of truth, the meaning of life, and the inevitability of death"—in other words the prevailing themes of age-work, life review, and transcendence (440).[2]

2

Warren opens *Now and Then* and its "Nostalgic" section with a sublime effort combining autobiographical insight and philosophical reflection, "American Portrait: Old Style." The poem first appeared in the *New Yorker* during the Bicentennial year, and the national atmosphere of celebration in 1976 may have something to do with Warren's perhaps ironical title. Warren never invokes nostalgia in the popular sense of "the good old days" warmly recalled; his recollection is related to the word's root meaning of a painfully remembered lost home.[3] The old-style portrait referenced in the title is not of Warren himself, but of his friend Kent Greenfield, another native son of Guthrie who escaped to the larger world of major league baseball—"the great American pastime" of their youth. Kent becomes K in the text, perhaps as a gesture toward privacy in this story of a failed American Dream, though this stylistic flourish also serves to abstract the recreated character from the real person. K also becomes a kind of double for the poet, and their individual deeds often are conflated in the several texts in which Warren recreates variations of Kent Greenfield, one of his most persistent portraits in both poetry and prose. In "American Portrait: Old Style," Warren's early alter ego also evokes both the matters and themes of age-work and life review because this text presents these old friends in mutual existence into their eighth decades on earth.[4]

Warren was three years younger than Kent Greenfield, but the two became friends when Warren's family moved next door to the would-be ballplayer in 1911 on what then were the outskirts of the town (Blotner 11). Because the precocious Warren was able to skip several grades at the small Guthrie school, the neighbor boys soon became classmates as well. Although the friendship between the budding scholar and the burgeoning athlete may seem unlikely, each admired in the other the qualities he lacked himself. Their awareness of these deficiencies might have created some degree of envy between the pair as well. Certainly, Warren's literary treatments of his friend prove somewhat ambivalent as they alternate between a romantic celebration of their youthful innocence together and a more realistic portrayal of their existence apart in adult worlds of disappointment and loss. Kent Greenfield first appears as Jim Hawks, a sort of Kentucky Huck Finn who grows into a small-town outlaw and dies violently in Warren's first unpublished novel, which he completed in 1934. A harshly realistic view of Kent Greenfield's career as a professional pitcher is presented in one of Warren's finest short stories, "Goodwood Comes Back," first published by the *Southern Review* in 1941. Although the title references the newspaper headline announcing Luke Goodwood's return to the big leagues after banishment for drinking, it also refers to his southern homecoming, where his vices lead to his death at the hands of his "white trash" brother-in-law.[5] His boyhood friend also makes a brief appearance in Warren's *Brother to Dragons,* where "R.P.W." recalls how "Kent" shoots a "Canady" goose and demonstrates that "the only / Thing in life is glory" (19). In the reminiscent prose of his later recollections, particularly the pictures of Guthrie in *Portrait of a Father* (1988), Warren again emphasizes this kinder judgment of Greenfield as an American innocent.

"American Portrait: Old Style" combines Warren's ambivalent visions of his friend, and thus of himself, in contemplations of childhood innocence from the perspective of adult culpability. The poet begins the "Nostalgic" section with his own life review, recalling the halcyon days of his friendship with Kent when neither of them were "big enough for the ballgame" and had to make their own adventures in the fields and woods that spread out "Beyond the last house, where home was" (339). By the conclusion of the poem, the more painful sense of nostalgia will emerge in the persona's loss of his youthful "home," along with its easy acceptance of what seemed a natural order of American life. Hints of defeat and death are soon discovered, "Past the marsh we found the old skull in, all nameless / And cracked in star-shape from a stone-smack," perhaps the detritus of some forgotten skirmish like the ones the boys feign in a gravelike "trench, six feet long, / And wide enough for a man to lie down in / In comfort, if comfort was still any object" (339). The persona sees these discoveries as traces of earlier settlements, and he imagines that "Pap must have died of camp fever / And the others pushed on, God knows where" (339). As surely as the young Warren's imagination was fired with the mythic history of "The Dark and Bloody Ground," a glance out his classroom's window also revealed a realistic Kentucky landscape with "no hope and no history" (339).

Instead, the boys have to invent their own imagined version of history, by hunting with "BBs and Benjamin" (an air gun) "the Buffalo," once the denizens of their region's wild "Cane-Brake" (339). Their trophies were in reality only their mothers' domestic chickens, and such pursuits, even if violent, do seem rather nostalgic in the popular sense. In romanticized imagination, however, these childhood hunts evolve naturally into life-and-death fights with "sly Shawnees" and brutal "Bluebellies," who are also fair game as racial and cultural others to be vanquished in the establishment and defense of their idealized home place (340). By the time of his last summer together with Kent, the persona is almost ready to understand what imagination really is, "The lie we must learn to live by, if ever / We mean to live at all" (340). And live they must, for "Times change. / Things change" (340). The poetic persona can still picture K as a godly figure from a Renaissance fresco, with "the sun on his uncut hair bright" while passing through their "ramshackle town," not to "some wild white peak dreamed westward" but to "The Big Leagues" (340). The ace pitcher's long decline described in "Goodwood Comes Back" is swiftly summarized here: "Yes, this was his path, and no batter / Could do what booze finally did: / Just blow him off the mound" (340). Warren is not really interested in baseball as a sport, but only in what it represents symbolically, a boy's game performed by grown men for money or an American dream become nightmare.

Warren's persona also recognizes the patterns of his own life in that of his symbolic double. "And I, too, went on my way, the winning and the losing, or what / Is sometimes of all things the worst, the not knowing / One thing from the other" (341). Now, with the hard-won wisdom of age, he does know "How the teeth in Time's jaw all snag backward," and that whoever enters the dark maw of time is lost—whether pitcher or poet (341). At the two friends' reunion at the persona's homecoming in search of his lost boyhood, now some six decades past, they recognize each other with difficulty. The retired farmer quiets his bird dogs, hesitates, and at last declares, "Well, for Christ's sake—it's you!" (341). Of course, the persona is no longer the same "you," no more than is his double. K still stands "All Indian-brown" and "nigh straight," though "the arms and the pitcher's / Great shoulders, they were thinning to old-man thin," mirroring the persona's own physical decline (341). Perhaps aware of this perception, K smashes an insulator atop a light pole with a stone, saying "'See—I still got control!'" (341). This incident is used in "Goodwood Comes Back," but it is based on an event before rather than after his baseball career according to Greenfield himself—another indication that this reunion is created, not recreated.[6]

"American Portrait: Old Style" concludes with Warren wandering through the fields and woods of his youth in early evening "toward sunset" under "the late summer's thinned-out sky" to complete his age-work (341, 342). In the locus of his imaginary hunts and fights, "Where old dreams had once been Life's truth," the gravelike trace of the once-storied trench has become only "a ditch full of late-season weed-growth" (341). Alone in the gathering shade, the poetic persona seems compelled to lie down in this depression and look up to see how the "sky moves, / Drifting on, drifting on, like forever, / From *where* on to *where*" (342).[7] These thoughts of eternity make him wonder "What it would be like to die" and to become "Like the nameless old skull in the swamp, lost" in the ceaseless motion of nature and the inexorable march of time (342). Warren wills himself back into the present, however, and ends this poem with an image of achieved selfhood, much like that represented by "a hard-won something" that the persona found earlier in "One-Mule Cart" (335).

> But why should I lie here longer?
> I am not dead yet, though in years,

And the world's way is yet long to go,
And I love the world even in my anger,
And love is a hard thing to outgrow. (342)

Even after reviewing his retreating life and contemplating his approaching death in the quintain stanza that concludes "American Portrait: Old Style," Warren is able to affirm his continuing love for his place and time in a fallen world by means of his poetic form. The traditional rhythm, repetition, and rhyme of this last stanza will become features of Warren's *Alterstil,* the late style he develops from the examples of poetic forebears including Hardy, Yeats, and Frost to express the hard-won sublimity of his age-work, life review, and transcendence.

3

After "American Portrait: Old Style," *Now and Then* presents a series of five comparatively brief narratives centered on symbolic aspects of Warren's youth as recreated in his age, makes a transition through the longer narrative that bridges his childhood and adulthood in "Red-Tail Hawk and Pyre of Youth," and finally concludes the "Nostalgic" section with three shorter narratives based on events drawn from his later life. Warren's arrangement of all ten poems in this section seems generally chronological, though differentiations of the younger persona's age prove slight in the poems about his boyhood. In all of them, he is pictured nearing the end of his boyhood and the beginning of his adolescence, at about age twelve or so. All of these selections are thus concerned with some rite of passage, either public or private, culminating in the symbolic rejection of his personal and poetic past in "Red-Tail Hawk and Pyre of Youth." Before reaching his major selection, Warren narrates a religious experience that moved his "twelve-year-old soul" in "Amazing Grace in the Back Country"; as its title implies, the poem concerns a moment of spiritual crisis for the adolescent persona in an inverted secular revision of a traditional conversion experience (343). It precedes "Boy Wandering in Simms' Valley," a narrative of a secular epiphany set amid the detritus of an abandoned farmhouse that reveals the transience of human life and love to its young persona. The "Old Flame" referenced in the title of Warren's next selection presents another of his late-life visits home, when he dimly recognizes a now frowzy grandmother who was once a local beauty and an object of his boyish infatuation some five decades earlier (345). The poem that follows, "Evening Hour," recollects a more private moment at the local cemetery when the adolescent persona for the first time recognizes his own mortality. "Orphanage Boy," the last of the briefer narratives preceding "Red-Tail Hawk and Pyre of Youth," also recalls "American Portrait: Old Style" in its realization of universal mutability through the persona's experience of a hired hand's grief at being forced to put an aging dog out of its misery with a shotgun.

Warren's autobiographical relation to the materials presented in these five briefer narratives is even more complicated than that evidenced in "American Portrait: Old Style." Old-fashioned tent revivals like the one described in "Amazing Grace in the Back Country," for example, were still common enough during Warren's Kentucky years, when he surely would have seen and heard them in Guthrie; however, his family's genteel education and liberal religion would have made his actual participation in them rather unlikely. These religious rituals must have fascinated the younger Warren, however, for he often recreates them in his fiction and poetry—most often in terms of a compulsive attraction to the spontaneous enthusiasm exhibited that is then succeeded by immediate rejection or by gradual backsliding. One rite that shares several important details with the one in this later poem can be found in Warren's earliest unpublished novel, most notably "an ex-railroad engineer / Turned revivalist" (342). Later, his short novel "The Circus in the Attic" (1946) employs similar comparative images of revivals and carnivals when its protagonist, Bolton Lovehart, though properly raised in Episcopal church, allows himself to be immersed in a creek-side Baptist ritual directly before he runs off with the circus at age twelve. Later, Jeremiah Beaumont, the more complex narrator of Warren's massive historical romance, *World Enough and Time* (1950), is saved at one revival and lost at another after he cavorts with an old hag in his zealous frenzy.

In "Amazing Grace in the Back Country," Warren's young persona is aware of the sexuality in both the carnival and the revival tents. At the former, he saw the "fat lady" and "Man-woman" from the freak show as well as "a brace / Of whores" marked by advancing age, "one with gold teeth and one / With game gam," but both with "a guaranteed brand of syphilis" (342). At the altar call in the revival tent, the boyish persona hangs back until importuned by "some old-fool dame / In worn-out black silk," but he finally runs off to be alone beside a spring in the woods—a scene almost exactly like the rejections of their baptisms on the part of Warren's fictional protagonists (343). The difference from those earlier fictions exists in Warren's point of view in "Amazing Grace in the Back Country," where the aging poetic persona now can question "what grace" he has received over the "long years" since "I was twelve years old then" (344).

"Boy Wandering in Simms' Valley" would seem to recall another trace of Kentucky geography from Warren's youth, if he had not told an interviewer that the abandoned farm it pictures was discovered while wandering a Vermont valley as an older man, many decades after he could have experienced the boyhood epiphany realized in the poem (Watkins 116). It seems the poet realized that his experiences in the deserted farmhouse revealing the transience of "human hope" would prove all the more poignant if assigned to his younger self as "Nostalgic" narrative than if presented as a philosophical idea from his later life as in the more "Speculative" poems (344). Perhaps the ease with which Warren transforms his adult experience into that of an imagined boy is based in the several other poems of literal life review that he finishes during this period. This restructuring of his narrative also encourages Warren to employ traditional poetic forms, six quatrain stanzas of mainly iambic lines regularly rhyming on an ABAB pattern, with the only concessions to irregularity in the variation of line lengths between four and six feet and the final summary stanza of a single extended line. Indeed, these traditional patterns of narrative and verse, as well as of image and theme, suggest the influence of the poet's New England forebear Robert Frost on this poem of his age, which Warren then reassigns to his youth in the upper South.

Warren's own New England poetry suggests Frost's use of his regional geography in his narrative pieces, including several that focus on the elder poet's frequent images of abandoned farmsteads in poems ranging from the early "Ghost House" (1913) and "The Black Cottage" (1914) to "The Need of Being Versed in Country Things" (1920) and "In a Disused Graveyard" (1923) during his midcareer, to "Directive" (1946), a later effort. In an interview, Frost intimated that the complex symbolism of "Directive" was also a poetic response to T. S. Eliot—his only rival as a twentieth-century American poet according to Warren (quoted in Parini 362, 382). Frost's forsaken farm does recall the desiccated landscape of "The Waste Land," but in "Directive" it is redeemed by "A broken drinking goblet like the Grail" that allows the persona to taste the cold, clear waters of the farm's natural spring (Frost 379). "Boy Wandering in Simms' Valley" works another interesting variation on these images of psychological loss and poetic recovery. The luckless Simms nursed his wife until her death and then shot himself, leaving his farm to sink back into nature; now the barn is down, and "The yard back to wilderness gone, and only / The house to mark human hope, but ready to fall" (344). Even though Warren's lines might as well be Frost's, instead of Frost's broken goblet with its suggestions of childhood long lost, Warren's boyish persona "Saw the old enameled bedpan, high on a shelf," a symbol of human waste and decline that leaves him dazzled by late summer's setting sun in the poem's concluding, single-lined stanza that echoes on into his age, "And stood wondering what life is, and love, and what they might be" (344).

The three brief narratives that follow—"Old Flame," "Evening Hour," and "Orphanage Boy"—are interesting in terms of age-work and life review, but none can match the poetic quality of the three that preceded them, a judgment supported by Warren's exclusion of them from his final volume of self-selected poetry in 1985. These three pieces seem almost like lesser versions of "American Portrait: Old Style," "Amazing Grace in the Back Country," and "Boy Wandering in Simms' Valley." For example, the persona's long-lost "Old Flame" shone as brightly in the pantheon of the poet's youth as his friend Kent in the opening selection of *Now and Then*. The nameless girl who infatuates the younger persona is, like Kent, a few years older than the persona and thus more physically developed and sexually attractive. Like his male ideal, she too trails clouds of glory while traipsing through town with the sunlight reflecting brightly from her twin black braids. From her too, the enthralled youngster learns that "glory's the only thing that matters," much as he does from his friend (345). Unlike in his relation to Kent, the persona remains only a secret admirer of this small-town beauty, never even speaking to her before he leaves the town for the great world. When they meet again after fifty some years on one of the poet's sentimental journeys home, his experience is immediately recognizable to anyone who has attended a class reunion. He does not recognize her even as she calls out "Why, it's you!" much as Kent did (345). With her "gingham, false teeth, gray hair," this "grisly old dame" mirrors the physical decline of Kent's age as well as his own, so that the beauty is become only a "pile of age-litter" (345).[8]

The darkening burial place that provides the backdrop for "Evening Hour" recalls the nocturnal setting that follows the revival in "Amazing Grace in the Back Country." In both, the maturing persona begins to feel his own mortality along with his first intimations of infinity. Warren opens "Evening Hour" by differentiating the terms "graveyard" and "cemetery," a distinction that John Burt cites as important to the cultural dichotomies of the poem in his notes to Warren's *Collected Poems* (813). The setting of "Evening Hour" recreates Guthrie's Highland Cemetery, a small-town version of the romantic fashion for landscaped burial places that flourished in nineteenth-century America, but this patch of earth also gives up artifacts that suggest it may have been an Indian burial ground. So the boyish persona haunts the place searching for ancient arrowheads, "Among shiny new tombstones recording the first-planted dead" (345). The youth is unaware of these ironies until one evening after "all // The lights of town had come on" (346). Now distanced from home, he is struck by "the crazy impulse . . . . . To lay ear to earth," like an Indian, listening "for what voices beneath might say" about both life and death (346).

"Orphanage Boy" is another narrative poem that pictures a burial place at eventide, and it also proves itself parallel to "Boy Wandering in Simms' Valley" in its evocation of boyhood's end by way of imagery intertextual with Robert Frost's narrative poetry concerning "farm hands," both hired and not. Teen-aged Al arrives from the orphanage to work for the persona's uncle on his farm as a "Hired boy if he got enough to / Call hire" (346). Given the profanity and smut he reveals to the younger persona, who seems to be summering at the farm as Warren often did at his Grandfather Penn's, one wonders if he can still be called a "boy" in any sense but as a label of his lower status in the social hierarchy of this agrarian community. At the isolated farm, Al's only close companion is "Bob, the big white farm bulldog," but when it is bitten by a copperhead" and sickens to the point that the uncle tells Al to put him down, this order becomes only another chore that a hired hand would be expected to perform in his employer's stead (346). As the uncle hands his shotgun to Al, "He never named Bob's name" (346). The persona then follows Al and Bob on their grim errand deep into the darkening woods. Later, he retreats home after the task is done, leaving the hired boy stricken by inconsolable grief (347). Al never returns to the farm, and it takes the persona a year to work up the courage to retrace his course in the woods to the place where he discovers the grave the hired boy dug for Bob. Like the revelation in "Boy Wandering in Simms' Valley," the orphanage boy's loss and grief provides this persona an insight into the grim realities of adult life more revelatory than all of his profane language and salacious innuendos.

4

"Red-Tail Hawk and Pyre of Youth," a significantly longer narrative in ten sections, begins with another of Warren's initiatory experiences, centers on a symbolic gesture of his manhood, and ends with an ambivalent vision of life, death, and the possibilities for transcending both. The poem becomes another sublime effort in Warren's life review and age-work, as well as the finest poem in *Now and Then.* Even a brief discussion will demonstrate the poem's shared sublimity with the best poems in the two preceding volumes such as "Rattlesnake Country," "Evening Hawk," or "One-Mule Cart." The poem's opening sections 1 and 2 present the poetic persona's youthful hunting of the red-tail hawk. This pursuit signals his maturation beyond that seen in the earlier narrative poems, for he is armed with "a .30–30," a man's weapon much more powerful than the Benjamin air rifle he sported in "American Portrait: Old Style" (347). His killing shot, "the act impossible but / Possible," seems at once volitional and fated—both joyous, "Heart leaping in joy past definition," and tragic, "in / Eyes tears past definition" (348). Indeed, his destruction of the creature will mark the rest of his life, as he seems to realize in sections 3 and 4. He returns from the hunt, hugging the bloody carcass "cuddled / Like babe to heart," to mount it as a trophy of his imagined manhood. Using tools like his "father's old razor," his first artistic recreation of the hawk marks his progress from childhood to adulthood (348). This process is minutely described, but for all the persona's artistic pains, the result is only a lifeless simulacrum of this once vital creature.

Section 5 becomes pivotal in the narrative as it summarizes the passage of the years between adolescence and manhood under the now sightless gaze of the mounted hawk perched in his bedroom study as a memento mori much like Poe's raven. Then Warren returns to Guthrie sometime during the early 1930s in section 6, "When my mother was dead, father bankrupt, and whiskey / Hot in my throat" (349). Sections 7 and 8 present the pyre for both the now bedraggled bird and for the persona's lost innocence in a sort of bonfire of the vanities into which he pitches the detritus of his earlier life. The penultimate section 9 ranges backward to the moment of their "commensurate fate" in his killing of the hawk (350). After this life review, the final section 10 accepts the final end of age-work as Erikson once put it in an epigrammatic formulation, "To be, through having been to face not being." The persona's imagined last moments in the ultimate operating room reveals his destiny symbolized in the red-tail hawk's resurrection, like the phoenix, "From the regally feathered gasoline flare / Of youth's poor, angry, slapdash and ignorant pyre" (350).

Although Warren later admitted that it was Kent Greenfield who made the miraculous shot and that he did not burn the stuffed bird but tossed it out with the rest of the trash from his parents' lost home, the red-tail hawk referenced in his title is derived directly from the poet's autobiographical experience (Blotner 442; *Talking* 296). The symbolic bird becomes the subject of this late poem by way of literary criticism, however. Warren dedicates "Red-Tail Hawk and Pyre of Youth" to Harold Bloom because the celebrated critic indirectly suggested its subject in his review of the 1976 *Selected Poems* by focusing on the poet's predilection for hawk imagery and by extension his hawklike poetic vision (*Talking* 239–40). In his 1979 review of *Now and Then,* the younger Southern poet Dave Smith agrees with Bloom and goes on to connect the hawk that haunts Warren's persona with both the artist Audubon's dead birds and Coleridge's dead albatross, subjects of his poetry in *Audubon* and his criticism in " A Poem of Pure Imagination." For Smith, Warren's hawk becomes his personal albatross created by a violation of nature paralleling that of the Ancient Mariner and which he will finally escape in the hawklike literary vision of what the bird comes to represent within his psychic life review.[9]

Certainly, Coleridge's poem provides one intertext for Warren's "Red-Tail Hawk and Pyre of Youth," but others suggest themselves as well. The dreamlike hunting of the hawk seems as implicitly indebted to Shelley as to anyone among the Romantics, and the poem explicitly provides a dozen others in the bonfire of books that serves as a pyre both for the hawk and for the persona's youthful literary dreams. In terms of Bloom's *The Anxiety of Influence* (1973), Warren's persona struggles to rid himself of both influences and anxieties as he approaches midlife. Warren's literary and personal friendship with Bloom began at Yale and blossomed in his enthusiastic response to the prominent critic's theories on influence and anxiety, in which the poet recognized his own conflicted relationship with T. S. Eliot (Bloom, "Foreword" xxiv). Although neither Coleridge nor Eliot are tossed into its flames, Warren's pyre seems fed by a heap of fragments, works the persona had stored against his personal ruin in the tradition of *The Waste Land:* a mélange of High Modernist sources from *Hamlet* and Milton to Baudelaire and Rimbaud, from the "mechanical" poses of Japanese pornographic prints to the literary posturing in "a book / Of poems friends and I had printed in college" (350). Strangely, in his later piece on Warren's hawk imagery, Bloom does not read this pyre poem as an agon with poetic forebears, assigning that role to his Wordsworthian effort "The Leaf" (1975): "Which is to say, it is Warren's rhetorical strength to have converted the Eliotian trope of orthodoxy" (Bloom, "Sunset Hawk" 202).[10]

5

As Warren's second sublime selection in the initial section of *Now and Then,* "Red-Tail Hawk and Pyre of Youth" might serve as an appropriate transition, not just from childhood to his adult recollections but from his "Nostalgic" narratives of realistically depicted initiations to his "Speculative" lyrics of philosophically considered contemplations. In the collection as published, however, Warren concluded the "Nostalgic" section with a trio of shorter poems—"Mountain Plateau," "Star-Fall," and "Youth Stares at Minoan Sunset"—that seemingly trace out the chronological pattern of his life between the imagined immolation of youth and the beginnings of age. Although the primary setting of "Mountain Plateau" remains uncertain, it presents a scene from some high country remembered later in Warren's life. "Star-Fall" perhaps recalls one of Warren's Italian sojourns with Eleanor Clark, in all probability during the 1950s, like the ones recreated in his first Pulitzer Prize collection of poetry, *Promises.* The title of "Youth Stares at Minoan Sunset" indicates its setting in the Greek isles and during the 1960s when Warren's son Gabriel would have been about the same age as his own youthful persona in the narratives that open the "Nostalgic" section. These last poems are all successful efforts, a critical judgment supported by Warren's inclusion of two of them, "Star-Fall" and "Youth Stares at Minoan Sunset," in his 1985 *Selected Poems.*

This related pair of poems and "Mountain Plateau" all really seem more lyric than narrative, however, as in each of them a single autobiographical image is frozen into a physical tableau that simultaneously advances some philosophical speculation about its meaning. These three pieces seem more akin to those that follow in the "Speculative" section and might well have been swapped with several included there. Warren probably presents them here to round out the "Nostalgic" section as a life review and to help balance *Now and Then* by an analogy with the equation of his title. Even with these last three selections, Warren's opening section contains only ten poems on twenty-three pages in his first edition; however, his second section presents twenty-seven poems on forty-six pages. Although Warren dropped his section titles when he reedited *Now and Then* in 1985 for his final self-selected omnibus collection, he included six poems on fifteen pages from the first section and only six poems on nine pages from the second.

Although I hesitate to question Warren as editor of his own work, the wiser course well might have been a more ruthless editing of *Now and Then,* as Warren himself apparently recognized within a few years. Too many poems crowd the "Speculative" section, and they include several that tend to duplicate one another and blur together, even under the most sympathetic and careful scrutiny. For these reasons—as well as for the fact that several selections in the second section only indirectly concern age-work, life review, or transcendence—my study will not attempt to discuss them all at length. Instead, I will consider the last three poems from the "Nostalgic" section next and then select only a few from the second, focusing on the six Warren reprinted in 1985, as examples of several groupings he attempts in the "Speculative" section.

"Mountain Plateau" is dedicated to James Wright, appropriately enough as it was first published in a special issue of the poetry journal *Ironwood* celebrating the younger poet's fiftieth birthday. Wright had begun his career as a poet by studying with John Crowe Ransom at Kenyon College, and his first collections of poetry were influenced by the poetic formalism of the Fugitive/Agrarians that characterized Warren's earlier poems. Like Warren, however, Wright turned to freer forms, looser structures, and more personal narratives in his later work. In Warren's collection, "Mountain Plateau" provides an example of similar changes in its juxtaposition of his earlier experience and later recollection of this landscape as a correlative for his spiritual isolation in the present. The poem's first five lines almost become a stanza but remain less formal, something like an artist's line sketch, as "pen strokes, tangle, or stub" to picture a crow on a black branch outlined against a blank snow field (351). The next verse section is the single word "Uttered" followed by another of a single line, "Its cry to the immense distance," which translates the visual image to one of sound (351). Five brief verse paragraphs then turn on the persona's declaration that the "landscape of my heart" now replicates that earlier scene, confessing that though "I have lived / Long," he is still unable "To make adequate communication" (351). Although Warren's poem in *Now and Then* makes only minor changes to his journal text, the dedication penciled into the collection's galley proofs suggests his new awareness of James Wright's death from throat cancer early in 1980 (Burt 739).

"Star-Fall" and "Youth Stares at Minoan Sunset" are both concerned with the difficulties of communication as well, like several poems gathered after them in the "Speculative" section. To those communication problems inherent in the natural distances of space and time, this pair of poems adds those of geography and history. "Star-Fall" finally involves transcendent visions, but its opening is rooted in the earth of "that far land," the Italian coast where Warren and Eleanor Clark sojourned before and after their marriage. Like his remembered Kentucky home, this setting likewise invoked earlier in *Promises* seems dark and bloody ground. The renovated coastal fortress where they live is replete with "castrated drawbridge where / For four bloody centuries garbage / In the moat's depth had been spilled / To stink" (351). The poem's persona and his love try to rise above the bloody flux of history, however, by reclining on the sea cliff, silently holding hands, and watching the night sky for the annual meteor showers of August. Warren is nostalgic here not only for nights of love but for the past glory of history and mythology ranging back to the classical world. For in astronomy these falling stars are called the Perseids, while in local legend they are associated with Vulcan, as Warren suggests in his image of them as "sparks in a shadowy, huge smithy, with / The clang of the hammer unheard" (352). When this celestial revelation proves too immense for contemplation, the couple turns from the sky to view how on a more human scale "Far off in the sea's matching midnight / The fishing lights marked their unfabled constellations" (352).

In the last of the ten poems in the "Nostalgic" section, "Youth Stares at Minoan Sunset," Warren recreates these balances of geography and history in imagery of sky and sea as he recollects a scene from a later era of his life. The youth of the title is not the poetic persona, but Warren's young son recalled from family travels in Crete only a few years earlier (Blotner 443). This adolescent's romantic elation, new "minted black" before the "great coin" of the copper sun, only serves to remind the poet that he has lost the youthful joy in nature revealed in Warren's earlier poems of reminiscence (352). As the writer had used the word "Cretan" in his drafts of the title and the text, his final choice of "Minoan" suggests not just the dark and bloody history of this island but the complex mythology surrounding Minos, the legendary monarch who gave his name to Crete's megalithic culture (730). We should remember that Warren evoked the Minotaur and its labyrinth in *Brother to Dragons* and also be aware that he will return to them for similar purposes in "Chthonian Revelation: A Myth" and "Looking Northward, Aegeanward: Nestlings on Seacliff," the two sections of "Mediterranean Basin" that become the "Prologue" to his penultimate collection, *Rumor Verified: Poems 1979–1980.*

6

The twenty-seven selections that comprise the "Speculative" section of *Now and Then* seem organized into subgroups of two, three, and four poems emphasizing thematic tensions persistent throughout Warren's poetry: dream and nightmare, communication and silence, love and loss, as well as life and death. Like most critical readings of this collection, mine is unable to discern a defining pattern among these small groupings aside from their consistent speculation on the inscrutability of life, the inevitability of death, and the possibility of transcendence. Multiple intertextualities pervade the entire second section, linking several aspects, not just of these subgroups but of their individual poems. In particular, my reading of the "Speculative" section will emphasize the six pieces Warren included in his 1985 *Selected Poems.* However, Warren begins his second section with a grouping of three poems he does not reprint—"Dream," "Dream of a Dream," and "First Dawn Light." All three speculate about the character of dreams, a theme that will reappear throughout the entire second section. These initial texts do not recall literal dreams as such, but each considers the relation of dream to consciousness in the life of its persona.

In the second stanza of "Dream," the poem that begins the "Speculative" section, Warren tells his readers, "I have read in a book that dream is the mother of memory" (353). The rest of the poem wrestles with the problem of remembering and understanding dreams by way of imagery echoing Genesis, the *Iliad,* and *Hamlet.* The poem concludes that "the dream is only a self of yourself," and this puzzling proposition will reverberate in several later poems about self-definition (353). Even the title of Warren's next selection, "Dream of a Dream," increases the complications of idea and image, though its poetic structure is both more discursive and traditional with its pattern of ten-line, regularly rhyming stanzas. The persona apparently dreams about an actual stream nearby, but he is unsure if this dream is merely a revision of another dream about the symbolic stream of time. In either case, the sound of a stream seems to whisper his name while showing "the glimmer and froth of self before it is gone" into the flow of life (354). On waking to the "owl's icy question," the persona is still unsure of what is dream and what is not (354). "First Dawn Light," which follows, repeats the same existential questions in "Last dream, last owl-cry / Now past" (354). Of course, the owl's cry is "Who?" and the answer to its overwhelming question is a definition of the self which the persona cannot supply, at least at this juncture. Although not one of the three poems that form this initial subgrouping seems in any specific sense autobiographical, they still suggest a more abstract and philosophical life review as part of the most difficult age-work—the realization of selfhood in the face of decline and death.

The two poems that follow the opening dream sequence of the "Speculative" section, "Ah, Anima!" and "Unless," reappear a few years later in the next *Selected Poems.* They are paired not just in image and theme but in their matching formats—unrhymed couplets with irregular lines of varied lengths. This pair reveals more nightmares than dreams. In contrast to the quiet darks and bright dawns of the initial subgroup, "Ah, Anima!" considers the nature of the soul against the backdrop of an overnight hurricane that haunts the persona's fitful sleep and fearful dreams with the prospect of the destruction that daylight will reveal. This consternation is seen in the exclamatory title that Warren immediately translates in his opening lines: "Watch the great bough lashed by the wind and rain. Is it / A metaphor for your soul?" (355). "Anima" is the Latin word for soul, of course, and the term was redefined by Jung to denote the essential kernel of self beneath the outer identity constructed in social context. Warren then compares the natural disaster represented by "the scything // Tail of the hurricane" with the human destruction revealed "On the great chart of history" (355). Indeed, this dark night of the soul seems one where the layers of cultural, social, and even physical identity are stripped away, so "you were nameless—oh, anima!" and ready to leave "The husk behind, and leap / Into the blind and antiseptic anger of air" (355).

This sheath of reality is stripped away once more in "Unless," the selection that can be paired with "Ah, Anima!" in terms of poetic theme, image, and format. Warren's opening couplet asserts that "All will be in vain unless" his reader realizes that "what you think is Truth is only // A husk for something else" (356). Warren's persona speculates that "something" might be called "energy," another meaning of the term "anima" in both its classical and contemporary uses. The Jungian night journey traced in the poem traverses a wasteland replete with "desert rocks / And Freudian cactus tall in moonlight" (356). This nightmare's operative image is a symbolic rattlesnake, however, a living creature that "Scrapes off the old integument" to leave it behind "translucent and abstract, like Truth" (356). Then "Clean and lethal and gleaming . . . Unhusked for its mission," the "fanged, unforgiving" serpent is reborn to prepare the reader for the moment when he will himself "Breathe with the rhythm of the stars," his face "stripped to white bone by starlight" to unmask the skull beneath the skin and the transcendence beyond this image of a death's head (356).

Interestingly enough, the title of the next poem that Warren retains from *Now and Then* for inclusion seven years later in his last *Selected Poems* is "The Mission." Although a pair of poems questioning human communication, "Not Quite Like a Top" and "Waiting," intervenes in the original collection, neither proves strong enough to save; neither does Warren save the pair on the failure of communication that follow "The Mission," "Code Book Lost" and "When the Tooth Cracks—Zing!" The mission that gives its title to the poem separating these two lesser pairs also involves communication and silence, begins in a dream that quickly becomes nightmare, and balances precariously between life and death. "The Mission" opens with "a dream of horses" recalled from a scene at nightfall outside a town in France years earlier (359). The awakened persona reflects that the horses "must be long dead" and probably slaughtered, for he remembers that "*La boucherie chevaline,* in the village / Has a gold horse-head above the door" (359). Winter moonlight makes him consider another animal now in a deathlike state, huddling "inside his fur like an invalid inside / A charity-ward blanket" (359). He then admits that like the dead horses, the hibernating bear, and even the frozen brook, "I, too, // Have forgotten the nature of my own mission" (359). "Perhaps that lost mission" proves fortuitous, for it causes the persona to consider transcendence in the poem's final stanza of a single long line—"The possibility of joy in the world's tangled and hieroglyphic beauty" (359).

The world's hieroglyphs are almost impossible to interpret easily, however, as demonstrated by succeeding subgroups of poems in *Now and Then.* As Warren confesses in the three poems that follow "The Mission," the code book is lost, the memory is no longer reliable, and one must question "is there a *now* or a *then?*"—as does the persona in "Sister Water" (362). This subgroup of pieces on the difficulties of communication and interpretation is succeeded by several selections about finding and losing love, some of which appear at least partially autobiographical. "Memory Forgotten" puzzles over the lost maternal love of Ruth Penn Warren; "Waking to Tap of Hammer" probes the growing filial affection for Gabriel Warren; and "The Smile" proves another loving homage to Eleanor Clark Warren. However, the more abstracted and perplexing "How to Tell a Love Story" and "Little Black Heart of the Telephone" are the only poems from this subgroup Warren saves for the 1985 *Selected Poems.*

The love story that gives its title to the first of these two pieces may have at least faint autobiographical reference for Warren, since love's beginnings are located in a memory of the persona's beloved "running ahead" amid "White surf and a storm of sunlight," before she reveals "a smile / Back-flung" (365). The beach setting and the bright imagery recall several of Warren's love poems for Eleanor Clark going back as far as *Promises,* his first volume following their marriage. The complex imagery and philosophical abstraction of "How to Tell a Love Story," however, make it seem particularly close to "Paradox" from *Can I See Arcturus From Where I Stand?* That earlier poem opens with virtually the same images and gestures: "Running ahead beside the sea, / You turned and flung a smile, like spray" (328). My reading of "Paradox" connects it both with the ancient philosopher Zeno's theoretical consideration of motion and change, as well as with the actual age difference between Warren and his younger wife that indicates she probably will outlive him. This philosophical and autobiographical paradox is extended in "How to Tell a Love Story" because the later poem spends most of its length arguing that the story of human love cannot be told fully until death concludes it. "Perhaps I can't say the first word till I know what it all means. / Perhaps I can't know till finally the doctor comes in and leans" (365).

Warren's title for the faintly traced narrative discernible in "Little Black Heart of the Telephone" suggests a possible love story, at least in its attribution of emotional responses to a material object, but a love story that aborts itself in its failures of communication. The poem opens with the ringing of an unanswered telephone heard "screaming its little black heart out" in a sound that seems to cry "*Nobody there? Oh, nobody's there!*" (365). The blackness assumed of the telephone's heart may seem problematic, at least until the contemporary reader realizes that the image Warren imagines here is one of the instruments of communication from his past, then almost universally black in color. From the opening stanza, the poetic persona identifies the outcry of his own sufferings, "I know how it feels / When you scream and scream, and nobody's there" (365). Yet when the ringing telephone is silenced for sleep, the persona still anticipates its screaming again—which he seems powerless to stop despite his presence in the same room. In other words, this message is one that he does not want to receive, "for I know how pain can't find words. / Or sometimes is afraid to find them" (366). Instead, the telephone's cry of "*Nobody there? Oh, nobody's there!*" is repeated and attributed to a more universalized humanity that gazes upon "stars lost in blankness that bleeds / Its metaphysical blood, but not of redemption" (366). Warren's persona worries that his dreams will be haunted by messages from the past. "Little Black Heart of the Telephone" ends with another stanza comprised of a single line of extended length, "In my dream I wonder why, long since, it's not been disconnected" (366).

The metaphysical darkness revealed in "Little Black Heart of the Telephone" blends into several of the selections that follow it in a subgrouping, or perhaps two, organized around the tensions of life and death. The next selection in the "Speculative" section, "Last Laugh," traces Mark Twain's mordant humor to the night when little Sam Clemens witnessed the autopsy that followed his father's untimely death. Ten quatrains of regularly rhyming iambic lines rehearse the humorist's biography; yet another concluding stanza of a single line describes how he watched his wife Livy expire a lifetime later, "And was left alone with his joke, God dead, till he died" (367). "Last Laugh" is followed by Warren's equally dark reaction to reading his first wife's obituary in "Heat Lightning," a poem in which he graphically recounts their passionate, though finally joyless, sexual couplings (Blotner 444). The title of the next selection, "Inevitable Frontier," suggests death, and it is replete with scatological as well as sexual imagery. "Heart of the Backlog," which then follows, begins with a reminiscent evening before a dying fire, but its naturalistic imagery of an owl and a vole as predator and prey in the snowfall outside recalls "Time as Hypnosis" from *Or Else*. In "Identity and Argument for Prayer," the persona approaches death with "Old hope, old pain, old evil, old good, / All long forgotten" along with his "old *I*" or self-identity (372, 373).

The final subgrouping turns back lifeward, at last, despite its persistent images of sunset, fall, and death that culminate in the concluding selection of *Now and Then*, the sublime "Heart of Autumn." In "Diver," another poem that seems suggested by the youthful activities of Warren's son Gabriel, images of seafaring and scuba diving again represent life's repeated patterns of departure and return. The following selection, "Rather Like a Dream," begins with an anecdote about the young Wordsworth reaching out to touch the solid forms of nature and ends with the aging persona left alone at sunset in autumnal woods to "wonder, / Wonder if I should put out a hand to touch // Tree or stone—just to know" (375). More images of fall follow in *Now and Then*'s penultimate pair of poems. "Departure" depicts the ineffable sadness of summer's end at a fashionable seaside resort, while "Heat Wave Breaks" describes a more dramatic end to summer in a mountain thunderstorm. These four selections prepare the reader, not just for the imagery of the volume's final selection, but for its daring attempt at transcendence of the natural cycles of day, year, and life.

Warren's final choice from *Now and Then* for his 1985 selected edition, "Heart of Autumn," ranks as one of his three sublime efforts in the volume along with "American Portrait: Old Style" and "Red-Tail Hawk and Pyre of Youth." In "Heart of Autumn," Warren's persona realizes not just the passage of the year but of his life while watching wild geese wheel southward across an autumnal sunset in their seasonal migration. This imagery is already familiar from his earlier poetry. Perhaps the most notable example is found in the first part of "Tell Me a Story," the concluding lyric of *Audubon,* where Warren's aging persona recalls the vernal passage of the wild geese he witnessed but could not comprehend as a youth: "Long ago, in Kentucky, I, a boy, stood / By a dirt road, in first dark, and heard / The great geese hoot northward" (266). In his poetic depictions of both spring and fall migrations, Warren seems to reprise the more sentimental roots of American Romanticism in poems such as William Cullen Bryant's "To a Waterfowl" (1821). Bryant employs the same images to reassure his readers that a higher power guides both the bird on its path to summer bliss and his persona on the long, lonely way through life. As we would anticipate, Warren's migratory poems discover no easy equations of natural and human cycles.

In "Heart of Autumn," a lifetime away from that earlier spring in Kentucky that ended *Audubon,* "fall comes" by way of "the northwest gap" in the mountains of Vermont (376). With it, "in perfect formation," come the "wild geese," down from the northern reaches of the Canada, "under gray cloud-scud and over gray / Wind-flicker of forest" (376). A few may fall to "the lead pellet," "Some stagger, recover control," but all press on as "*V* upon *V* arrows the season's logic" (376). Even though "None / Knows what has happened," the persona also must ask himself in late life, "Do I know my own story?" (376). By way of comparison, "At least, they know / When the hour comes for the great wing-beat," as well as "the imperial utterance / Which cries out for distance" (376). Each one is symbolic of transcendence, a "Sky-strider, / Star-strider," and they all "in their nature know / The path of pathlessness" along with "the joy / Of destiny fulfilling its own name" (376).

By way of contrast, the persona admits that "I have known time and distance, but not why I am here" (376). Even if he has trod the human "Path of logic, path of folly," both prove the same universal dead ends in the long run (377). Warren's poetic personae throughout *Now and Then* have stood at this same place with "face lifted now skyward" and thus starward, "Hearing the high beat," much like his boyhood self in "Tell Me a Story." For the first time, if in the last poem of the collection, this impasse is overcome through a "Process of transformation" (377). Such imagined change is part physical metamorphosis and part psychological transcendence. His "arms outstretched in the tingling" anticipation of wings soon are matched by "tough legs, // With folded feet" (377). More important, the autumnal emotion impacts his heart "with a fierce impulse / To unwordable utterance," something akin to the wild cries that annunciated the summer pilgrimage of the wheeling geese. Warren's resolution proves no easy entrance into nature, however, having no allegorical equation to human nature like Bryant's in "To a Waterfowl." Rather it is "the sounding vacuum of passage . . . Toward sunset, at a great height" (377).

If sunset and sky height are familiar images of death, Warren's passage here remains only a "vacuum"—an absolute emptiness within space to use its dictionary denotation and the great void looming at the end of life in its poetic connotations. The life review that concludes with the final selection of *Now and Then* thus replicates Butler's paradigm, and we are reminded not just of Erikson's formulations about the wisdom to be earned by confronting eternity, but of Tornstam's speculations about psychological transcendence in the face of age and decline, death and nonbeing. This new direction toward transcendence in Warren's work will culminate in his last collection, *Altitudes and Extensions,* but such was the rush of Warren's late productivity that two other collections would intervene in only seven years, *Being Here* and *Rumor Verified,* the subjects of my next two chapters.

4

Autobiography and Age-Work

Being Here: Poetry 1977–1980

> All peril past,
> He westward gazes, and down, where the sun will brush
> The farthermost bulge of earth. How soon? How soon
>
> Will the tangent of his sight now intersect
> The latitudinal curvature where the sun
> Soon crucial contact makes, to leave him in twilight,
>
> Alone in Glory?
>
> —"Eagle Descending"

1

Because simply existing becomes something of an accomplishment in itself for a septuagenarian poet, the title of Warren's new collection, *Being Here,* becomes subtly significant given his concerns with age-work and life review. The volume's subtitle, *Poetry 1977–1980,* also appears important in its equally understated suggestions. The alert reader will notice that its span of years includes that of Warren's previous collection, as *Being Here* does include some pieces published within the chronological limits of *Now and Then: Poems 1976–1978,* and this time span also overlaps with that of *Rumor Verified: Poems 1979–1980.* This seeming difficulty once again demonstrates how carefully Warren chose his selections to fit his particular purposes for each individual collection. We also should note that *Being Here* provides Warren's only use of "*Poetry*" rather than "*Poems*" in the subtitles of his collections. Considering the distinction Warren draws between these two terms in his most important theoretical essay, "Pure and Impure Poetry," his subtitle for *Poetry 1977–1980* must be more than mere happenstance.

James H. Justus demonstrates this distinction of *Being Here* by citing Warren's epigrammatic formulation in "Pure and Impure Poetry": "Poetry wants to be pure, but poems do not" (108). Then, after noting that the collection's three epigraphs are concerned with time, Justus concludes, "*Being Here* also betrays a yearning for one kind of perfection—the purity of timelessness—even in the midst of doubt that it exists" (109). In my view, Warren implies that in artistic theory poetry always aspires to the purity of the ideal, though in artistic practice poems always compromise with the impurity of the real. In New Critical dynamics, these tensions between the "pure" and the "impure" create sublime poetic texts, as Warren famously demonstrates in his seminal essay on Coleridge's *The Rime of the Ancient Mariner,* which he subtitled "A Poem of Pure Imagination" (1946). Warren's poems incline always toward the impure matters of experience, of course, though in his autobiography and age-work, including *Being Here,* he is forced to confront the pure abstractions of nonbeing and transcendence.

Despite the many elations of Warren's personal and professional life over the two years that separated *Now and Then* from *Being Here,* he also experienced several intimations of mortality—both his own and others. Just months after *Now and Then* was published, Allen Tate died at age seventy-nine, following several years of lingering illness. Warren attended his old friend's funeral in Nashville, of course, adding his personal sorrow to the communal grief of those aging Fugitive/Agrarians who still survived. Only a few months after *Being Here* was published, Warren himself was diagnosed with "enlargement and adenocarcinoma of the prostate"—the same conditions that caused the death of his father at age eighty-six (Blotner 457). Between these distressing occasions, however, Warren happily celebrated his seventy-fifth birthday in April of 1980, receiving well wishes not just from family and friends but from the larger literary and academic communities. In June of that year, he traveled to the nation's capital to accept the Presidential Medal along with fellow southern writers Eudora Welty and Tennessee Williams, among other artists (Blotner 452). When *Being Here* appeared that summer, it received much praise, not just in literary journals but in popular publications such as *Newsweek,* where a long article enthusiastically proclaimed Warren "America's dean of letters" (Blotner 453).

Being Here was not Warren's only poetic publication during this period, however. Revisiting his personal as well as his professional past, in 1979 Warren finished a revision of his *Brother to Dragons: A Tale in Verse and Voices,* first published in 1953. A revised edition for theatrical presentation had appeared in 1976, directly following a performance of it on National Public Television in which Warren took the part of his own aged father (Blotner 421). In later interviews, Warren revealed that he had always been dissatisfied with the earlier text in which he felt he had "wandered into a . . . trap of blank verse" and that revisions made for the stage inclined him toward a freer poetic format (*Talking* 337). As with any part of his later work, Warren's revisions of *Brother to Dragons* after more than three decades functions as both age-work and life review in terms of matter and theme as well as of form and style.[1]

Warren told an interviewer that his new *Brother to Dragons* "is no different philosophically," despite the fact that it "is very different technically—in rhythm (the important thing) and in organization" and that it had undergone "a lot of cutting" (*Talking* 338). Many Warren critics, however, have argued that this new version of one of his fundamental works is altered profoundly by exactly these several changes. One major source of this textual transformation is found in Warren's age-work and life review. In the original work, published by Warren at age forty-eight, Thomas Jefferson seems a distant father figure challenged by Warren's protagonist, the autobiographical "R.P.W." Thus, Jefferson becomes a foil for Robert Franklin Warren, who also appears there in his own person. In the revised text, published by Warren when he is fast approaching Jefferson's life span of four score and three, the monumental figure is humanized by his paternal relation to a nephew, Meriwether Lewis. Warren's children were born after he finished the first *Brother to Dragons,* and it seems that three decades of fatherhood have changed the writer's view of filial and parental relations, helping him to reconcile with both real and surrogate fathers.

Even a brief comparison of the opening pages in the 1953 and 1979 texts reveals how much Warren's changes from his earlier, more formal poetic style to his later, looser lines affect his characters and themes. In the earlier opening, Jefferson cannot speak even three lines of blank verse before R.P.W. interrupts him with five lines of riposte. In the later version, Jefferson is given an opening speech in thirteen lines of varying lengths, while R.P.W. has only two to answer him. In the original *Brother to Dragons,* the two figures then debate the fulfillment of "the triple boast" inscribed on Jefferson's gravestone, including his authorship of the Declaration of Independence, the American foundational text (5). In the revised *Brother to Dragons,* Jefferson concedes that his epitaph rings hollow as he kneels to see his reflection in the underworld stream of Lethe and recognize that "it is only human" (5). As in many of Warren's later poems, selfhood is discovered in the mirrored image of a paltry patriarch. Jefferson goes on to ask in newly written lines, "What else had I in age to cling to / Even in the face of knowledge?" (5). He concludes that "Even after age and the tangle of experience," he hopes the boast might be true.

> So, in senility
> And moments of indulgent fiction I might try
> To defend my old definition of man. (5)

Warren's opening page of revisions suggests how much the rest of *Brother to Dragons* is transformed by his age-work and life review, and many pages that follow confirm these developments. For just one important example, Warren's final page also is revised thoroughly, when he cuts both a somewhat overstated thematic summary and an account of his final return to his own father, who died in 1955 after the first edition.

2

Although Robert Franklin Warren disappears from the conclusion of the 1979 *Brother to Dragons,* he is not far from his son's mind during this period, for just a year later he reappears in the opening selection of *Being Here.* "October Picnic Long Ago" is not simply the first poem in Warren's new collection; it is set off in italics from the selections in the book's five numbered sections and contrasted with a concluding poem similarly differentiated, "Passers-By on Snowy Night." In the prose "Afterthought" to his new collection, Warren indicates that each poem was intended as "a bracket to enclose the dimly envisaged tangles and complications of the main body" and thus both "were composed well before the book had begun to assume anything like its final content and structure" (441). Warren's revelations demonstrate not just the organizational importance of these first and final selections but their thematic significance to the "shadowy narrative" the poet posits here as the structuring principle of his new volume (441). Earlier, I extended this "shadowy autobiography" that Warren mentions in the "Afterthought" to his Eriksonian age-work, especially in terms of Butler's life review and Tornstam's transcendence. Thus the five sections comprising the body of *Being Here* represent the major stages of the persona's life—childhood, youth, maturation, age, and decline and death.

Warren also singles out two more poems in his "Afterthought," "Empty White Blotch on Map of Universe: A Possible View" and "Ballad of Your Puzzlement," the focal offerings of the book's third and fifth sections, respectively. He then goes on to define each of these pieces as "an introduction to a section" and to describe each as "a kind of a backboard against which the poems of the section are bounced" (441). "Ballad of Your Puzzlement" also has been referenced in my introductory chapter in regard to its parenthetical subtitle suggestive of life review, "(*How not to recognize yourself as what you think you are, when old and reviewing your life before death comes*)" (423). This puzzling poem then presents an expressionistic montage of surrealistically dreamlike fragments from a more universalized autobiography, one bearing at first glance little relation to either the author's life or to a literary ballad. Warren's "Afterthought" also puts forward complicating considerations of "Empty White Blotch on Map of the Universe," which is only "A Possible View" after all. Warren characterizes this vision as "a parodic and disintegrating account of the history of man's striving for spiritual values and a sense of community, with only a defeated and pathetic romantic sexual yearning left in the end" (441). *Being Here,* he tells us finally, evolved "thematically, but with echoes, repetitions, and variations in feeling and tonality" in tension with a structure ordered by "a shadowy narrative" or "a shadowy autobiography" (441). Warren concludes his "Afterthought" in terms of artistic age-work and autobiography, insisting that "it may be said that our lives are our own supreme fiction" (441).

Most earlier criticism comes to somewhat similar conclusions about *Being Here* by way of Warren's "Afterthought." In the first full-scale study of the writer, James H. Justus echoes Warren by stating that *Being Here* "is built into five sections that comprise the 'shadowy autobiography' of the poet from childhood (section I) through old age (section V)" (104). Warren's biographer believes that in the new volume, "he was chronicling what it had been like to be a man alive . . . looking back in the book's five segments from childhood to years beyond the allotted biblical span" (Blotner

453–54). In his recent introductory study of Warren, James A. Grimshaw Jr. implies an even greater range of vision to *Being Here:* "The poet passes in this volume along the continuum of time from childhood innocence to a mature acceptance of life's road through the future" (163). Other critics complicate Warren's narrative pattern with various thematic complexities. In an important early essay on the volume in 1985, Peter Stitt concludes that "the structure of *Being Here* is both linear and circular"; linear in its "shadowy autobiography" but circular in Warren's coalescing of "thematic concerns" (225). More recently, Randolph Paul Runyon accepts Stitt's trope of circularity but posits a different linear structure by linking each poem to the next within "life's long sorites" as formulated by Warren in "Aspen Leaf in Windless World" from the collection's final section (*Braided Dream* 160). My approach to *Being Here* builds on these earlier insights, but it traces the structural tensions between the poet's autobiographical life review and his philosophical age-work by means of the clues that Warren provides in his "Afterthought."

3

Warren's revelation that he composed his poetic "brackets" for *Being Here,* "October Picnic Long Ago" and "Passers-By on Snowy Night," before he fully organized the collection indicates something of their overall structural and thematic significance. "October Picnic Long Ago" is clearly autobiographical and slightly nostalgic, like Section I, which follows it, while "Passers-By on Snowy Night" is generally universal and clearly speculative, like Section V, which it follows. Although the remembered picnic takes place in autumn, its imagery evokes a golden Indian summer suggesting the prelapsarian innocence of its six-year-old persona that is echoed in the other childhood reminiscences of Section I. In contrast, the snowy night of the book's final poem might well be the winter solstice itself, the nadir of the seasons' natural cycle that evokes the conclusion of human life reverberating back throughout *Being Here* from the considerations of decline and death in the darker speculations of Section V.

Although Warren's birth family is the subject of the group portrait presented by "October Picnic Long Ago." it also becomes a picture of a more innocent age in national terms as well, like a photograph in a faded album with its period details such as the mother's long skirt and the father's high-button shoes. Nothing captures this pervasive feeling better than the hired horse and buggy that transports the family into an edenic countryside, "*That being before the auto had come, or many*" (381). It is as if this more natural mode of transport aligns them with the spirit of the countryside as they leave their weekday world behind on their Sunday excursion. The hypnotic rhythm of hoofbeats function like a metronome to order Warren's regular, if extended lines—both as they enter the natural world, "*Out of town,* clop-clop, *till we found a side-lane that led / Into woods,*" and as they leave it, "*and she gaily sang / As we* clop-clopped *homeward*" (381). Warren's regular rhymes in seven quintet stanzas (ABABB) also underline this sense of a lost golden age of the past "*where gold leaves flicked a fairy shadow and light*" as if in Romantic lyrics (381). At last, "*steered by a witch's sleight,*" they cross a small stream and enter into a magical place where all their dreams might come true (381).

After five stanzas, even the aging persona who recalls this long-ago picnic may yearn for some sort of transcendence through his recollection. In particular, he remembers his parents' daylong conversation and hopes that it continues somewhere, "*Perhaps in some high, cloud-floating, and sunlit land,*" that seems a universal projection of their gold glade in the midst of Kentucky's "Black Patch" (381). "*But picnics have ends*" the penultimate stanza announces, and the sunset of the final stanza heads them toward home "*while the shadows, sly / Leashed the Future up, like a hound with a slavering fang*" (381). Of course, this naturalistic image of time as devouring beast is projected by the aged persona, as the sleepy little boy of six, who "*didn't know what a Future was,*" drifts off in the buggy, hearing only his mother's "*bird-note burst . . . as she sang*" (381). In another signature of his late style, Warren ends "October Picnic Long Ago" with a single, set-off, and fragmented line that echoes the final one of the last full stanza—"*And she sang*" (381). As we will discover at the conclusion of this chapter, "Passers-By on Snowy Night" is even more tightly and traditionally organized to present its bleaker picture of the human passage through the cycle of nature toward death in its images drawn from a midwinter night.

The poem that opens and introduces Section I, "Speleology," is another childhood reminiscence, like "October Picnic Long Ago," and it also serves an introductory function, not just in relation to the developing order of the pieces in the first section from youth to age but to the maturing visions in the other four sections. “Speleology” also proves close to “Passers-By on Snowy Night” in terms of theme and meaning, as well as of image and symbol. In the course of “Speleology,” Warren's autobiographical persona develops from the innocent child of six first glimpsed in “October Picnic Long Ago” to a boy of twelve who experiences nature's first insinuations of his own mortality. Warren assured Floyd Watkins that the cave described here is real, so “Speleology” has a realistic base in the limestone karst and water-carved caverns of the Black Patch (165). At the same time, however, Warren develops the symbolic possibilities of his cave as both womb and tomb in images of the subconscious and of death.[2]

After discovering the “cave-mouth” at six, Warren's persona explores it again each year, as he “peered in, crept further” (382). At twelve, a new flashlight emboldens him to penetrate deep into the archetypal cavern. Resting on a ledge high above a subterranean stream, he snaps off his light to know “darkness and depth and no Time” (382). The faint lullaby of the water's flow echoes until the youthful persona realizes his own selfhood even in the midst of nature; he thinks “*This is me,*” then asks, “*Me—who am I*?” (382). Wakened from his dream of nature as the flashlight slips from his grasp, he hears “a song like terror” as nature's other anthem; even after securing the flashlight and illuminating the “slicing and sluicing” stream, “water winked, bubbles like fish-eyes” (382). The ironic intent of this subterranean wink is the fact that cave fish are eyeless and blind, very much like the cave cricket the persona discovers earlier. The final stanza then moves “years later, past dreams” to the aged persona recalling these early insights and repeating them again, “*This is me*” and “*Me—who am I*?” (382). “Speleology” concludes, like “October Picnic Long Ago,” with a stanza of a single line pointing uncertainly ahead: “And in darkness have even asked: *Is this all*? *What is all?*” (383).

The other poems gathered as Section I replicate the directions of “Speleology” by extending the experiences of their autobiographical personae further into their physical and psychological development. For example, the title of the second selection, “When Life Begins,” suggests both as its boyish persona learns about life and death in the shadow of his grandfather's monumental wisdom. The young Warren enjoyed just this sort of relation to his maternal grandfather, Gabriel Thomas Penn (1836–1920), to whom *Being Here* is dedicated. An officer in the Confederate cavalry in his young manhood, the matured man was a successful tobacco farmer and broker until the Tobacco Wars of the early twentieth century reduced his holdings to a small farm in Trigg County, Kentucky, where Warren spent the summers of his boyhood. His grandfather reappears often in Warren's poetry and fiction, more often as Warren himself approached the age old "Tom" Penn had achieved when he served as his grandson's informal guide into the mysteries of life and death. In its Civil War scenes of death and destruction, "When Life Begins" proves typical of the old man's lessons in the progress of life and death; for example, a shell burst over a battlefield is likened to "A day-star over new Bethlehem" (384). Hearing the old man's tales from the southern mythos, "The boy sat and wondered when life would begin"; unknown to him, "Time crouched, like a great cat, motionless"—the first of many images of similar beasts stalking him through the labyrinth of the future in *Being Here* (384).

"Boyhood in Tobacco Country" hearkens back to the same period in Warren's life, but its scene is set in autumn and is recalled from nearer home in Todd County, Kentucky. Walking alone at sunset, this boyish persona senses the turning of the seasons toward fall in the scent of tobacco-curing fires and the sight of moonrise obscured by their smoke. He declares, "darkling I stand," but, without an appearance of Thomas Hardy's "Darkling Thrush," he "yearns for a grief" worthy even of the poor "whip-o-will's" cry. (385). Warren uses the typical southern spelling for this night bird onomatopoetically named for its plaintive call often associated with death in folk traditions. Although now far removed in time and space from his boyhood home place in the Black Patch, the aged persona relives the same emotions as he senses once more that "Arrogant, eastward, lifts the slow dawn of the harvest moon" calling forth his earlier emotions now a lifetime later. Again, he knows "Oh, grief! Oh, joy!" despite the indisputable fact that at present "The dark roof hides the sky" (385).

The whippoorwill's is only one of the many bird calls that Warren employs as an aural image in *Being Here*, a motif that most often represents the ambiguous messages of nature. In the next selection, "Filling Night with the Name," that name is the whippoorwill's, and it is pronounced thrice over by the night bird as nature's sad commentary on a withered farmwife's last rite of passage that is referenced in the poem's subtitle,

"Funeral as Local Color." Likewise, a loon's raucous laughter wakes him from a nightmare drawn from his youth in the following poem, "Recollection in Upper Ontario, from Long Before." The extended narrative recollected in his dream concerns death and mourning once again, but here it is presented in the naturalistic description of an old woman struck by a speeding express train at the railroad junction near the persona's hometown a lifetime earlier.[3] An owl's "same old gargle of question" then suggests the persona's puzzled ambivalence in both boyhood and age about who should feel guilt for her horrific demise; the bird's call compels "your conscience ask if it's you who—*who-who*— / Did whatever it was" (386).[4]

"The Moonlight's Dream," which comes next in the section, continues the motif of the personal past transformed by a dreamlike recollection, here with the visual magic of moonlight. While wandering in his vision, Warren's persona pauses "while a whip-o-will / Asserted to the moonlight its name," though he is frozen in time, "nameless and still" (389). "The Only Poem," which follows, also recounts a recurring dream, one in which Warren as a young man realized his growing separation from his loving but possessive mother. In presenting the "facts" behind the dream, Warren recounts how before leaving Guthrie for graduate school in California he went with his mother to see the infant daughter of friends who was being kept by her maternal grandmother.[5] His mother's joy in that baby and her sorrow at his departure embarrass him then and now for he knows: "Success or failure—what can alleviate / The pang of unworthiness built into Time's own name?" (390). Only a brief consideration of his "unaimed, pubescent" grief and joy in "Platonic Drowse" separates "The Only Poem" from Warren's consideration of his mother's death in "Grackles, Goodbye" (390).

This final selection of Section I is another bird poem, of course, but here these migrating flocks of iridescently black creatures are both recalled from the past experiences of the poetic persona and observed once more in his old age. Indeed, the reappearance of these common birds in their cyclic migrations allows them to function as memento mori for the aging Warren, much like the migrating geese in "Heart of Autumn," the final selection of *Now and Then*. Like that poem, this one recalls nineteenth-century American Romantic poetry in both matter and form. If anything, "Grackles, Goodbye" is even more traditional in its metrical format—five quatrains of nearly regular lines varying between five and six feet and rhyming ABAB. At least one of Warren's critics has complained about rhymes that "create awkward lines" in his later poetry; in my view, this seeming awkwardness here supports the poet's ironic speculations on the traditional pieties of sentimental nature poetry (Blotner 454).

"Grackles, Goodbye" is partially located in the present, for as boy and man Warren's persona has marked the turn of the seasons when the "Black of grackles . . . pepper the blueness of distance" (391). In this poem, the past is accessible in a waking "trance of realization" induced by the fading bird calls as "The flock splays away" (391). Unlike William Cullen Bryant's contemplation of migratory flocks as symbols revealing a guiding hand behind nature, Warren's departing grackles quickly "are lost in the tracklessness of air"—much like times and people past (391). Transported in his vision, Warren first remembers "gold light" in the mountains of his manhood, then "yellow leaves" on the lawn of childhood, much like those on the family outing in "October Picnic Long Ago" (391). His mother's hand held his while he played with bright leaves whose natural color contrasts with the "obscene fake lawn" used as a grave cover at her funeral (391).

Warren was but twenty-six at the time of his mother's untimely death at the age of only fifty-six, and the many times he reconsiders his initial loss in his poetry demonstrates its psychological importance to him—even in his age. In the very face of death, whether his mother's in the past or his own in the future, Warren annunciates only the valediction suggested by nature. The poem's final stanza opens with a reiteration of its title, "Grackles, goodbye!" (391). If the "sky will be vacant and lonely," after their passing, then he will be reassured by the "horde's rusty creak" in another spring, "Confirming the year's turn and the fact that only, only, / In the name of Death do we learn the true name of Love" (391). Thus, Warren ends with just the suggestion of transcendence that motivated one of his mourners to choose "Grackles, Goodbye!" as one of the selections to be read at his 1989 memorial service.[6]

4

Much like the opening section that began in boyhood, *Being Here*'s Section II opens in later youth to reiterate the autobiographical order of the overall collection. Memories of Warren's own young manhood are recalled in the first of the seven selections that comprise this second grouping, but the half-dozen other poems that follow proceed to parallel feelings of cosmic bewilderment as his persona matures. The introductory poem, "Youthful Truth-Seeker, Half-Naked, at Night, Running down Beach South of San Francisco," seemingly dates to Warren's years of graduate study at the University of California in Berkeley, but it also looks back to "The Only Poem" in Section I, where Warren left his mother to begin his journey into maturity. Although the other poems in Section II concern other places and times in his own life (and perhaps of his son's life in the concluding "Sila"), they project his youthful puzzlement into the present of the poet contemplating his uncertain future in his increasingly difficult age-work. Despite his half century of maturing experience, Warren's life review can discover no easy answers to the questions raised by the ambiguous tuitions of nature he first experienced in his youth, especially those of transcendence.

The long title of Warren's opening poem in Section II not only connects it with his experience of California as a young man but also with the physical and psychological aspects of his extended development toward a mature identity. His youthful persona seeks for some insight into life and truth by immersing himself in nature, as he races shirtless down the beach and falls helpless on the shore where the waves touch the sands under a fog rolling in to obliterate the beach. The particulars of this Romantic quest seem typical enough of a graduate student in English, one whose "world" is bounded by "Poetry, orgasm, joke," but the poem also connects that search to his earlier and later experiences in its ultimate failure (392). The timelessness of "life's instancy" is reiterated in imagery of stars and birds where "constellations strive, or a warbler whets / His note," and later in different images of daylight shrouded with gray fog or "white-night Arctic light" that reverberates throughout the several winter poems (392). Here, nature seems unable to communicate "a truth the heart might speak" (392). Unlike earlier interpreters of sea or shore in "lines that bring tears to the heart," such as Walt Whitman or Matthew Arnold, Warren seems to hear or to see "No word? No sign?" (392, 393). After imagining dawn lighting the beach once again, his persona is left to inquire in the poem's last line, "if years later, I'll drive again forth under stars, on tottering bones," when he runs his race with death (392).

Let me postpone consideration of the next selection in Warren's ordering of Section II, "Snowshoeing Back to Camp in Gloaming," in order to connect it with the two concluding winter poems of this section, "Preternaturally Early Snowfall in Mating Season" and "Sila." This tactic allows me to link "Youthful Truth-Seeker, Half-Naked, at Night, Running down Beach South of San Francisco" with the third poem of the second section, "Why Have I Wandered the Asphalt of Midnight?" much as Warren does in his 1985 *Selected Poems*. Their long titles, dark imagery, and unanswered questions generally connect these two poems; more specifically, they are paired geographically by the fourth rephrasing of the question of the title in the second poem: "Why should I wander dark dunes till rollers / Boom in from China, stagger, and break / On the beach in frothed mania . . . ?" (395). The five examples of his wanderings that order this poem seem to extend throughout the persona's lifetime, but they are gathered in a final question "why, all the years, and places, and nights, have I / Wandered and not known the question I carried?" (395). As if in answer, the phrase "Yes, sometimes, at dawn" affirmatively introduces three brighter, more transcendent images of sunrise (395). This balance of night and day is maintained in the pair of poems that follow, "August Moon" and "Dreaming in Daylight." The late summer evening in the first poem reveals familiar nocturnal images: moonlight and star shine; dark wood and pale path; and the interrogative cry of "the great owl," as well as nature's "darkling susurration" that "Might—if only we were lucky—be / Deciphered" (396). In the second poem, similar conclusions are achieved as nature reveals only the eyes of hidden beasts on a woods walk where daydreams prove daunting as nightmares.

"Snowshoeing Back to Camp in Gloaming" and "Preternaturally Early Snowfall in Mating Season" form a natural pairing of winter poems, ones seemingly based on Warren's late-life excursions into various mountain ranges, if perhaps augmented by his imagination. An initial connection of the two poems can be found in the most striking words in their titles, "Gloaming" and "Preternaturally," words that are not repeated in their texts. The first term means twilight, of course, but with just the suggestion of archaism by way of Scots ballads or Romantic lyrics. In the poem it introduces, Warren's persona is making his weary way homeward at evening across a bleak winter landscape, seeing dead leaves that seem like "Old words forgotten in snowdrifts" (394). The only sound, however, is heard when "the crow in distance called," evidently announcing the final descent of dark, for the persona "knew / He spoke truth" (394). The poem then pivots on a short line consisting only of the apostrophe "Oh, Pascal!" (394). Although the philosophical references here might be many, Warren probably is suggesting the great thinker's precautionary "wager" or "gambit," wherein he concludes that the benefits of belief inherently outweigh those of doubt (Grimshaw 164–65). As if to corroborate this reading, Warren turns from the empty darkness to a remembered scene where "Beautiful faces above a hearthstone bent / Their inward to an outward glow" (394). He imagines his return in warm images of homecoming, as "one gaze / Will lift and smile with sudden sheen / Of a source far other than firelight—or even // Imagined star-glint," imagery much different than that of "Passers-By on Snowy Night" (394).

Although the physical movement of "Preternaturally Early Snowfall in Mating Season" is much the same as that discerned in "Snowshoeing Back to Camp in Gloaming," the philosophical direction of the poem is much different in its harsher naturalism. Paradoxically, this "preternaturally" premature snow portends some of these differences in its suggestion of an almost malevolent spirit lurking behind the brighter aspects of nature. Although the initial snowfall of the season may arrive earlier than normal in these mountains, the natural ritual of mating still obtains for the beasts of this wild, and it suggests a less optimistic vision of life than we see in the conclusion of the first winter poem. As noted in my discussion of *Or Else,* Warren imaged the first snowfall of winter on the western landscape of the Nez Perce Pass between Idaho and Montana in "I Am Dreaming of a White Christmas: The Natural History of a Vision." There it images death and transcendence much as in Robert Frost's poems such as "The Onset" (1921). That poem may be "quintessential Frost" for Cleanth Brooks, but he could be speaking of Warren when he remarks the older writer as "characteristically, the poet of autumn, of impending winter, of darkness to come" ("Robert Frost" 1859).

"Preternaturally Early Snowfall in Mating Season" proves a good example of Warren's variations on Frost's poetic legacy. Although the first few snowflakes were sprinkled on "gold-fading beech leaves" in sunlight that showed "remote indifference," that night revealed "no stars" and the next day "no sun" (398, 399). The result is "Grayness diffused," and it foretells "the real thing coming, and soon" for Warren's persona (399). One thing reassures him as he makes another camp, "snowshoes in tote," a bit of "Pure luck" in light of the blizzard that begins overnight (399). However, the persona is wakened twice: first by snow falling on his face and later by a buck and doe thrashing together amid the "ecstasy of storm" (399). Even with his snowshoes, it takes him two days "to get out / And rations short the second," so that he is left with only "the simple awareness of Being" after his ordeal (399). Thus, "being here" is enough to suggest "the guessed-at glory" of home to Warren's persona, though he must face another night of "gloom" when "fatigue and hunger" make it hard for him "to get a fire going" (399). Whatever homecoming awaits, it seems much different than that of "Snowshoeing Back to Camp in Gloaming," while both poems again anticipate "Passers-By on Snowy Night," the concluding selection of *Being Here*.

Section II of the collection finishes with the long narrative "Sila," in which Warren reiterates the imagery and symbolism of the preceding winter poems while returning to the persona of a young man initiated into an indifferent natural universe, much as in the opening selection from his own California experience. The identity of Warren's persona and the location of his setting are more problematic here, however. "Sila" is an "Eskimo" word for something like the elemental life force, suggesting the far north, but the snowscapes pictured may be in the western mountains or perhaps northern New England. The latter setting is plausible, if only because Warren's biographer indicates that the young persona is in fact Warren's grown son, who appears in another instance of the poet's projecting of his own life experiences into those of his progeny (Blotner 455). At the same time the striking title and Warren's long epigraph from the *Larousse World Mythology* explaining it lend an air of the universal and the timeless to his narrative. Although reminiscent of the other winter poems in this section, Warren's narrative presents much more than raw nature in its setting.

The unnamed young protagonist is exploring on cross-country skis accompanied by his "tawny great husky," named Sila in homage to its northern origins (400). As the poem opens, the persona is arrested by a "ruin of old stonework," evidently the traces of an abandoned farmstead that he thinks must date "*Two hundred years back*" (400). At the moment of taking his own place in the world, this youth wonders that another as young as himself may have lifted these stones in place to mark the start of his mature life. Looking at a gravestone to give a name and a date to this story from the past, the young man unleashes the husky. It plunges into raw nature, flushing and felling a doe hidden in a snow-covered deadfall. Wrestling his pet off its prey, the protagonist meets the dog's "eyes blue as steel" only to realize "that instant, / All eons of friendship fled" (401). The symbolic beast has shown itself, and this revelation of Tennyson's nature, "red in tooth and claw," is fully realized when the young man must cut the throat of the doe to spare it suffering. An elemental force compels him to taste its warm blood on his knife in a sacramental union with "something at last / That he'd never before known" (402). He can only cry out "Oh, world!" because he knows "No name for it—no!" though "its" name is really Sila both literally and symbolically (402). Warren plays one last trick with time, projecting his young protagonist "some sixty years later" to his deathbed when he will recall this initiation into first knowledge of the world's true nature (402).

5

Warren opens Section III with "Empty White Blotch on Map of Universe: A Possible View," a rather difficult poetic effort that he characterizes in his prose "Afterthought" to *Being Here* as a sort of sore thumb, "not only peculiar in style, but as having meanings quite contradictory to the tone and intent of the work as a whole" (441). The blank vision of the universe implied in the title is undercut, however, when the subtitle posits this reading of the universal map as only one possibility. As Warren goes on to tell us, the poem presents "a parodic and disintegrating account" of the human situation within the natural universe (441). Warren's "history" of human development begins with "man's striving for spiritual values and a sense of community," but it ends with "only a defeated and pathetic romantic sexual yearning" (441). Warren concludes that this selection is also intended "as an introduction to a section chiefly concerned with the issues ironically raised in the poem" (441).

It may seem that Warren sufficiently explains "Empty White Blotch on Map of the Universe: A Possible View" in his "Afterthought," but his generalizations remain strangely abstracted. It is only when illustrated by this poem's and this section's concrete images that they become meaningful for Warren's age-work and life review. In its central position, the third section of *Being Here* represents midlife and its inevitable crises. The ten additional selections that comprise this grouping generally support this reading. In particular, the sixth, or middle, poem, "Part of What Might Have Been a Short Story, Almost Forgotten," references Warren's troubled first marriage and its ultimate demise in what became his most obvious midlife failure. As in the first two sections on his childhood and young manhood, the progression of Warren's personae through his middle years is not completely linear, as it moves backward and forward between earlier and later memories. Therefore, the opening poem of Warren's third section stands out like a "sore thumb" precisely because of its abstracted and universalized vision of the conflicts and failures of middle age.

Tensions between abstract and concrete in the poem begin with Warren's title, where the universe is imaged as a map in which the world appears as an empty blank. A map is a text analogous to a poem, of course, one that represents a larger reality and interprets it for a reader. Warren's imagined map recalls one of those early world maps drawn in the age of exploration on which empty white spaces represent terra incognita. In Section III as a whole the human world is terra incognita for Warren, however, who expands his trope by locating his poetic persona Crusoe-like on a desert island. He is cast away on an uncharted coast not by a Shakespearean tempest, but by "a father's lust" that thrusts him into the world (403). Like Prospero's, "this island is full of voices," though the persona cannot make contact with these singers or translate their lyrics into language he can understand (403). He does find "a ruined cairn raised by lost aboriginals" but can discern no spiritual meaning in it (403). Instead, he turns back to scraps of human culture in his memory such as "orations from school I pronounced to the squalls / Of gulls and tern-laughter" as a "comic charade," or pathetic rituals such as a self-crucifixion that ends with "*lama sabachthani*" (403). Still alone on his God-forsaken isle, Warren's persona crawls back into his cave, hears the surf beat on like a "monody," and dreams of sea voices able to communicate "like pain, [in] their love-stung cry" (404).

In the ten other poems comprising Section III, Warren's speculative formulations in his "Afterthought" and his concrete images in "Empty

White Blotch on Map of the Universe: A Possible View" are reiterated in personal revelations elucidated by autobiographical details. For example, Warren's persona recalls the winter poems of Section II when explaining the purpose of snowstorms as "coverings-over, forgettings" in the second poem of Section III, "Function of Blizzard." The snow whitens concrete realities such as "Black ruins of arson in the Bronx," while he wonders in his personal confession what "Item of the past I'd most like God to let / Snow fall on" (404). In the next selection, "Dream, Dump-Heap, and Civilization," Warren connects a dream of decapitated kittens projected from his past, a garbage dump in "Norwalk, Connecticut" observed in his present, and a philosophical question to contemplate in the future about his earlier complicity with evil—"Is civilization possible without it?" (405). The "Vision" that follows in the poem of that title does not function to let "Truth be revealed" but so its persona will realize the "truth" inherent in "the first / Illicit meeting" from his past and a life-threatening surgery in his future (406). "Globe of Gneiss" provides another vision of the world as blank space in the image of this "great globe," in a sense another symbol mapping nature in metamorphic granite, "harder / Than steel" and "poised" by a prehistoric glacier on a New England mountainside to no human purpose (407).

A wonder formed by unknowing forces of nature over eons of time in the West is presented in "Part of What Might Have Been a Short Story, Almost Forgotten," the pivotal sixth poem of the third section. This narrative of a trip to visit the Shoshone Falls of the Snake River in Idaho during the 1930s proves the longest of the eleven in this grouping and the most significant in terms of both Warren's own midlife crisis and the universal human failings that he consistently images as great beasts, real or imagined, silently waiting there to spring upon future victims. Warren remembers the drive over "rough roads" nearly a half century earlier in a quest for "Nature's beauty" on the part of a couple unspeaking in their separate contemplations (408, 409). Presented here in Warren's irregular octosyllabics, the great falls recasts the globe of gneiss from the previous poem, "as tons of water / Glinting like steel, if steel could flow, / Plunge over geologic de- / bris to darkening depth" (408). Its thundering roar soon sends the woman back to the car, as "Noise gave her headaches," while the man is "drawn to the / Brink, gaze frozen downward" into the terrifying abyss

(408–9). Late sunset and first stars draw the persona's vision upward once more, only to see a mountain lion—"On the slant of a / Skyward-broken stratum, among / Sparse scrub, it crouched" (409). He is frozen in fear until the creature, "With insolent, / Contemptuous dignity," leaps into "blank darkness past / Lip of the chasm" (409). Driving again with his silent companion on "roads poor-mapped," Warren's persona projects the future, wondering "what beast might, waiting, be" (410). That "metaphysical" creature he equates with the "foetal, fatal truth" which the couple "witlessly concealed / In mere charade, hysterical // Or grave, of love" that he had forgotten until this later age-work and life review (410).

As if in reiteration of the truths discovered amid the revelations of raw nature, in the next poem Warren observes other crises of middle age in the seemingly civilized trappings of a "Cocktail Party," perhaps one he might have attended between his divorce and remarriage. His persona observes how, even in "the haze of alcohol," the "gage of the girl's glance" invites "a faint / Stir, as of a beast in shadow"; realizing "the horror of Truth," he puns at the last, it "lies in wait" (410). Literal beasts appear in the next selection, "Deep—Deeper Down," a short narrative about shooting "cotton-mouth" snakes in Louisiana with a male friend; they strive "To purge the earth of evil" in this daily ritual of male bonding "For spring and all summer" until the friend's "wife drove back"—though his own mate never appears (411).[7] "Sky," the short poem that follows, is concerned with a storm rather than a literal beast, but its symbolic subject is "What most we fear"; however, its "true name is what we never know," much as the young protagonist of "Sila" discovered (412). Metaphorical beasts are introduced in the penultimate poem of Section III, "Better Than Counting Sheep," but rather than these dull creatures, Warren's persona counts "All those ever known who are dead now," until "your heart / Howls with the loneliness of a wolf," in a notable instance of both age-work and life review. The final beast poem in the third section of *Being Here* would seem to date to the early years of Warren's second marriage when the newlywed couple lived on the Italian coast. Its title is "The Cross," its subtitle is "(*A Theological Study*)" and its beast is a tiny monkey drowned on the previous night (413). Warren's persona discovers the pathetic remains on the beach among the detritus of a seasonal storm—taking time to tell him "*ciao*," to bury him in "a scraped-out hole," and to make him a "little cairn on top" (414). The cross of the title is described in the penultimate line, "Two sticks tied together to prop in the sand," and the theological study is implied in the final line, "But what's the use of that? The sea comes back," bringing with its waves successive iterations of natural annihilation and metaphysical emptiness (414).

6

The fourth section of *Being Here* approaches Warren's situation in the book's present of 1977–80 by considering the onset of old age, the imminence of death, and the possibility of nonbeing. Once again, Warren begins with an abstract statement of these human problems in his first selection, "Truth," but he goes on to more concrete realizations of them in the nine additional poems that complete the grouping. The single word of Warren's title is reiterated nine times within the 151 words comprising "Truth," in capitals each time as befits its abstraction. Warren's concrete images also attempt to transform his intellectual formulation of "Truth" into more intuitive emotions, so that his readers are presented with multiple truths that resonate through the other poems that follow. The variations that Warren plays on the definition of "Truth" are indicated by his structuring of the poem; it consists of twenty-three unrhymed, irregular lines in seven stanzas of one to seven lines. "Truth" appears as the subject of nine of Warren's ten sentences and as the initial word in eight of his lines, creating a notable instance of his fondness for anaphora that drives home the poet's insistent search for a universal "Truth," while acknowledging that no single truth exists, only its various subjective alternatives.

The opening line of "Truth" establishes this understanding of Warren's subject as he tells his reader that "Truth is what you cannot tell," though he will try to do so in this poem and the nine others that come after it (415). The burden of age-work is presented in the second line, "Truth is for the grave," a variation on Warren's theme that death defines life, which reverberates throughout this poem and section (415). Although death is eternally unchanging, in life "Truth" often seems as ephemeral as "the flowing shadow" or "the downy feather" (415). "Truth" also proves amorphous as both "the trick that History" plays over and over again or "the Serpent's joke" that the Deity seems somehow to countenance (415). "Truth" can be heard, if not understood, both as the "whisper we strive to catch" or "the scream of a locomotive" that we fail to heed (415). Warren consistently pulls "Truth" closer and closer to death, however, concluding that it is at once "the long soliloquy / Of the dead" and "what would be told by the dead / If they could hold conversation / With the living" (415). In the final line of the poem, "Their accumulated wisdom must be immense," Warren affirms the value of age-work and life review in their implied dialogues with the dead (415).

Although no point-for-point correspondence exists between the nine definitions and images Warren reveals in "Truth" and the nine other selections that complete the section, the imagery and meaning of the initial poem often reappear in them. For instance, "On into the Night," Warren's second selection, finds the only truth of nature in its cyclic changes, imaged here by a transforming sunset in autumn as perceived by his aging persona. At the "downward slope" of afternoon, shadows of the woods become "an image of Time's metaphysic," much like the more ephemeral shadings of "Truth" in the previous poem (415). Nature remains silent in the face of human questioning, "Like film in silence being unspooled" (416). At dusk, "the prick of appetite" animates the bat to "scribble // . . . lethal script on a golden sky," the bear to "utter his sexual hoot," the thrush to throb "its last music," and the owl to ask its "mystic question" (416). In a night now silent again after nature's "glut," Warren's persona cannot decode these natural emanations any more than he can the beat of his own heart, whose "merciless repetition" declares "Its task in undecipherable metaphor" in the last stanza comprised of only this single line (416).

Nature's cryptic silence is reconfigured in the next poem, "No Bird Does Call," in which Warren's aging persona remembers a natural retreat of his youth, again as if he is watching a silent film. This bower, "beech-bounded, beech-shrouded," would be a forest chapel in a lyric from the era of American Romanticism, but even here the persona cannot find peace after fleeing "the bustle of men" (416, 417). When he awakens from his dream, "it seemed then that years— / How many?—had passed," as if he were a twentieth-century Rip Van Winkle (417). In the final line of the poem, however, Warren's persona reflects that many years after this youthful flight, "when I wake in the night to remember, no bird ever calls" (417). This sort of inscrutable silence Warren names "the old stoicism of Nature" in "Weather Report," the ironically titled selection that forms a clear pairing with "No Bird Does Call" (417). The report that follows in this poem is not one given about the weather, but one delivered by the weather, as raindrops seem to tap in code on the roof that separates Warren's persona from nature. He deciphers this message as "*Today is today,*" but he asks himself, "Have I read it aright?" (417, 418). For corroboration of his reading, the persona listens for the "warblers" who "poured out their ignorant joy" to yesterday's sunny afternoon (417). Today, he sees one silent bird, "rain-slick like old oil," its beak "unmoving as death" (417, 418). In spite of this enigmatic silence emanating from nature, Warren's persona imagines he hears how the "earth grinds on," but he questions even this perception at the last (418).

Nocturnal rain creates the aural imagery of "Tires on Wet Asphalt at Night," the fifth poem in Section IV. Sleepless in the dark, Warren's persona hears the "*swish-hiss*" made by the tires of a passing car, and he imagines its occupants as "A man and a woman" illuminated only by the "cold dimness of gauge-lights" (418). This invented couple seems another instance of the distanced pairs that Warren often projects from his first marriage. In his imagination, the woman perceives his own darkened bedroom windows as "Two dead eyes that nobody has closed," while the persona then follows the couple home to their bedroom and the mechanical love-making that only reinforces their separateness (418). At some subliminal level of consciousness, Warren's persona also identifies the swishing and hissing of the tires on the wet road with the "faint but continual" sound of waves lapping a "beach-patch" discovered on one of his Mediterranean sojourns long before (418). He feels compelled to climb down into this cove, "crag-locked and pathless," another natural retreat like the caves and bowers remembered earlier in *Being Here* (418). The persona's problem is not so much his descent to this retreat in late afternoon, but his ascent from it in early evening that leaves him "exhausted, face-down, arms outflung," and shaking either in fear of or love for the natural world around him (419). Again, Warren concludes with a stanza of a single extended line, this one linking the two sets of images recalled in his reaction to the night sound of tires on wet asphalt, "I wish I could think what makes them come together now" (419).

The two poems that follow after "Tires on Wet Asphalt at Night,"

"Timeless, Twinned" and "What is the Voice that Speaks?" form another obvious pairing—again in their concerns for the meanings of silent and speaking voices. In the first of the pair, Warren's persona is contemplating the beauty of an autumn day marked by "one white / Cloud," "an azure which / Is called the sky," and a "gold drench of light" (419). Yet "No voice / Speaks, since here no voice knows / The language in which a tongue might now rejoice" (419). Although the persona fears that he is drowning in the flood of silence that results, both nature's and his own, he still identifies himself with the "lonely, autochthonous" cloud and clings to "our single existence, timeless, twinned" (419). In contrast, there are many answers to the question asked in the title of "What is the Voice that Speaks?" Some are the voices of nature, including the tongues of a "laurel leaf" or a "*coluber constrictor*— / Black racer to you" (420). The question of identity posed by "the great owl" is invoked once more, "the one you've never, in anguish, been able to answer" (420). In reply to this query about self-identity, the final image of natural sound, "the wolf-howl" in its "desolate timbre," recalls "Better Than Counting Sheep," from the previous section (420). For the human voices in response to his own that Warren's persona remembers in this poem—those of a blind beggar mocked, a dying mother disdained, a divorced wife scorned—all suggest his lonely isolation in self and selfishness (420). Recalling the first poem of this section, Warren asks, "What tongue knows the name of 'Truth?'" (420). He answers his own question with the second line of his final couplet, "All we can do is strive to learn the cost of experience" (420).

The paired poems "Language Barrier" and "Lesson in History" also seem to be efforts toward understanding that steep price of experience in regard to communication failures. In "Language Barrier," the problem proves more personal, and it has a more positive aspect that prefigures similar poems in the fifth section of *Being Here* and in the two later collections. The difficulty perceived here by Warren's persona is comprehending the hints at transcendence that nature intermittently reveals. In the mountain imagery of "Language Barrier," patterns emerge that will become increasingly common in Warren's later poetry, when his personae at last realize that nature is trying to communicate some aspect of "glory" (421). While enjoying a mountain landscape composed of white snow, blue water, and dark stone, Warren's persona asks himself "What grandeur here speaks?"

(421). He answers his own question by asserting that the natural world is certainly a "language we cannot utter," and it may not be "a language we can even hear" (421). Recalling this grand scene years later in a dream, he wonders once again at "that old altitude, breath thinning again to glory, / While the heart, like a trout, / Leaps" (421). Through a long night, he is unable to understand nature's great revelation, much less translate it; instead, he is reduced to listening to the "creatures of gardens and lowlands" around his home. In a single-lined final stanza, Warren's persona concludes on an optimistic note: "It may be that God loves them, too" (421).

The difficulties of "Lesson in History" are both more universal in their concerns and more pessimistic in their implications. Warren begins by declaring in his opening line, "How little does history manage to tell!" (421). As examples, he cites problems involving less important yet more personal details in the lives and deaths of a half-dozen historical figures. This diverse gathering includes, in order of appearance: Judas Iscariot, Daniel Boone, Marshall Cambronne, Charlotte Corday, Hendrik Hudson, and Anne Boleyn. Warren's persona also raises similar questions about the reader and a friend. In the reader's case, they include incomprehension of another natural landscape, this one composed by "a corner of moonlit meadow, willows, sheen of the sibilant stream" (422). In the concluding couplet, the persona asks who will know "what long ago happened there?" or "what, in whisper, the water was trying to say?" (422).

The tenth and last poem in the fourth section, "Prairie Harvest," employs a much different landscape to project the same sorts of questions asked but not answered in "Language Barrier" and "Lesson in History." However, Warren's seasonal setting at evening in autumn after the great reaping reprises the theme of age once more. At this late stage of day, year, and life, the reader identifies with the poetic persona through Warren's use of second person. Perceived as standing alone on the prairie and contemplating the seemingly endless reaches of raw nature, the reader registers the red sunset "over forever miles of wheat stubble" and, as the air cools, notes "blue mist / For uncountable miles of the shaven earth's rondure arises" (422). In "last high light the bullbats gyre and twist," though their cries fade "in the world's emptiness," and the only sound heard is one's own heartbeat (422). When the evening star at last appears in the darkening sky, the same one "the Kiowa once stared at," the ultimate question of age-work and autobiography repeats itself in Warren's closing lines, "can you devise / An adequate definition of self, whatever you are?" (422). These questions of identity and transcendence echo throughout Section IV, as we have discovered, so we should not be surprised when they reappear in the fifth and final section of *Being Here.*

7

In his "Afterthought" to the collection, Warren indicates that "Ballad of Your Puzzlement" functions as a poetic "backboard against which the poems of the section are bounced" (441). Therefore, it seems surprising that the poem comes second in the order of Section V. His first selection is "Eagle Descending," a poem dedicated "*To a dead friend*" in its subtitle (423). That friend was Allen Tate, who died in 1978, and "Eagle Descending" was first published in 1979 by the *Vanderbilt Poetry Review,* appropriately enough (Blotner 456). Warren's elegiac effort thus becomes a perfect choice to start the last section of *Being Here,* concerned as it is with death and human preparation for it. In this sense, "Eagle Descending" serves as a prologue to the fifth section much as "October Picnic Long Ago" functions as the preface to the volume and "Passers-By on Snowy Night" as the poetic epilogue for it. "Eagle Descending" seems closer to the concluding poem in image and theme, of course, and these two sublime pieces then bracket the ten poems that make up the book's final section, including the introductory "Ballad of Your Puzzlement."

First of all, we should recognize that "Eagle Descending" proved problematic for Warren in more ways than its placement in this collection. Tate was perhaps his oldest friend, and he was probably his closest colleague as a poet, though some personal and professional estrangement seems to have developed between them in their later years. Tate was several years Warren's senior and in declining health for many years, but his death must have been both an arresting personal loss and a striking reminder of the universal human condition. Only a few years earlier, Warren could not complete a poem for a gathering in honor of Tate's life at his seventy-fifth birthday; later he seems to have some difficulty deciding whether his poem on the senior poet's death was finally successful (Blotner 420). Warren did not include it in the 1985 *Selected Poems,* and he not only excised it but marked it "not good" in preliminary notes he made in preparation for another selection of his poetry in 1987 (Burt 754). As Warren usually judged his own work well, his conclusion about the poem is puzzling and perhaps suggestive of some personal conflict. In my view, "Eagle Descending" remains among the very best of Warren's great avian poems, and surely it must be included as one of his strongest efforts in the later canon.

Other Warren critics, most notably Harold Bloom, corroborate my ranking of "Eagle Descending" among the poet's very best work. In his magisterial essay, "Sunset Hawk: Warren's Poetry and Tradition," Bloom situates his subject at the intersection between sublime lyric and tragic modes as influenced by traditions extending from the ancient classics through the Romantics to High Modernism. For his examples Bloom turns to Warren's bird poems, particularly his several later works concerned with hawks as personal symbols, some addressed in my earlier chapters. Bloom's selections include "Eagle Descending" as a variation on Warren's imagery of flight and one that in his judgment "suddenly gives us perfection" ("Sunset Hawk" 74). Bloom also declares "Eagle Descending" "an elegy worthy of its subject," connecting Tate and Warren through T. S. Eliot's *Ash-Wednesday* as a "precursor poem" influential on both poets and their poetry ("Sunset Hawk" 74). Although Bloom concludes that Warren's elegy proves more classical than Christian, he does not completely connect "Eagle Descending" with Tate's essential classicism.

As the most learned classicist among the Fugitive/Agrarians, all traditionally educated in the ancient languages and literatures, Tate is represented both significantly and appropriately by the ancient imperial symbol in "Eagle Descending." Warren's images of flight, so often invoked to realize his own hawklike vision, combine here with the imagery of altitudes and extensions developing in his age-work. Although the classical katabasis, or descent into death, is suggested in Warren's title, in his first stanza, "The eagle rides air currents. . . . With spiral upward now, steady as God's will" (423). Indeed, it is the living, the earthbound, "Who downward sink" with the descending sun (423). The three sentences that comprise stanzas 1 to 3 all begin with "Beyond," and this repetition stresses the eagle's ascent above both mountain peaks and cloud columns (423). In the third stanza, however, the eagle's vision transcends earthly geography to encompass the classical landscape of the afterlife: "he stares at the plains afar / By ghostly shadows eastward combed" (423). This mythic reference is reiterated as the fourth stanza opens, "No silly pride of Icarus his!" (423). As he wings westward, the eagle is past all peril of sinking down, despite the setting sun that will leave him alone (423). As Bloom puts it, "That Sublime will survive the fading of twilight," but no analysis is equal to the sublimity of Warren's four concluding lines ("Sunset Hawk," 75):

> The twilight fades. One wing
> Dips, slow. He leans.—And with that slightest shift,
> Spiral on spiral, mile on mile, uncoils
>
> The wind to sing with joy of truth fulfilled.

For me, this last line represents the poetic sublimity Bloom imputed to "Eagle Descending" in much more than its perfect meter, for the thematic tensions between intellectual truth and joyful emotion in the elegy are perfectly suitable both to the life and death of its subject as well as to the age-work and life review of its author.[8]

Although "Eagle Descending" proves appropriate for a preface to Section V, Warren's positioning of "Ballad of Your Puzzlement" as its second selection does not preclude its functioning as the sort of introduction suggested in his "Afterthought" or in his parenthetical subtitle to the poem itself, "(*How not to recognize yourself as what you think you are, when old and reviewing your life before death comes*)" (423). At the beginning of this chapter, I indicated that this lengthy subtitle underlines the concerns of age-work and autobiography that pervade *Being Here,* but it also introduces the images and themes of preparation for death that will distinguish this fifth and final section. In his "Afterthought," Warren puts it exactly in this way: "This section is, of course, concerned with the reviewing of life from the standpoint of age" (441). The section models the theme and structure of *Being Here,* just as "Ballad of Your Puzzlement" models the theme and structure of the section.

The strangeness of "Ballad of Your Puzzlement" as an introductory selection is implied ironically in its very title, for it proves neither ballad-like in form nor transcendent in matter. In fact, the poem's puzzling effects arise from the piece's filmlike structuring and nightmarish substance. However, the film style suggested in it is not contemporary with the poem;

rather, it recalls the expressionistic qualities of the silent movies Warren would have known in his boyhood. The silent film's juxtaposition of static tableaux and frenetic motion is captured in Warren's poetic form; again, he employs tercets, twenty-six of them, this time in lines of three or four feet. Like the most artful among the silent classics of the silver screen, Warren's poem replicates a sort of waking dream in which his persona is transformed into a kind of double or shadow of his conscious self. At the same time, "Ballad of Your Puzzlement" follows the overall pattern of the collection from youth to maturation to aging and death.

Warren begins "Ballad of Your Puzzlement" in an anticipatory mood, proclaiming in its first line, "Purge soul for the guest awaited," while adding in the next stanza, "Put your lands and recollections / In order, before that hour" (423). This awaited hour would seem to be the end of age-work, while the "recollections" might be conclusion of life review—both in death. The reader is identified with this vision of life and death by the writer's use of second person, "For you, alas, are only // Recollections" (423–24). These "recollections" are realized "Like a movie film gone silent," lacking even the traditional explanatory titles, "With a hero strange to you // And a plot you can't understand" (424). This unfamiliar protagonist is first described as a young man "with a passion for Truth" imaged in terms of an acrobatic performance on "the fated / And human high-wire of lies" (424). As in expressionistic film, "scene flicks to scene without nexus," transforming innocent youth into midlife murder, "Where the blade, flash bright in darkness, / Slides slick to the woman's heart, / To the very hilt" (424). After the hero kneels, "Alone, alone at prayer," evidently in confession, he is seen again, "old now and stooped," making a contrite gesture toward a "loathsome beggar" (424–25). In the last scene of his movie, he has become a tramp himself, a "Chaplinesque" shadow in a barren landscape where he "Trudges on, alone, toward sunset" (425).[9] Death comes as the screen goes dark, yet with "blackness / Slashed by stab-jabs of white / That remind you of lightning bolts // At night, at a storm in the mountains," that might be seen realistically as the unwinding of the film's white-marked leader or symbolically as a slight suggestion of possible transcendence that will mark the poems of this fifth and final section (425).

The first of these poems, "Antimony: Time and Identity," operates as a philosophical restatement of the themes Warren realized through the filmic imagery and psychological symbolism presented in "Ballad of Your Puzzlement." Antimony is defined as the logical contradiction of two things that seem equally true, of course. For example, time and identity may seem equally real for us, but the fact remains that time eventually contradicts individual identity. In the poem, Warren implies the span of years that brings him to this logical impasse, but he condenses it into one night's quiet canoeing on a mountain lake ringed by dark forest. The persona sees only the stars and hears just the sounds of nature, until, "As consciousness outward seeps, the dark seeps in" and "the self dissolves," and he is left to "wonder if this is I" (426–27). Then, he is brought back to life with the first beams of dawn that illuminate the future in "the blueness of distance" and the past in "scraps of memory," hanging "on a rusting barbed-wire fence" (427). The poem's seventh and final section consists of a single couplet, obliquely rhyming: "One crow, caw lost in the sky-peak's lucent trance, / Will gleam, sun-purpled in its magnificence," which once more seems to suggest possible transcendence even in the face of time and death (427).

The paired poems that come next in the fifth section, "Trips to California" and "Auto-da-fé," return to longer passages of time in regard to autobiography and history. The trips recollected in the first of these poems are not focused by California except as Warren's frequent destination during the days of his first marriage in the 1930s. Most of the piece is spent depicting the nearly biblical ravages of the Dust Bowl on the Great Plains, in a preview of his later poem "Going West." The sight of a dead mule suggests to the poetic persona the earlier slaughter of the buffalo, and those images in turn imply the whole blood-soaked reality of the westward impulse in American history. Just as California is the "mother / Of dreams," personal and historical, the persona now learns that "Reality past may be only // A dream too" and that the future grows inexorably from the "Dark humus of history or our / Own fate" (428). The title of "Auto-da-fé" translates innocently enough as an act of faith, but the most infamous instances of its application are the fearful judgments of the Inquisition, particularly the sentence of death at the stake. Warren's persona seems to see the most famous historical examples of this dire fate reaching some sort of human "Truth" through the "Beauty of body" transfigured "When flame licks like a lover" (429). He extends this sexual metaphor by translating the scream of pain into poetry "purer / Than even the cry, ecstatic, torn out / At the crisis of body's entwinement" (429). This final imagery also takes the poem back to remembered experience and to the sources of human revelation Warren treats in his poems of his fifth section.

"Aspen Leaf in Windless World" and "Acquaintance with Time in Early Autumn," the paired poems that come next in Section V, combine natural images with philosophical concepts. As Randolph Paul Runyon astutely observes, the two pieces are connected by physical imagery of living and dying leaves as well as by the logical concepts of sorites and paradox (*Braided Dream* 160–61). The aspen leaf of the first title, one that "waggles" even in a windless world, is only the first of the poem's several images representing the "unworded revelation" of nature that proves too indistinct to "decipher" (430). This imagery includes: the "Arabic scrawl" of sea foam on a beach; the "flight of birds," the tree toad's "quavery croak"; and the "sub-sob" of "wind in the cedar" (430). Warren unites all of this inscrutable imagery in the logic of his penultimate stanza: "What image—behind blind eyes when the nurse steps back— / Will loom at the end of your own life's long sorites?" (430). The single leaf in the second poem is an image more easily comprehended, for both the persona and the reader, of the annual onset of autumn and the inevitable commencement of age. Warren opens with an apostrophe in a mock-heroic style, "Oh, leaf, // Cling on! For I have felt knee creak on stair" (431). Yet the "air unmoving" provides a "golden paradox" on this early autumn day, as the "flame-red" leaf lets itself fall at last to meet its "shining destiny" (431). Paradoxically, the implied acceptance of an inevitable fate on the part of this last aspen leaf becomes an index of joy for the aging poet who watches it "descend to water I know is black" with no fear of annihilation and then contemplates his own possibilities with a more ordered mind (432).

The austere imagery and intellectual symbolism of these paired "leaves" within Warren's book is succeeded by a pairing of autobiographical pieces, "Safe in Shade" and "Swimming in the Pacific." Though separated by "Synonyms," a seven-part sorites of silences and sounds, the two poems flanking it are so close in both matter and form that they are better considered next as a pair. One feature they share is an intertextuality with earlier selections in *Being Here,* respectively, "When Life Begins" from the first section and "Youthful Truth-Seeker, Half-Naked, at Night, Running down Beach South of San Francisco" from the second. "Safe in Shade" and "Swimming in the Pacific" differ from those earlier poems, however, in that their angles of vision, their viewpoints, look backward toward childhood and youth, not forward to maturity and age. For example, the places of the grandfather and the boy in the appropriately entitled "When Life Begins" are reversed in "Safe in Shade." The first poem is really about the grandfather as seen by Warren's persona, while in the second the old man is more a symbol of what the persona has become "in / That paradox the world exemplifies" (433). In age, the persona wants to know "Where is my cedar tree? // Where is the Truth—oh unambiguous— / Thereof?" (433). Likewise, in the earlier analogue to "Swimming in the Pacific" Warren sees everything through the perspective of the young man; even in the earlier poem's last line, it is the youthful persona who wonders if he will repeat his ocean plunge in his age. In the later poem, Warren views the young protagonist as an earlier self left behind on the shore as he rises from the sea "in my twilit nakedness" to consider again the questions of youth "on the sand supine" (437). He has found an answer in a mature love for his wife, so that in the "grayness" he can "see your face, slow, take shape. // Like a dream all years had moved to" (437).

Although "Night Walking" is the last selection of Section V, it also forms a pair with "Passers-By on Snowy Night," the final poem of the collection. The pieces are comparable in that both feature problematical passages in the dark, the first in early autumn and the second in midwinter, while both offer at least a glimmer of hope for the unfathomable future represented by the darkening night. The two poems do contrast in length, as "Night Walking" is over twice as long as "Passers-By on Snowy Night"; for the most part this difference develops from the doubled characters in the first who both are presented in greater complexity. The major difference between the two poems, however, is the identity of these characters; in the longer poem, they are Warren and his grown son, while in the shorter one they are only the persona and an aged passerby. "Night Walking" thus proves appropriate for the conclusion of the book's final section; Warren's persona is able to sense future continuity through the night journey of the son that provides the father some solace in his own preparation for death. Perhaps the most puzzling aspect of the young man's night passage is his sleepwalking, which the persona implies from a similar incident years earlier in Greece. The younger man's somnambulism may represent either the image of life as a dream that Warren so often presents or perhaps an image of death as a slumber from which the sleeper may somehow wake. As if in recognition of these possibilities, the father decides not to interfere with the son, because he realizes that "All else is his—and alone" (439). In other words, the young man has his own life to live, his own quest to undertake, whether in nocturnal dream or daylight vision.

In "Passers-By on Snowy Night," Warren focuses more fully on his poetic persona, who is paired with an undifferentiated other addressed in the second person and quite possibly standing for the reader within the poem's narrative logic. Warren's tactic seems right in regard to his intention, articulated in his "Afterthought," that this final poem functions as "a bracket to enclose . . . the complications of the main body" of *Being Here* (441). As we have seen, the volume opened with a poetic preface set off by its italics, "October Picnic Long Ago," a golden idyll of Warren's childhood that ended with the onset of evening and its shadowy implications for the future. His future then is realized in the five sections of the collection representing childhood, youth, midlife, age, and preparation for death. That future darkness has drawn closer to Warren's persona in "Passers-By on Snowy Night," a poetic coda for *Being Here* set off by its presentation in italics like the prefatory "October Picnic Long Ago."

As if to emphasize the finality of this vision, Warren's structure is extremely tight and traditional in the poem, comprising six quatrains of irregular tetrameter lines that do rhyme regularly in an ABAB pattern. Thus, the opening line, "*Black the coniferous darkness,*" stands in a dark contrast to the second, "*White the snow track between*"; this pattern is emphasized in the answering rhymes, "*starkness*" and "*lean*" predicated of the "*moon, skull-white*" and the "*upper ledges*" of the mountains (439). In the second quatrain, that moon seems to regard mountain and man with "*equal indifference,*" as "*you trudge to* whither *from* whence" (439). These paired and alliterating archaisms underline the symbolic nature of this winter night's journey that started "*somewhere,*" perhaps "*long before daylight withdrew,*" with "*the dream of a windowpane's glow / And a path trodden to invite you*" (439). Although the persona allows "*there may be such place,*" the "*mocking moonlight*" as yet reveals only these passersby, "*Alone*" to each other: "*I wish you well in your night / As I pass you in my own*" (439). Then the sixth and last stanza makes a final predication of their mutual predicament.

> *We each hear the distant friction,*
> *Then* crack *of bough burdened with snow,*
> *And each takes the owl's benediction,*
> *And each goes the way he will go.* (439)

A benediction, or a "good word" from its Latin roots, has both secular and religious import as a well-wishing or a blessing, but, as we have heard it echo so often in Warren's poetry, the only word the owl produces is its interrogative "Who?" Thus, even in this late stage of his journey, Warren is still trying to answer life's vexing inquiries about self and identity. More important, he also is urging us as his readers to prepare for our inevitable age-work and life review when we will be tested with just such overwhelming questions about the possibilities of dissolution or transcendence. These mortal uncertainties and their sublime formulations in the blessed benedictions of poetry will appear again in Warren's next volume of poetry, *Rumor Verified: Poems 1979–1980*, as we will discover in the succeeding chapter, but they will have their finest articulations in his final collection, *Altitudes and Extensions*, some five years later.

5

Mortality and Eternity

Rumor Verified: Poems 1979–1980

Pray only
That, in the midst of selfishness, some

Small act of careless kindness, half-unconscious, some
Unwitting smile or brush of lips, may glow
In some other mind's dark that's lost your name, but stumbles
Upon that momentary Eternity.

—"Small Eternity"

1

In September 1981, not quite a year after the publication of *Being Here,* Warren's collection of forty-four new poems from the years 1979 and 1980 appeared under the cryptic title of *Rumor Verified.*[1] This telegraphic formula from an earlier era also serves as the title of the volume's thirteenth selection, itself an enigmatic effort that concludes with "the verification / That you are simply a man, with a man's dead reckoning, nothing more" (457). Warren's use of "dead reckoning" here includes both the denotation of the phrase as a means of navigation to a future position from one in the present and its connotations as the absolute sum total of all human endeavors in death. Warren is ever more aware of life ending in *Rumor Verified,* as we might expect to find in his ongoing age-work. Even as Warren continues his personal life review in the poems of his new collection, however, he seems to intuit many correspondences to and convergences with those of others including family, friends, and forebears. If mortality seems the only absolute that anyone really can verify in life, in these poems the very fact of death still evokes rumors of wisdom, eternity, and transcendence for Warren.

The year that separated *Being Here* from *Rumor Verified,* one that saw his seventy-sixth birthday, confronted Warren with sequences of events both disheartening and encouraging. Old friends continued to pass away with what must have seemed increasing regularity, including Katherine Anne Porter and Caroline Gordon in 1980 and 1981, respectively (Blotner 458–59). Although both Porter and Gordon were somewhat older than Warren, the long years of physical and psychological decline for two women once vibrant and creative could not bode well for his own prospects in old age. Between their painfully attenuated deaths, the burdens of his own years must have increased exponentially when the urological complaints common at his age were diagnosed in his case as the same prostate cancer that had caused his father's death some three decades earlier. Like Robert Franklin Warren before him, the writer bore his affliction stoically, focusing instead on other, more positive developments in his life.[2]

Warren's continuing series of achievements included his new books, most notably *Jefferson Davis Gets His Citizenship Back* (1980), and new adaptations of old ones, such as a deluxe thirty-fifth anniversary edition of *All the King's Men* and Carlisle Floyd's opera based on the same novel (though titled *Willie Stark)* that debuted at Washington's Kennedy Center in 1981. His continuing honors included several birthday and anniversary celebrations, in particular ones at the University of Kentucky and Vanderbilt University (Blotner 458). In the spring of 1981 Warren was among the first recipients of a MacArthur Prize Fellowship; often called a "genius award," appropriately enough in his case, it provided five years of support and allowed him to devote his full attentions to his two final volumes of poetry, *Chief Joseph of the Nez Perce* and *Altitudes and Extensions.* In personal terms, Warren's sculptor son Gabriel married painter Ana Maria Flores-Jenkins in 1980, while his daughter Rosanna, now an established poet, married Stephen Scully, a classical scholar in 1981 (Blotner 452, 465–66).

Rumor Verified met with a generally favorable response when published in the autumn of 1981, and the collection has continued to enjoy the respect of Warren scholars and critics since then.[3] Most readers noted an increasing gravity of subject and style in *Rumor Verified* as a collection, and many of them, myself included, find a renewed sublimity in many of its individual selections. For example, Joseph Blotner believes that "this volume contains more fear and awareness of death, with a greater acceptance of limitation and sense of closure than any of its predecessors" (462). Likewise, Victor Strandberg concludes that *Rumor Verified* "derives its distinctive unity and power from the intensity of its meditations on mortality—a natural theme in the poet's eighth decade" ("Robert Penn Warren" 440). With a sense of final things, Randolph Paul Runyon locates the literary achievement of *Rumor Verified* in its intertextual relations with Dante's *Divina Commedia,* the source of Warren's epigraph for the volume (*Braided Dream* 90–94). If *Rumor Verified* contains fewer truly sublime poems than other late volumes, I find it about their equal in the overall quality of its forty-four selections.

Earlier criticism is less in agreement about the collection's structural unity, however. *Rumor Verified* is divided into six sections differentiated by roman numerals and brief titles that are bracketed by a numbered prologue and a coda. The volume's major critics—including Joseph Blotner, Victor Strandberg, and Randolph Runyon—all find Warren's gatherings in *Rumor Verified* to be both topical and sequential. James A. Grimshaw Jr. correctly contrasts the divisions here with the chronological ones in *Being Here* as "kinds of philosophical questioning . . . of nature, God, love, memory, time, and self-knowledge" (170). In my view, Warren's eight sections are formed by four pairings on paired and then re-paired topics: time in I, "Prologue," and II, "Paradox of Time"; space in III, "Events," and IV, "A Point North"; mortality in V, "If This Is the Way it Is," and VI, "But Also"; and eternity in VII, "Fear and Trembling," and VIII, "Coda." In all of these configurations, the human concerns compared and contrasted are universal matters of age-work, autobiography, and transcendence.

2

As we have discovered in his earlier collections, defining the relation of actual "time" to abstract "Time" remains a persistent task of his age-work for Warren. In the paired opening sequences of *Rumor Verified,* the writer posits another attempt at a definition—in this instance as paradox. Before this paradoxical consideration of Time as an abstraction in Section II, Warren concretizes the issues of time as a human reality in Section I. This prologue consists of a two-poem sequence subtitled "Mediterranean Basin," in which both parts are based on Warren's visits to the Greek islands some years earlier. The poet's consideration of the past here is not simply personal, however, as he involves the prehistory of the region in the paired poems that the sequence comprises—"Chthonian Revelation: A Myth" and "Looking Northward, Aegeanward: Nestlings on Seacliff." Warren's titles both recall the ancient mythos in their classical diction. "Chthonian" is derived from the Greek noun for "earth," and the adjective was generally associated with the mythological underworld and its shadowy deities who were the darker counterparts of the shining Olympians. The Aegean, Homer's "wine-dark sea," was named for Aegeus, mythic king of Athens and father of Theseus who perished in its depths when he mistakenly believed his son destroyed by the Minotaur. In both these poems, the brief sequences of their contemporary narratives resonate against the distant ages of classical myth and ancient history to recreate what Warren calls, "the agony of Time" (447).

Within the context of this short sequence, Warren's diction invokes the classical sense of his phrase, for abstract "Time" reveals the "agon," or death struggle, of the self within the passage of time. In the first poem's surface narrative, a contemporary couple quest along a volcanic seascape for a hidden beach cave of "mystic and chthonian privacy," known only to them (445). Their penetration into this "cave-shade," significantly the product of seismic "earth-agony," is presented in imagery and symbolism recalling that of the explorations in "Speleology" from *Being Here.* In the late afternoon, they make love, doze off, and then wake to swim "A kilometer toward the headland, then home" (446). The images of the day as a dreamlike trance transform it into some ancient ritual that realizes the "hermetic wisdom" gained in their katabasis, or symbolic descent into this timeless underworld (446). Despite "the darkling drag of the nameless depth" as they swim away, like the human burden of time, they hear "the gull's high cry / Of mercilessly joyful veracity" with "Eyes starward fixed" (446).

If the dark sea journey in the first poem of this pair verifies the rumor of death, it also lends credence to golden legends that transcend time. The second poem observes the same sea cliffs along with their avian nestlings in the light of this wisdom newly won from the ancient sources. Looking "Aegeanward" and musing on "How long ago galleys—slim, black, bronze-flashing—bore / Northward too," the poem's personae connect timeless myth with ancient history (447). Thus, the screaming nestlings of the seabirds recall both the human and the geologic history of the Archipelago in the earthquakes and eruptions that darkened the sun and felled the "rooftree or keystone of palaces" (447). These terrors were at first credited to the chthonian deities who could be placated only by blood sacrifice, so that at last

> Priest's grip drew backward curls of the king's son until
> Throat-softness was tightened, and the last cry
> Was lost in the gargle of blood on the blade. (447)

Offerings were in vain, as cities, both mythical and Minoan, were buried in ash or drowned in the sea by the natural and human forces that united to create this stark seascape. If the survivors understood little of these catastrophes at first, they "slowly, began" to realize them "In new ignorance, the agony of Time" (447).

The agonistic struggle between real "time" perceived as the "impure" flux of diurnal events and "Time" understood as a "pure" ideal provides the defining paradox in the second section of *Rumor Verified.* In fact, Warren uses "Paradox of Time" as the titles of both Section II and its second selection, itself a sort of subsection comprised of three separate poems. Both Section II and its tripartite subsection counterpoint speculative or philosophical age-work considering Time as a concept with particular and nostalgic observations of time drawn from the flow of the past in the poet's autobiography. The initial selection, "Blessed Accident," provides an intertextual introduction to the relation of time to Time by imaging midlife for its personae as "*Nel mezzo del camin*" or "In the middle of the way," in my rendering of Dante's famous opening of the *Commedia* (448). This allusion recalls Warren's epigraph for the volume, the final three lines of the *Inferno* where Dante and Virgil emerge from the subterranean cavern of the underworld to contemplate the stars at the beginning of their purgatorial ascent toward paradise.[4] In his irregular, unrhymed couplets, Warren's imagery portrays the past as a long, hard journey up a mountain trail to a point where the persona surveys his life choices and tries "to distinguish between logic / And accident" in paths taken or not (448). Even though "complacency in the logic of / Your conduct of life" allows for the future "possibility, doomful, of joy," the likelihood "of God's palsied hand shaking // The dice-cup" makes whatever bit of imagined wisdom one achieves in age but another "blessed accident" (448–49).

Poem I, "Gravity of Stone and Ecstasy of Wind," Warren's initial panel in the smaller triptych also presented under the general title of the five-part section, employs "The paradox of Time" as the second line in the third of his tightly organized, if irregularly rhyming quatrains. Moreover, the poet defines its paradoxical "doubleness" by contrasting Time as symbolized by a "benign, arrogant" western star with time as represented in "your tenement / Of flesh" (449). Yet "fleshly glory may gleam" if an old man will "Sit on the floor with a child," hear its "laugh," and see its "life-arch" in order to learn a "vision" that will "atone / For all folly now left behind," like that on Royal street years earlier (449). As Warren's final lines instruct us: first, "Learn the gravity of stone"; then, "Learn the ecstasy of wind" (449).

The second panel, II, "Law of Attrition," likewise opens with the difficult lessons to be learned from the material universe.

> Learn the law of attrition,
> Learn that the mountain's crag-jut,
> In that attitude of pride,
> Knows the sledge and gnaw of seasons,
> Each in its enmity. (450)

In this image, the attrition is a literal wearing down of the proud mountain crag across "aeons" of geologic time, though the same process obtains in the briefer span of human life (450). This second selection here proves even more speculative and abstracted than the first as it ultimately images the equally proud persona worn down to "A single, self-possessed grain / Of sand on an unmapped strand," like that in the earlier "Empty White Blotch on Map of Universe: A Possible View," reflecting distant starlight with "indifferent joy" (450, 451).

The final panel of Warren's paradoxical triptych, III, "One I Knew," begins abstractly enough with another image of a "snow-peak," again arrogant in its glory, like the great dead, "Who once stood / Erect and prophetic in / Age's long irony" (451). The poem then becomes more personal, and thus more interesting in my view, when Warren turns to an individual exemplar: "I knew / One once, old, old, alone / In his unselfed, iron will" (451). Although the other elder is never named, he is identified easily enough as the poet's father, Robert Franklin Warren (Burt 814). The most obvious clue to the aging man's identity is "the cancer of which / Only he knew," his "precious secret" (451). This hidden tumor had been referenced by Warren in earlier poems, notably in "Reading Late at Night, Thermometer Falling" from *Or Else.* In "One I Knew" the growth is not that of the earlier poem, "big as a horse-apple," but one beautiful as "The bud of a century plant" (314, 452). Although its unfolding signals "The agony of the end," after the dying father collapses over an unfinished letter to his living son, it also reveals a sort of transcendent glory when "The shimmering / White petal—the golden stamen— / Were at last, in triumph, / Divulged" (452). A reader who is aware of Warren's biography must wonder how much his own mortal affliction influenced reconsideration of his father's before him, and how much the poetic power of "One I Knew" derives from this development.

The three remaining selections in the second section of *Rumor Verified* form a kind of triptych rather like that of "Paradox of Time." Two speculative pieces, "Small Eternity" and "Basic Syllogism," are balanced by more personal nostalgia in the concluding poem, "Sitting on Farm Lawn on Sunday Afternoon." All three consider the work of memory, but it is more abstract and general in the first two, more concrete and particular in the autobiographical reminiscence of the third. Even their titles suggest their differences. The nouns "Eternity" and "Syllogism" are redolent of philosophy and logic, but they are modified concretely by the adjectives "Small" and "Basic." The definition of that "Eternity" with which Warren concludes the first poem again reflects his differentiation of time and Time (453). Although we can conceive of "Eternity" as a philosophical construct, the only way in which we know it is in fleeting memories of the past. As he concludes, "Time / Is a wind that never shifts airt," or compass point; the wind of change always blows from the past to the future, though both exist only in the present (453). As the aged learn when trying to recall names and faces in reviewing their lives, "Memory dies. Or lies," so that the possibility of eternal transcendence still seems as small as Warren's title hints (453). In the second selection, "Basic Syllogism," the aging persona considers "how soon the sun / Its basic syllogism enacts" in the sunlight and shade of a bright autumnal afternoon (453). The tripartite logical syllogism is replicated in both the poetic structure of regularly rhymed quatrains and the imagery of birth, growth, and death as discovered in the cycles of the day, year, and life.

Once again, "Sitting on Farm Lawn on Sunday Afternoon," the concluding selection of this section, presents similar elements in more personal terms. The poem is itself a memory of memories; the aging poet contemplates a scene from his past in rural Kentucky, one in which those who were then his age now recalled their own lost years. "The old, the young—they sit," while "the afternoon muses onward" in early autumn, for "only a few maple leaves / Are crisping toward yellow" (454). Although "the limpid year uncoils / With a motion like motionlessness," the winds of time past are inalterably bearing all present into the obscurity of night, winter, and death. Even their dead "kin who in dark now hide" sometimes "weep / At wisdom they learned too late" (454). In his own old age, the persona asks himself, "Is all wisdom learned too late?" (454). His question recalls the one posed earlier in "Rattlesnake Country, "*Is* was *but a word for wisdom, its price?*" (293). None of those present on the farm lawn that lost Sunday afternoon know the answer to that question, nor do they "yet know all / The tales and contortions of Time"—any more than the poet himself does, "alone, / In another place, and hour" (454).

3

Time is named as the subject of the second section in its title, but space is only implied in the titles of the third and fourth sections of *Rumor Verified*—III, "Events," and IV, "A Point North." Although all human events reveal themselves in the course of time, those narrated in these two paired sections emphasize a spatial continuum both abstract and autobiographical in terms of distances and directions—East and West in Section III, North and South in Section IV. Indeed, this spatial patterning is reinforced by several titles of the individual selections, most notably both sections' initial poems—"Going West" and "Vermont Thaw." Warren's persona is literally driving from the East to the West across the Great Plains toward the Continental Divide in the first, while in the second he describes a northern thaw following a southern front. Both selections prove intertextual in theme, as Warren links time and space in psychological journey of "Going West":

> The land
> Beyond miles of distance, fled
> Backward to whatever had been,
> As though Space were Time. (455)

The capitalizing of "Space" seems to equate it with the universalized "Time" of Section II, drawing a distinction between the actual miles recorded on his car's odometer and the human odysseys represented by the crossings of these "Great Plains" (455). At the beginning of Section IV in "Vermont Thaw," Warren references that western experience by defining the current of warm air from the South as "something like / The wind in the Far West they call the *chinook*" (464). In both poems, as well as in the two gatherings of pieces they introduce, Warren seems to conflate geographical direction and distance with natural and human cycles, as we will see in a closer reading of these texts.

Warren uses "Going West" to introduce the seven poems that comprise the third section of *Rumor Verified* because it provides the most successful example of his spatial approach. The poem may recall one of Warren's long drives across the country in the 1930s, though it also may have developed from his more recent interest in the West because of his new poetic project on Chief Joseph. It proves significant that absent the poet's offhand comment that this day was "oh, long / Ago" even a careful reader could not discern whether the piece is set in past or present (455). Warren is not concerned here with time and chronology so much as with space and geography. This orientation in terms of direction and distance is realized in Warren's opening lines: "Westward the Great Plains are lifting, as you / Can tell from the slight additional pressure / The accelerator requires" (455). His course is set toward a West that bears both national and psychological symbolism as the last locus of the American Dream and as the traditional terminus of an individual life.[5]

Both understandings of the West are present in Warren's sublime narrative. On the one hand, "Going West" becomes paradigmatic of the American Westering experience, as Warren encapsulates his archetypal journey in a pivotal stanza of only a single line: "This is one way to write the history of America" (455). Ironically, his searching of the far horizon for snowcaps "like a vision," is interrupted by the "bloody explosion" of a pheasant smashed against his windshield as he speeds ever westward. Warren's research on the Indian wars had confirmed that the history of the American West could be imaged by "The whole land forward, forever, / All washed in blood, in feathers, in gut-scrawl" (455). His reaction to this startling event also has a more personal meaning as well, for he must clamp "the wheel with a death grip" to steer out of a fatal wreck (455). When his car finally comes to rest, he cannot clean his windshield completely, so that by evening the "Red sunset now reddening to blood streaks" masks the still distant mountains from his view (456). Nearly a half century later, the event returns to haunt him in a dream where he can recall the blood-smirched windshield but not "the imagined / Vision of snowcaps" it blots out (456). In other words, "Going West" proves a spatial variation of Warren's ongoing life review and age-work in both personal and cultural terms.

The half-dozen poems that follow after "Going West" in Section III all involve events more concerned with spatiality than with chronology. Even "Rumor Verified," this section's third poem, which also lends its title to the whole collection, traces the life span of its implied persona in terms of places rather than times. As suggested earlier in this chapter, the rumor in question concerns mortality, and once it is verified the persona might as well disappear from his accustomed seat of privilege to sneak "Into El Salvador, or some such anguished spot" to make amends for his past (457). There, he could "pray with the sick, kiss lepers // . . . hold / A cup of cold water for the dying man to sip," so as to "learn wisdom" (457). In other words, he could do something much like age-work. The poems before and after "Rumor Verified" seem to be located in places past and present recalled in Warren's autobiography.

Warren wanders his present home in "Nameless Thing" and tries to confront the immanence of death there, while in the "Sunset Scrupulously Observed" from his sundeck he reads a small vision of eternity into the ascending jet trail highlighted against a darkening horizon The three poems that complete the section are each set in a particular place from Warren's past. "Minneapolis Story" connects his memory of a dying transient discovered in a Christmas Eve snowstorm years earlier with the more recent death of a friend, perhaps John Knox Jessup, to whom the poem is dedicated. Western mountains are again recalled in "Mountain Mystery," though it is difficult for reader to discern if their greatest mystery is the tension between memory and mortality, or between love and loneliness. The "Convergences" named in the title of the final selection of this grouping emanate from Warren's youth in Kentucky, but they also reverberate down to his present home in New England. Walking along the local railroad line, the poem's youthful protagonist encounters a tramp, "Wolfish and slit-eyed," who threatens him much as other outcasts did in Warren's earlier narratives, whether in stories such as "Blackberry Winter" or in poems such as "Recollection in Upper Ontario, from Long Before." The young Warren watches the transient disappear in the distant convergence of the tracks as they enter the dark maw of a railroad tunnel. Now the aging Warren wonders if "the track I was doomed to go / In my biologic flow" is now rushing him toward death, "that black hollow / Which led where you cannot know" (463).

The overall title of the next section, IV, "A Point North," refers to Warren's setting in terms of his rural retreat referenced in the title of its first selection, "Vermont Thaw," though the four poems gathered in this section also are unified by the yearly passage of nature as suggested in the title of the second selection, "Cycle." The remaining two poems of this grouping contain seasonal references in both of their titles as well—"Summer Rain in Mountains" and "Vermont Ballad: Change of Season"—so that this quartet of poems considered together reiterates the four yearly seasons as a metaphor of the human life cycle. In their order as presented here, the four selections progress from early spring to early summer and then from late summer to late fall, though winter is immanent in all of these seasonal transitions, much as death is in all of life's seasons. We noted earlier how this nagging hibernal consciousness in Warren's poems often proves intertextual with Frost's poetry, and Warren's unease during all seasons here seems particularly appropriate in terms of Frost's northern New England.

In "Vermont Thaw," the dripping of the unusually early snow melt becomes strangely disquieting for the persona, so that he negatively answers his own interrogative review of the rapidly changing seasons: "Can you comfort yourself by thinking of spring? / Of summer's fecundity . . . Of gold and flame // In benediction of autumn? Of snow's first / Nightwhisper? . . . No" (464–65). Such is the case in the seasonal poems that follow. In "Cycle," Warren describes an uncommon heat wave at a northern summer's zenith, and concludes another seasonal inventory with the inevitable end of the cycle: "But I know that snow, like history, will come"—or perhaps arriving like death (465). "Summer Rain in Mountains," likewise, "may be a code" signaling a cool front from Canada that disturbs a party on the poet's "sun-deck" and a "secret warning" of winter that leaves him in need of a whisky (466). A day of cold rain marks the transition from fall to winter in "Vermont Ballad: Change of Season," a poem in which Warren makes more explicit connections with age and death, as he is now "Three quarters now of a century old" (467). Warren's literary ballad concludes a dozen intricately rhymed triplets with a couplet of attenuated lines revealing a double figure much like ones we have met before in his poetry.

> In this section such a man is not an uncommon sight.
> In rain or snow, you pass, and he says: "Kinda rough tonight."
> (467)

Just such a stranger appeared earlier in "Passers-By on Snowy Night," the poem that serves as a coda for *Being Here.* Much as in that earlier incarnation, here Warren as poet is still trying to complete his own age-work and life review.

4

The existential truth that we each must choose our own track through the cycle of life provides an effective transition to the varied considerations of natural mortality included in the next two sections of *Rumor Verified,* V, "If This Is the Way it Is," and VI, "But Also." The relation of these paired sections is implied by their titles: mortality determines the end of any individual life, but the cycles of the day and of the year also suggest some possibilities of rebirth, transcendence, and eternity. Warren's ordering of his individual selections within these fifth and sixth sections reveals other meaningful comparisons and contrasts. The seven poems of Section V are arranged in three pairs concluding with a coda in "If," a piece that begins four of its five stanzas by reiterating the section's general title, "If this is the way it is" (474). Although Section VI, "But Also," is comprised of seven selections as well, its comparisons and contrasts are complicated by a subsection titled "Glimpses of Seasons," in which four poems again compare the annual cycle of the year to that of human life. In his overall organization of *Rumor Verified,* Warren contrasts his certainty about mortality in the fifth and sixth sections with his ambivalence about eternity in the five poems of Section VII, "Fear and Trembling," and in the single poem, also titled "Fear and Trembling," that SectionVIII, "Coda," comprises.

Given Warren's insistence on a coda to conclude *Rumor Verified,* my analysis of the sections " If This Is the Way it Is" and "But Also" will underline the importance of their final poems. The arresting title of the seventh and last selection in the fifth section, "If," as well as Warren's repetition of the section title as the initial line in four of its five stanzas make the poem seem one intended as a kind of coda.[6] Warren's opening line declares that "If this is the way it is, we must live through it"; for even in the face of death, life must go on (474). Despite the "nightmare" images in this irregular stanza, the poetic persona also acknowledges that "bliss can seem more absolute than a clock's / Last tick in a dark-shrouded room" (474). Warren continues his language of transcendence in the second stanza, urging us to lift our gaze past sea and crag, "until the soul is absorbed / Into the blue perfection of unnamable distance" (474). The longer third stanza then returns to nocturnal imagery in a memory of "The dark and unpopulated / Piazza Navona" in Rome, where Warren at midlife puzzled over a childhood dream that, like a "discarded newspaper" on the piazza, carried "yesterday / Into tomorrow" (474).

The brief fourth stanza was added to the text as finalized in *Rumor Verified* (Burt 769). It begins "This was only a trivial incident of / My middle years," and both setting and diction here recall Dante's "*nel mezzo del camin*" from the earlier selection "Blessed Accident" (474). Warren makes a pair of smaller yet still significant changes to what becomes his fifth and final stanza; first, he alters our ultimate need in life from "A new definition of Self" to "A new concept of salvation" (Burt 769). Also, he adjusts his final phrase about the symbolic seascape of eternity from "the blind depth of groan, or fulfillment" to the more colloquial "blind depth of groan out yonder" with its connotations of something distant yet still within the range of vision, much like eternity itself (Burt 769).

The three other pairs of poems that Warren includes in Section V are all reflected in and completed by "If" as a kind of coda. For example, the first line of his final poem, "If this is the way it is, we must live through it," is suggested in the title of Warren's opening selection, "Questions You Must Learn to Live Past." In this first selection, more questions of eternity arise at a father's deathbed, in the remembered face of a childhood friend now dead, and with a snake's autumnal shedding of "its old integument" as it "Slips down to curl in some dark, wintry hole, with no dream" (468). This emblematic hibernation, or annual sleep, in "Questions You Must Learn to Live Past" finds comparison and contrast in the nocturnal and eternal slumbers of the second and paired poem, "After Restless Night." In it, Warren tells his reader that life is only "a rumor we might as well take at face value" (469). If the persona believes that rumor of life will be verified in regard to himself and his wife at dawn, he also remembers that his dead parents are now sunken in a sleep so deep that there is "no distraction to their frozen agon" (470). The struggles of his father's and mother's past lives are frozen both literally and figuratively by their mortality, as both are locked now in "the noble indifference of Eternity" (469).

The next two poems in Section V, "What Was the Thought" and "Dead Horse in Field," are paired in their considerations of the simultaneous attraction and repulsion their personae feel for physical decay. Once again, the "thought" referenced in the first title seems to be the same amorphous dread of dissolution that has been encountered earlier in much of Warren's age-work. His persona here should be contented to doze in his warm bed and contemplate his faithful wife, healthy children, and material possessions. Instead, the nagging consideration that they all will be lost at the instant of his death sneaks its way into his consciousness like a mouse creeping "Along a baseboard, hungry in the middle / Of the night, in a strange house" (470). After Warren's persona finally sleeps, he is awakened by the domestic cat; it bears a dead mouse, the embodiment of his unfocused anxiety: "There, blood streaking the counterpane, it lies— / Skull crushed, partly eviscerated," like the detritus of a nightmare (471).

"Dead Horse in Field" presents even more compelling physical evidence of mortal decay in the dead body of a much larger animal, but in its artistic complexity the second poem in this pair also offers a few clues concerning eternity. Warren's persona is forced to shoot his two-year-old thoroughbred when it breaks a foreleg galloping through a mud hole at the far edge of his property. Before he can arrange to bury the carcass, he sees "gorged crows" rising from their "beneficent work" that begins by gouging out the dead creature's eyes; "Next day / The buzzards" flock, drawn by "The sweet stink" to start the more serious labor (471). By evening, however, all the carrion birds "swing black in nature's flow and perfection, / High in sad carmine of sunset" (471). In a few months, the stripped skeleton will become "That intricate piece of / Modern sculpture, white now / By weather and sun, intricate, now / Assuming in stasis / New beauty!" (471). After a year, the cycle of nature will reveal itself in "The green twine of vine, each leaf / Heart-shaped, soft as velvet, beginning / Its benediction" (471). Warren follows this contemplation of death and life, of nature and art with two single line stanzas: the first is short and declarative, "It thinks it is God"; the second is elongated and interrogative, "Can you think of some ground on which that may be gainsaid?" (471). These final lines seem to imply at least the small possibility of some sort of divine immanence in natural, if not in human life.[7]

As if in consideration of his concluding suggestion, Warren's next selection is titled "Immanence," and a similar sense of immanent revelation pervades the paired poem, "The Corner of the Eye." In the first poem of this final pairing in Section V, Warren's poetic persona is unable to divine whether such immanence is "benign—or inimical" (472). The "eviscerated" mouse from "What Was the Thought" reappears when this sensed immanence "Plays cat-and-mouse with you, veiled, unrevealed," like a "teasing enigma" (472). Its most frightening aspect would be if "The swollen Immanence turns out to be all," because then no possibility of transcendence could exist (472). If so, the individual "Yet yearning, torn between fear / And hope, yet ignorant, will, into // The black conduit of Nature's Repackaging System, be sucked" (472). Warren's capitalized phrase here suggests a sort of philosophical naturalism much different from "nature's flow and perfection" as observed in "Dead Horse in Field."[8]

Analogous imagery drawn from literary naturalism can also be discovered in "The Corner of the Eye." The immanent entity here may be just a poem as it emerges into the poet's consciousness, or perhaps something much more disquieting. This dread thought "may be like a poor little shivering fieldmouse" frightened by the utterance of an owl, again recalling the dead mouse in "What Was the Thought?" (473). The owl's guttural questioning also recalls "Dead Horse in Field" when it is compared to "the grind of a great file the blacksmith sets to hoof" (473). Although, like Henry

James's psychological image in *The Beast in the Jungle* (1903), the future may lie in wait, "breath rarely heard, fangs dripping"; it may be "merely a poem, after all" (473). Perhaps it will be a poem like "If," the coda of Section V, also prefigured by the images of ocean waves, discarded newspapers, and midlife crises iterated in "The Corner of the Eye."

The ambivalence in regard to life and death discovered throughout V, "If This Is the Way it Is," and reiterated in its coda, "If," is extended in VI, "But Also," though in the latter's ten poems Warren's emphasis shifts ever so slightly toward the tentative considerations of eternity to be found in the final two sections of *Rumor Verified.* As in Section V, Warren seems to arrange the selections in his sixth section as pairs that are paired in turn. This pattern proves even more complicated in Section VI because Warren focuses it around a subsection of four poems subtitled "Glimpses of Seasons." Warren's careful structuring of this section is demonstrated in his thorough reediting of the poems written earlier. As first published by the *Southern Review,* "Glimpses of Seasons" includes just the first three sections that reappear in *Rumor Verified*—I, "Gasp-Glory of Gold Light"; II, "Snow Out of Season"; and III, "Redwing Blackbirds." In his initial editing of his new collection, Warren retained this tripartite pattern, but in his final version of the text he relocates a separate poem that earlier had preceded the subsection as its fourth selection, IV, "Crocus Dawn" (Burt 769–70). Warren's reconstituted subsection balances a pair of autumnal poems with a vernal pair, and thus he is able to end "Glimpses of Seasons" even more positively. Warren's editorial change also pairs the poems "What Voice at Moth-Hour" and "Another Dimension," which precede the subsection, and divides the four poems that follow it into two more pairs—"English Cocker: Old and Blind" and "Dawn" as well as "Millpond Lost" and "Summer Afternoon and Hypnosis."

Given the pivotal role of "Glimpses of Seasons" in Section VI, my analysis will consider it before these other pairs of poems. Once again, Warren's employment of the seasonal cycle recalls Frost's contemplations of the changing seasons, especially his poems in which the end of the season seems immanent in its birth, such as his well-known "Nothing Gold Can Stay" (1923). The Frost text is a spring poem that begins with the image of yellow leaf buds, which prefigure the golden leaves of fall with which Warren opens I, "Gasp-Glory of Gold Light." Even as Warren appreciates the fulfillment of "gold maple," he recalls the "Now forgotten green-bough loop" and reviews the "fat leaf-droop" and "first reddening rondure of August" (476). Summer, it seems, "Forgets to define / The mathematics of Time," even if the poet cannot do so, balanced as he is on "the knife-edge of no-Time" (476). In fact, trying to comprehend the cycle of seasonal change is like trying "to think, at the same moment / Of the living and the dead" (476). Poem II, "Snow Out of Season," recalls several of Warren's own poetic snowscapes, as well as Frost's "The Onset," a similar poem about the first snow of a long winter in northern New England. In contrast to the golden day of Warren's first poem in this cycle, this October "dawn / Was nothing but swirl of snow-dimness" and "boughs hung heavy, white only, no crimson / Of maple, no willow by destiny yellow" (477). Against "this myth of nothingness," one "White in lethalness," the only spots of color and vitality Warren's persona can discover are the red dogwood berries, like "Uncountable jewels flamed" to "make the heart leap" with joy—even in an aged observer (477).

April presents analogous spots of color in the regularly rhymed quatrains of Poem III, "Redwing Blackbirds," whose return symbolizes spring for Warren's poetic persona as much as autumn is represented by other birds of black in "Grackles, Goodbye" from *Being Here.* Like those earlier flocks, the sound of the returning redwings is "rusty," as if they might be the very creaking of the earth turning with the seasons (391, 477). The black birds' "gut-grabbing cry / That calls on life to be lived gladly, gladly" for Warren's persona in early spring resonates even in his autumnal dreams, "seasons later, sleet coding on pane" (478). Waking, the aged persona wonders, "Next year will redwings see me, or I them, again then?" (478). Although Poem IV, "Crocus Dawn" was added to "Glimpses of Seasons" late in Warren's reediting of *Rumor Verified,* this rough sonnet disguised as seven separated and unrhymed couplets proves an apt conclusion to his glimpses of the seasons in its elision of spring with dawn and ultimately with the promise of rebirth even in age. Warren's image seems more psychological than physical, a "premise of promise" derived from the faint purple of dawns from youthful days to help him make it through the nights of age (478). As in Warren's other dark nights of the soul, sound effects include "a heart that flutters vacantly" and "The tiny mathematical tick that is your only // Benediction in darkness" (478). Yet "After / Darkness," the benediction, or blessing, of Warren's poem is found in its title image, "Oh, crocus dawn, // May our eyes gleam once more in your light before / We know again what we must wake to be" (478). Perhaps, even the big sleep of death may end in a radiant dawn enlightening and awakening us from its darks.

Just as the two pairs of poems in "Glimpses of Seasons" imply the cyclic courses of day, year, and life, the half-dozen poems Warren gathers in the three pairs that make up the rest of Section VI, "But Also," relate to varied aspects of those natural cycles—most significantly to dawn, spring, and rebirth. Although the initial pairing, "What Voice at Moth-Hour" and "Another Dimension," are memories of twilight and midday respectively, both remembered scenes seem literally set in spring but in figurative youth and midlife. Evening is "moth-hour" only because the persona once stood in a Kentucky orchard where "the white / Petals of apple blossoms were falling, / Whiter than moth-wing," another Frost-like premonition of winter (475). The possible pun in the poem's title seems to identify a "moth-er's" voice calling "*It's late! Come home*" in its last line, though the imperative tone may suggest that the command is his father's (475). In either case, it is now too late in the persona's life for sentimental nostalgia as he prepares for his last great passage to his final place of rest. Likewise, "Another Dimension" recalls part of an earlier journey abroad in its opening lines, "Over meadows of Brittany, the lark / Flames sunward" (475). At midday and midlife, the persona describes a spring landscape again portending winter, as "Dividing fields, long hedges, in white / Bloom powdered, gently slope to the / Blue of sea that glitters in joy of its being" (475). Although the lark ascends to "an altitude where only / God's ear may hear," the persona now can believe himself "redeemed" when he recalls seeing it "flare upward," while he "strained to hear, sun-high, that Platonic song" (475, 476). Warren closes with a stanza of but a single line, "It may be that some men, dying, have heard it," that suggests the possibility of "Another Dimension" to human existence still to be explored even at the exact moment of death (476).

The four poems that complete "But Also" fall into two pairs linked by imagery derived from the cycles of day, year, and life. The subject of "English Cocker: Old and Blind," for example, is described in five traditional AABB couplets that reveal the aging animal's "old faith" while facing "the abyss" (479). Perhaps more important, Warren's human persona finally recognizes in his failing dog "The kinship of all flesh defined by a halting paradigm" (479). The following selection, "Dawn," comes to a conclusion similar both to "English Cocker: Old and Blind" and to "Crocus Dawn," when Warren hears a crow caw not to signal the light of day but to invite the persona to prayer in the shadow of endless night; "Dear God . . . Will I find it worthwhile to pray that You let // The crow, at least once more, call?" (480). "Millpond Lost" is another poem of bright autumn recalling poem I, "Gasp-Glory of Gold Light," in its imagery and "English Cocker: Old and Blind" in the regularity of its ABAB stanzas. Here, the millpond mirrors a September landscape much as Warren's memory replicates a Kentucky scene from his youth. His final, unrhymed couplet of extended lines rescues this effort from mere nostalgia: "In darkness, I've tried to imagine the pond after such time-lapse, / Or name the names of the boys who there shouted in joy, once" (481). A third piece in regular ABAB stanzas, "Summer Afternoon and Hypnosis" brings Section VI to a close as a kind of poetic coda recalling "If" in the preceding section. At the zenith of the diurnal, annual, and human cycles, Warren's persona rises from his trance on a beautiful summer afternoon to seek "the roof whereunder you find enhoused / The mystery of love's redeeming smile" (481). He is going to his final resting place, both literally and figuratively, as if in answer to the earlier call "*It's late! Come home.*"

5

If the paired sections considering mortality, V, "If This Is the Way it Is," and VI, "But Also," progress toward an initial consideration of eternity as an essential element of life review, then the pair of sections that conclude *Rumor Verified,* VII, "Fear and Trembling," and VIII, "Coda," must reconsider mortality as a later stage of age-work under that aspect of eternity. Earlier rumors of wisdom, integrity, and transcendence seem much closer to verification in the six poems of these paired sections, especially in terms of traditional religious images and symbols as well as of allusions to and intertextuality with biblical passages. Clearly, the defining phrase for both Sections VII and VIII becomes "Fear and Trembling," the title both of the seventh section and of the single poem presented in the eighth section as a coda for the entire volume. This phrase evokes the book title of *Fear and Trembling* (1843), Søren Kierkegaard's famous meditation on the mystery of faith as figured in the story of Abraham and Isaac (Blotner 553). However, I believe that Warren invokes the scriptural source of that earlier title in Paul's epistles, "work out your salvation with fear and trembling" (*Philippians* 2:12). While Kierkegaard applies Paul's words to God's testing of Abraham's faith, Warren takes a wider view of salvation history, one that includes another Pauline allusion linking the third and fourth poems in Section VII, "Twice Born" and "The Sea Hates the Land," as we will see. In a very general sense then, Warren seems to contemplate something like salvation in the human meaning of this late work, at least in psychological if not in religious terms.

As remarked earlier, Warren does not provide his reader with anything resembling traditional "wisdom literature" in the traditions of the later Wordsworth, the American Fireside poets, or even his New England forebear Frost. To the end of his days Warren described himself as a "yearner" in terms of belief, but at the same time he remained a self-proclaimed "nonbeliever" in regard to the revealed truths of religion, to borrow his own dichotomous formulation (*Talking* 213). The first selection in Section VII, "If Ever," establishes exactly this sort of dichotomy in his role as both elder and poet. The poem opens in a marked contrast to the implied redemption in love that concludes "Summer Afternoon and Hypnosis" by asking, in regard to death, "can love at the end, have an end // That is absolute?" (482). Warren then goes on to question exactly "what exists in the grab-bag of pastness?" or in "that dark, seething vastness // That was your life?" (482). His diction becomes more classically stoic, however, as he continues to peer into "that vatic darkness," the mysteries of which remain obscure even to the "vates" or prophetic poet (482). Warren then wonders if "all things," Janus-like, "wear / Two faces" alternatively representing "hope—or despair," Doom—or promise," or "the future, or history" (482). "If Ever" ends with the poet's advice to "plunge into / Cold shock of experience" like "a mountain lake and let / Stroke, after stroke, sustain you" at these exhilarating altitudes of your self-defining existential efforts.[9]

If the cold plunge into existence that Warren suggests in "If Ever" becomes a kind of natural baptism, then the consumption of edible fungi counseled in his next poem "Have You Ever Eaten Stars?" seems a sort of communion with nature. In confirmation of their symbolic connections, both of these sacraments are presented at the higher altitudes of human experience—within "a mountain lake" in the first, and within "A glade on a bench of the mountain" in the second (482). "Have You Ever Eaten Stars?" is subtitled "A Note on Mycology" (mycology being the scientific study of fungi), and it is divided into two sections, titled "Scene" and "Question." Warren added the brief titles along with the text of the second subsection when he revised the poem for *Rumor Verified* after its initial publication in the *New Yorker* (Burt 771). Warren's revisions only serve to emphasize the sacramental imagery that connects "If Ever" and "Have You Ever Eaten Stars?" as prefigurations of his final volume, *Altitudes and Extensions.*

Warren's description of his scene in the mountain glade evokes a chapel of nature like those of the nineteenth-century Romantics. Here, trees "meet / In peace" around a "hollow, . . . soft, centuries old" where a "grass blade / So biblically frail" receives a single "sunray" that is on its "noontide visitation" (482). The setting is a naturalistic one, however, where "all in that cycle's beneficence / Of being are slowly absorbed" back into "What once fed them" (482–83). After a fall rain, Warren's persona becomes part of this process when he finds "earth black as midnight sky" now "studded with / Gold stars," really "bright golden chanterelles" in "A glade-burst of glory" (483). The earlier version of the poem ended at this point with a stanza of a single line, "Later I gathered them into a basket" (Burt 771). In his revision, Warren changes "them" to "stars," transforming his simile to a metaphor (Burt 771). His image becomes a symbol in the initial line of the new subsection, "What can you do with stars, or glory?" (483). Warren answers his own question directly, "Eat. Swallow. Absorb," if not the heavenly stars then their earthly sacramentals (483). Eaten with the right spirit, they let "flesh be more preciously / Gratified," and "brain glow / In its . . . Skull-sky," and "heart / Rejoice" in "seeing life as glory" (483).

The pairing of these first two poems, "If Ever" and "Have You Ever Eaten Stars?" indicates that the next two poems in Section VII might be paired as well, and once more the most vital connections are found in the religious images and scriptural allusions of "Twice Born" and "The Sea Hates the Land." The title "Twice Born" reflects the baptismal imagery of "If Ever," while its vivid "blaze of vision in the dark hour" recalls the biblical story of the burning bush (483). After a midnight storm with "thunder blundering among mountains," the persona assumes that his luck saves him from a natural peril until "one last and greatest crash" and "a flash dazzling the dark of the room" (484). Like Saul on the road to Damascus, he suddenly realizes that "God / Was not mocked by any easy assumption," much as Paul would conclude later in *Galatians* 6:7 to his fellow converts (484). The symbol of the persona's new vision is "A great dead pine, / Fifty yards off, a torch sky-high now" (484). This "God-ignited torch" not only fills the room with "a faint flicker" but with a "calm sweetness," as Warren's persona back in his bed realizes that the storm is only a "metaphor for what, long back, I / Had undergone," the restless life he can now review in the peace of age (484).

"The Sea Hates the Land" opens in a similar mood by asserting, "Be not deceived" (484). This is a second allusion to the verse referenced in "Twice Born," which reads, "Be not deceived; God is not mocked: for whatsoever a man soweth, that shall he also reap," in the English of the King James Version. The text proves a helpful one for a meditative review of life as the work of age, and Warren develops this one in the imagery of sea and shore he knew from Melville and Conrad, both his earlier critical subjects. Recalling "If Ever," Warren again instructs his readers to "Swim seaward, stroke steady, breath deep," so that the conscious self is thus "Absorbed in the innocent solipsism of the sea" (485).

"Afterward," the fifth and final poem of Section VII, "Fear and Trembling," then functions as a sort of "afterword," or perhaps coda for the section, while it also prefigures "Fear and Trembling," the lone selection of Section VIII, "Coda," which ends the volume. "Afterward" pivots on a naturalistic vision of eternity that reflects not only the poem's earlier imagery but also the four other poems in this section. Warren uses the preposition "After" to introduce a half dozen clusters of meaning that range from the abstracted "After the promise has been kept, or / Broken" to six lines of concrete memories stirred by the obituary of a long forgotten lover (485). Other iterations of mortal limitations include Warren's repeated images of forlorn sunset, shameful memory, and lonely insomnia. Midway in the poem, its persona posits "the unimaginable expanse of polar // Icecap, stretching forever in light of gray-green ambiguousness" as "if this // Is the only image of eternity" (485–86). In the rest of this poem, Warren asks his reader to contemplate other natural and human symbols, including "menhirs, monoliths, and all / Such frozen thrusts of stone," "a nameless skull, by weather uncovered or / The dateless winds," and "a great cactus . . . thorny and black, in ritual unresting" against a moonlit "forever sky" (486). The poem ironically contemplates "a conversation of mutual comfort" with these symbols of mortality, perhaps in hope of teasing out slight suggestions of eternity (486).

"Fear and Trembling," the only selection in Section VIII, "Coda," continues this contemplation of mortality but in a sublime poetic meditation that concludes *Rumor Verified* with more than a suggestion of human transcendence. Indeed, four of Warren's five regular quatrains counsel meditation. In the first, the silence of the forest at a late-summer sunset suggests that "It is time to meditate on what the season has meant" (487). Warren then opens his second stanza by asking, "But what is the meaningful language for such meditation?" (487). The pivotal third quatrain seeks a new idiom in the silent contemplation of nature, of the wood "where high leaves / Against sun, in vernal translucence, yet glow with the freshest / Young tint of the lost spring" (487). In the first line of the fourth stanza, Warren's poetic persona wonders, "Can one, in fact, meditate in the heart, rapt and wordless?" (487). This line of questioning is continued in the last quatrain stanza, where the ABAB pattern of the first four is transformed to ABAA, setting up the final stanza of a single extended line ending in the last B rhyme. Warren begins this final sentence of five lines by echoing the opening of the previous stanza, "Can the heart's meditation wake us from life's long sleep . . . ?" (487). His answer is coded in images of intellectual complexity and poetic sublimity. If life's labors prove "foolish and fond," then "only at death of ambition," or in the contemplation of mortality, "does the deep / Energy crack crust, spurt forth, and leap /? From grottoes, dark—and from the caverned enchainment" (487). This subterranean energy implies the archetypal power of the subconscious, of course, but it also recalls Warren's epigraph from *Inferno* where the mortal poet Dante and his immortal mentor Virgil emerge from the infernal caverns to make their way toward the purgatorial mountain while contemplating the eternal beauty of the heavenly stars.[10]

In these last half-dozen poems of *Rumor Verified,* as in most of its contents, Warren assumes the true task of the poet in age, not simply penning verse in his later years, but writing poetry that probes the meanings of past and future, of life and death, with an integrity of vision that remains consistent from his initial commitment to his final achievement. As we have seen, Warren never spares himself in his quest for the most profound kinds of meaning to be discovered in the final stages of human and artistic development. No easy version of Erikson's age-work or simplified account of Butler's life review are discovered in Warren's later collections as they make their progress toward his final closure with Tornstam's psychological transcendence. If *Rumor Verified* is not the strongest of these later works, perhaps because of the aging poet's urge to publish the findings of his quest under the deepening shadow of his mortality, it still proves an important one both in its overall poetic quality and in its quiet, yet consistent evolution toward the natural transcendence evident even in the title of Warren's final self-selected gathering of poetry from 1985, *Altitudes and Extensions,* which forms the focus of the chapter that follows.

6

Sublimity and Transcendence

Altitudes and Extensions: 1980–1984

> Yes, stretch forth your arms like wings, and from your high stance,
> Hawk-eyed, ride forth upon the emptiness of air, survey
> Each regal contortion
> And tortuous imagination of rock, wind, water, and know
> Your own power in creating all.
>
> —"Delusion?—No!"

1

Unlike the swift evolution of *Rumor Verified* in less than the year before its publication in 1981, Warren would take nearly four years to publish his final collection, *Altitudes and Extensions,* as the introduction to his fourth and last self-selected volume, *New and Selected Poems: 1923–1985*. The reasons for the longer gestation period of this concluding work are several. Warren's new volume appeared on his eightieth birthday, and its selections seemingly required more time and effort to accommodate the ongoing age-work and life review necessitated as he confronted ever more closely the inevitability of death and the possibility of transcendence. Debilities of age and illness also began to slow Warren's phenomenal poetic productivity. Although his prostate cancer largely remained in remission through his seventies, Warren suffered from severe osteoarthritis, which he handled with characteristic stoicism "'by not paying much attention to the pain'" (Blotner 475). Warren also dealt with the continuing infirmities of family and friends, particularly of Eleanor Clark's vision problems and the rapid decline of his only brother Tom from emphysema. Milestones included the birth of his first grandchild in 1982 and the ultimate death of his younger brother in 1985 (Blotner 468, 476).[1] In addition to these and other personal issues, Warren published the third and last of his longer poetic narratives, *Chief Joseph of the Nez Perce,* in 1983, midway between his last two collections of poetry, *Rumor Verified* and *Altitudes and Extensions.*

Like *Brother to Dragons* and *Audubon* before it, *Chief Joseph* becomes part of both national and personal epics, as Warren once again traces the shadowy parallels between the biography of a complicated historical personage and his own complex poetic autobiography. Warren's two other long narratives marked important transitions in his development as a poet. In 1953, *Brother to Dragons* announced Warren's midcareer return to poetry after a decade's silence, while *Audubon* in 1969 signaled the beginning of his poetic age-work and autobiography as reflected in the overall title of my study. At the midpoint of this later stage of his poetic career, Warren also published a substantial revision of *Brother to Dragons* in 1979, altering the relations of its central father figures and their surrogate sons as discussed earlier. Through Warren's revisiting and revising many of these same images and ideas, *Chief Joseph* thus becomes another interesting and important, if somewhat neglected, longer narrative in the poet's age-work.

Warren critics have only begun to trace the problematical parallels among *Brother to Dragons, Audubon* , and *Chief Joseph.*[2] If the two earlier narratives exemplify Warren's inherently pessimistic outlook on the human condition and American culture, the latest one progresses to the more positive visions of both self and society increasingly evident in his later life and works. *Chief Joseph* is perhaps the most important of Warren's three longer poems in relation to his ongoing age-work, not just because of its place in the chronology of his poetic development but also due to its despairing cultural analysis and its redeeming personal insight. Connections with Warren's ironic view of American history are obvious from its three epigraphs, which contrast Thomas Jefferson and William Tecumseh Sherman with Chief Sealth, to its darkening close on the battlefield at Snake Creek in Montana, where in 1877 Chief Joseph at last surrendered to the Army of the United States. The narrative moves from the natural innocence of the Nimipu, or "The Real People" as they called themselves, when encountered by Lewis and Clark, to the courage of the Nez Perce, as their white antagonists named them in their resistance to treaty breakers forcing them from their traditional homelands. Most of the narrative concerns the daring of their epic run for freedom in Canada, where they sought to join Sitting Bull, "Who now sat safe by the 'skirts of the old lady Queen,' / Far Northward" (502).

This historical chase, widely celebrated in the popular media during the year of its centennial in 1977, is not Warren's thematic emphasis, though it may have been his original starting point.[3] As always, Warren is a skillful storyteller in verse, but even more than his two earlier narrative poems, *Chief Joseph* is a work of complex intertextuality. From his triple epigraph forward, Warren juxtaposes the historical documents themselves with his imaginative version of the story as presented through a multiplicity of narrative viewpoints. Three narrative voices predominate: Chief Joseph's telling his own story, an impersonal narrator's reciting textbook history, and Warren's own retelling how he traced Chief Joseph's footsteps, both figuratively and then literally, on a pilgrimage into geographical and historical wilderness. In turn, Warren's overall narrative divides itself into three elements: Chief Joseph's inner development, the recorded history of the period, and Warren's poetic reaction to both in the contrasting of past and present, of youth and age, and of innocence and experience. Chief Joseph in exile is very much the fallen American Adam, but by pure force of will he returns from a prison camp in Oklahoma to the northwestern mountains—though not to his traditional fatherlands in the Wallowa country. Visited by the rich and famous, those who in the historical narrator's apt phrase "slick-fucked a land," Chief Joseph remains aloof, living stoically and preserving the vision of his fathers in his personal age-work (520). Some two decades after his death in 1904, Chief Joseph's people finally were allowed to return his remains to his home place.

Warren's story does not end in death and burial, however. In his final section, the author, speaking now for himself, narrates his personal search for Chief Joseph. In a drive reminiscent of his exploration of the historical setting of *Brother to Dragons* in Kentucky more than thirty years earlier, Warren visits the historical battlefield at Snake Creek in Montana accompanied by two younger poetic colleagues. His imagination recreates not just the desperate fight but Chief Joseph's reluctant surrender to save the women and children from the destructive fury of rifled cannons and Gatling guns. History provides Warren the poet with Chief Joseph's famous final speech: "From where the sun now stands I will fight no more forever" (523). Warren ends with his own words, however, ones which recall the visionary conclusions of both *Brother to Dragons* and *Audubon*, a new vision, but one which once again balances the contests between irony and belief in the lives of Jefferson and Audubon. In *Chief Joseph,* Warren's concluding lines prove somewhat more positive, perhaps even optimistic:

> But suddenly knew that for those sound
> Of heart there is no ultimate
> Irony. There is only
> Process, which is one name for history. Often
> Pitiful. But, sometimes, under
> The scrutinizing prism of Time,
> Triumphant. (525)

If Jefferson, Audubon, and Chief Joseph all died without the promised lands of their personal visions, Warren, as both creator and character in his later narrative poetry recovers a grander bounty in the heart of American nature by transcending counterfeit culture and inauthentic selfhood to discover natural beauty and to understand human bravery.

As noted above, Warren turns westward ever more frequently in the age-work and life review of his later fiction and poetry. Perhaps the most interesting aspect of Warren's West is his personal reversal of continuities of geography and history inscribed as innocence and corruption in the traditional cultural narrative of the region. Warren inverts the American cultural paradigm; his West is first fallen and then redeemed when he penetrates farther into its landscapes and further into its history. This pattern may be discerned, for example, in the geographical, historical, and thematic progression of Warren's three long narrative poems—*Brother to Dragons, Audubon,* and *Chief Joseph.* At last, Warren accepts the West as "a place to come to" that permits the grandest efforts of the human spirit in life review and age work and validates the assertion of possible order and meaning in the face of inevitable death and dissolution.

2

Chief Joseph also provides a useful introduction to *Altitudes and Extensions* in the comparison of their settings, themes, and, meanings. The most immediate consideration is Warren's use of western landscapes in his new collection, especially in its opening section, which is then balanced in Section II by a selection of poems set in and around Warren's more familiar locales in the East. In the remainder of *Altitudes and Extensions,* Warren remains as aware of history, in both its individual and cultural aspects, as he is of geography. The third section of the volume is comprised of a single narrative, "New Dawn," a realistic account of the nuclear holocaust at Hiroshima in light of America's amnesia about its past, and one reminiscent of the historical revisionism in *Chief Joseph.* "New Dawn" is followed in Section IV, appropriately enough, with three poems that all take place in literal or figurative dusks, echoing the collection's initial selection, "Three Darknesses." Warren organizes the remaining twenty-seven of his forty-eight poems into four sections that can be considered as two pairs under rubrics familiar from discussion of other collections—"Nostalgic" and "Speculative" from *Now and Then* and "Space" and "Time" from *Rumor Verified.* The concluding Section IX of *Altitudes and Extensions* then presents the sublime lyric "Myth of Mountain Sunrise" as its single selection and as a brighter epilogue contrasting with the darker opening selection and section.

Most critics who consider the overall structure of *Altitudes and Extensions* at all draw this same contrast. Victor Strandberg traces the volume's dialectical imagery "From the first poem, 'Three Darknesses,' to the terminal 'Myth of Mountain Sunrise'" ("Robert Penn Warren" 442). Randolph Paul Runyon also implies their connection by way of Warren's poetic sorites (*Braided Dream* 81–84). James A. Grimshaw Jr. makes the additional point that "although Warren does not designate poems as preliminary and coda in this volume, 'Three Darknesses' and 'Myth of Mountain Sunrise,' respectively, could easily serve in those capacities" (Grimshaw 182). Aside from contrasting its first and last selections as a progression from darker to brighter themes, the critics do not much consider the organization of *Altitudes and Extensions.* Strandberg sees "a dialectical pattern of images [that] gradually produces an extraordinary final effect of rejuvenation" ("Robert Penn Warren" 442). Runyon locates his view of the later collections in terms of dialectics of texts in a psychological sorites extending to *Altitudes and Extensions* (*Braided Dream* 19–25). Grimshaw is more concerned with the divisions of the volume, grouping the first six sections under the rubrics of "hope" and "love" and contrasting the final two sections in terms of "decline" and "endurance" (186, 189–90).

In my view, Warren's tripartite opening selection in *Altitudes and Ex-*

tensions contrasts the West with varied landscapes, as if to point out its differences from the other seven poems comprising this initial section. The settings of Warren's tripled darks include a zoo in Rome on an early spring morning, the tropical Black Snake River at nightfall, and an American hospital at midnight. In the Roman zoo, a great bear's persistent pounding on the metal door "to a dark enclosure" represents the persona's own intellectual efforts "to enter into the darkness of wisdom" (529). The psychological darkness that falls on a yacht anchored in a jungle inlet and its alienated passengers seems descended from a tale by Conrad. The darkened hospital room on a night before an operation, "trivial" but suggestive of "The real thing" to come with age, is even more terrifying, and the persona seeks solace in an "an old-fashioned western" on a television set (530). American myth may assert that "Winchester fire . . . virtue will triumph" in this chase, but *Chief Joseph* has shown the irony of such a conclusion. However, Warren ends "Three Darknesses" by invoking the natural innocence of a transcendent western landscape, "The snow peaks / Float into moonlight. They float / In that unnamable altitude of white light" (530). If only in its small screen simulacrum, this brighter vision of the West assures the persona that "God / Loves the world"—at least "For what it is" (530).

In its contrasting of real and recreated western landscapes and their symbolic significances, "Three Darknesses" proves the introduction to Section I as well as to *Altitudes and Extensions.* This initial poem thus pairs not only with the last one in the volume, "Myth of Mountain Sunrise," but also with the final one in this section, "Far West Once." The remaining six selections then are presented in three rather evident pairs: "Mortal Limit" and "Immortality over the Dakotas," "Caribou" and "The First Time," as well as "Minnesota Recollection" and "Arizona Midnight." John Burt's extensive description of Warren's intensive tinkering with the order of both *Altitudes and Extensions* and *New and Selected Poems: 1923–1985* reinforces a conclusion that the arrangement of poems within sections is as important as that of sections within the overall volume (786–87). As we have seen, Warren pays careful attention to his opening and closing pieces, most often placing his strongest efforts in these symbolic situations."Far West Once," for example, is far and away the finest of the eight pieces that Section I comprises, and it is the only one approaching poetic sublimity in my view. The poem's individual achievement is complemented, of course, by its intertextuality with "Three Darknesses." In the final poem, mountains of the West that were only imagined during earlier stages of age-work in the opening poem are confronted in their full reality much closer to the end of the poet's life in "Far West Once." Beholding the great western peaks once more, perhaps for "'The last time'" as the aging persona says aloud to himself, he anticipates a time when this immersion in nature will be recovered "only in memory" (536). This sense of the last things pervades the age-work of *Altitudes and Extensions,* for example in the final poems of Sections IV, V, and VII—"Last Walk of Season," "Last Meeting," and "Last Night Train," respectively. Like this whole volume, however, "Far West Once" unfolds toward a higher understanding of the human condition in some of the traditional last things—Death and Resurrection, if not Heaven and Hell.

At sunset, facing the inevitable "blast of darkness—the target me," Warren's persona tries to commit this moment of "shadowy gorge" and "aspen leaf gold" to memory, along with other moments of "noon-plain . . . / . . . old rattler's fat belly" and "night-crouching cougar's eyes," storing all of them against the coming dark in "Heart-hope, undefinable, verging to tears / Of happiness and the soul's calm" (536–37). This climb would not be his last mountain excursion, for in other mountain camps he often recalls it.

> Or waking under nameless stars,
> Have heard such redemptive music, from
> Distance to distance threading starlight,
> Able yet, as long ago,
> Despite scum of wastage and scab of years,
> To touch again the heart, as though at a dawn
> Of dew-bright Edenic promise, with,
> Far off, far off, in verdurous shade, first birdsong. (537)

This sublime final stanza thus brings Warren full circle to his youth in Kentucky, his midlife trips to the West, and his old age in the mountains of New England as he conflates past, present, and even future dawns within "Far West Once."

Warren's familiar organizing tactic of pairing poems in dualities of theme and meaning is revealed once again in the tripled pairs that are found in the remainder of Section I. For example, parallels become obvious in the titles of the first two—"Mortal Limit" and "Immortality over the Dakotas"—as well as in their altitudes—a hawk's flight "over Wyoming" as observed by the earthbound persona and "the tiny glow" from "a little Dakota town" at dusk as seen through a jetliner's "two-inch-thick plane-window glass" (530, 531). These paired selections prove rather different in other respects, however. In form, "Mortal Limit" is one of Warren's sonnet variations, this one in the regular English rhyme pattern but presented in looser and longer lines. Its totemic bird again represents the seeming immortality of nature; the hawk first rises "past gray jags / Of mercilessness" that mark "the Tetons," though they are but one range that "gold eyes see" as "a last scrawl of light" (530, 531). The thinning atmosphere at this altitude returns the great bird as well as its observer to a "dying vision" of the "mortal limit" from the title (531). Both man and hawk must return to what the final couplet calls: "The breath of earth? Of rock? Of rot? Of other such / Items, and the darkness of whatever dream we clutch?" (531).

"Immortality over the Dakotas," the paired piece, takes the more discursive form of five stanzas of five and six irregular and unrhymed lines, in which the "semisomnolent" persona can pontificate in Latinate diction as "Dark hurtles past" at this high altitude about his seeming salvation after "a quick dip / In the Lamb's mystic blood" (531). Then "far, far down / . . . a glowworm" of light recalls an actual Dakota crossroads where he had stopped for gas on a western excursion years earlier, a place that seemed irrevocably lost despite its "Baptist church (Red brick)" (531). Pressing closer to the aircraft portal, the persona imagines an aging Dakota farmer, just informed of his mortal illness by the town doctor, standing in the dark because he is afraid to enter his house and tell his waiting wife of his mortality. Instead, he watches the lights of the jetliner crossing the sky in its simulation of a passage to immortality. Warren leaves unstated the fact that what his persona really could see in the dark glass is his own face, so that the imagined western agriculturalist, perhaps reminiscent of Tom Warren, who ran the feed mill in Guthrie, becomes a brother figure who represents the poet's own intimations of "Immortality over the Dakotas."

Warren's next two poems, "Caribou" and "The First Time," also form a very unmistakable pair with their basic connection in their common subjects. "Caribou" is the Native American name for the North American reindeer, while "The First Time" concerns its persona's initial encounter in the wild with "wapiti," the Native American word for the North American elk. The aerial observation of the caribou herds in the first poem may locate it more recently in western Canada, where Warren traveled in the 1970s; the first words of the second are "Northwest Montana," indicating that Warren recalls his first sighting of the "bull wapiti" on his western vacations in the 1950s (533). In both poems, Warren's persona needs others as mentors to guide him into the mysteries of nature that he is then left to interpret on his own. "Caribou" includes a biologist and two pilots, while the altitude of their perspective on the reindeer herd reminds the reader of "Immortality over the Dakotas." Instead of penetrating blackness, however, the persona must employ "binoculars" to peer into "the white anonymity" of nature where the animals instinctively "breathe destiny" (532). Left to his own devices, the persona reveals in the penultimate stanza of a single line, "I have lost the spot. I find only blankness," perhaps an empty symbol of his own destiny. The smaller band of elk in "The First Time," "One great bull, / Six cows, one young," are observed on foot under the earthy guidance of "Old Jack," an aging cowboy who says of the bull, "Now ain't he a pisser?" (533). Warren's persona views the proud bull within a natural tableau profiled against snows of a far range, "Balanced and noble . . . in that bronze-tinged emptiness" of a western sunset (533). Thus, the great elk becomes another totem of ennobling nature, like Warren's hawks and eagles, all extending themselves "in philosophic / Arrogance against / God's own sky" (533–34). "The First Time" is also notable for its contrast with the several "last" encounters in *Altitudes and Extensions,* evident here from the poem's title forward to its conclusion.

"Minnesota Recollection" and "Arizona Midnight" announce specific western settings in their titles, and these paired poems prove intertextual, not just each with the other, but with several selections in this first section of *Altitudes and Extensions.* The exact nature of the "Recollection" in the first poem's title remains problematic here, as the text's narrative of an immigrant grandfather lost in a Minnesota blizzard seems to be based on literary rather than personal sources. In any case, this death in Minnesota recalls the dying farmer of the section's third selection, "Immortality over the Dakotas." The startling disappearance of this old man under white-out conditions also suggests the same sort of disturbing existential emptiness the persona encountered in the "unshadowed vastness" of Canada in "Caribou" (532). When "Old Sugfred" does not return from his evening chores, his extended family become a makeshift rescue party, and they almost are lost themselves in the indifferent immensity of nature symbolized by the fearful storm. Then "first flame of the prairie dawn" reveals a frozen corpse, "Snagged on a barbed-wire fence," but the old man's "face was calm" with "an innocent expression" (535).

The Frostian contrast of black night and white snow observed in "Minnesota Recollection" presents an immediate contrast to the desert blackness of "Arizona Midnight," but it also recalls how Warren's persona lay awake contemplating a Montana midnight in "The First Time." There he is aroused by "some distant howl" to reconsider his totemic encounter with the great elk (533). In contrast, the "grief of the coyote" that wakens him to "the blankness which / Is Arizona at midnight" has its "only answer" in "My own grief, for which I have no / Tongue," at least as yet (536). The last dark just before dawn also recollects the initial "Three Darknesses," with its image of a desert night on the television screen. In both desert settings the most striking symbols are "Black / Stalks of cacti"; in the movie scene of the section's initial poem they loom darkly "like remnants of forgotten nightmares," while the "single great cactus" dimly seen against the "Arizona Midnight" of the penultimate selection presents "Its own necessary beauty" like a dream vision of dawn (530, 536).

As we discovered earlier, the first section's final poem is located in a West more symbolic than real, the traditional land of the last sunset with which it opens, though it closes at midnight with its persona, considering "Edenic promise" (537). If the geography of the West never fulfilled its historical promise of an American Dream in Warren's view, then at least its natural grandeur provides a place to review his life in relation to epics both national and individual. This aspect of Warren's age-work becomes even more apparent in the half-dozen selections separating the section's initial "Three Darknesses" from the final "Far West Once." "Mortal Limit" and "Immortality over the Dakotas," "Caribou" as well as "The First Time," and "Minnesota Recollection" and "Arizona Midnight" are paired by settings and events, as well as by themes and meanings, poetic aspects that will be reiterated in both comparison to and contrast with other selections throughout the other eight sections of Warren's new collection.

3

The second section of *Altitudes and Extensions,* for example, compares with Section I in terms of organization but contrasts with it in regard to setting. Once again, Section II contains eight selections organized as three pairs of poems framed by introductory and concluding pieces, though the settings here are Warren's more typical ones in the Southeast and New England rather than in the West. Perhaps for this reason, Section II is focused by autobiography, not by the ultimate age-work of one facing imminent decline and death. While the "Rumor at Twilight" whispered in the title of the opening selection seems to concern the inevitable mortality discovered in Warren's penultimate collection, *Rumor Verified,* it is suffused here with momentary recollections from a lifetime. Such is certainly the case with the final poem of the section, "Snowfall," where a series of memories are developed in a more ordered and extended fashion. Between the framing poems, Warren presents three pairs not quite as obvious as those in Section I—"Old Dog Dead" and "Hope," "Why You Climbed Up" and "Literal Dream," as well as "After the Dinner Party" and "Doubleness in Time." Under close scrutiny, all the poems in Section II demonstrate a double focus in chronology as each persona experiences in the present both recreations of his past and intimations of his future in terms of mortality and transcendence.

In "Rumor at Twilight," the first of three nine-line stanzas opens with its persona's unfocused "crepuscular / Agitation," perhaps the sort of free-floating anxiety that increases with age and becomes in extreme cases the so-called "sundown syndrome" often associated with senile dementia. The oncoming night is imaged as "a dark cave" once explored in youth despite cave bats hanging like "Dark fruit" overhead with "Droppings / Of generations soft underfoot" (538). This strange psychological association puzzles the persona because "no particular / Financial worries" come to mind as he stands in his yard after a family dinner. "Moments of memory" continue to punctuate his present unease, however, "like the phosphorescent" flashes of fireflies in the shrubs or the dark flights of bats above the maples (538). The last line of the second stanza questions the reality of these recollections, "Can you really reconstruct your mother's smile?" (538). In the third stanza, the fast-falling dark recalls a boy "drunk with . . . / . . . the massiveness of moonrise" (538). All of these images from memory—a bat-haunted cave, a mother's smile, and a moonlit lane—have appeared in earlier poems, of course, and they will reappear in the selections which follow in Section II as well as in the rest of *Altitudes and Extensions.*

"Old Dog Dead" and "Hope," the first of three pairings that become the body of Section II, are structured by similar flashes of memory impinging on the darkness of the present. This pair also reinforces the pattern in its thematic balance between pessimistic and optimistic visions of the human situation that will be reversed and then reiterated in the other two pairings that follow. The aged English cocker that the persona has put down in "Old Dog Dead" could be an autobiographical reference to the last of the Warren family pets. Rosanna Warren, who was particularly fond of her dogs and wrote a precocious children's book about them, seems to be the girl child remembered in her joy at the gift of the puppy fifteen years earlier (Blotner 353). When Warren's persona imagines the old dog's anonymous grave in the woodlot behind the veterinarian's office in Vermont, he thinks how "Far off a little girl, little no longer, would, / If yet she knew, / Lie in her bed and weep / For what life is" (540). What strikes him most, however, is that now the beloved pet, next the faithful father, and finally the girl child herself at last become an "old woman," "Now alone," will all be lost in what the last line of the poem describes, in a favorite formulation of Warren's, as "The unlabeled detritus and trash of Time" (540).[4]

As its title indicates, "Hope," the selection paired with "Old Dog Dead" in Section II, takes a more optimistic view of the persona's position in the late autumn of his life. Although the first of its four six-line stanzas opens at sunset much like "Rumor at Twilight," here "the orchidaceous light of evening" ennobles "the lowliest hedge-leaf" with its "purpling shadow," spreading its "spectral ash" after the "the magnificent disaster of the day" (541). In the irregular lines of the second stanza, "gold light" illuminates the colors of "the maple leaf" in a "last glory" heightened by dark spruces that "seem rigid in blackened bronze" (541). As the "first star petals" in the "transitional light" of stanza 3, "cinders in the west die," as though "the world has its last blooming" (541). Even after "a last bird twitters, the last bat goes" into the falling darkness of the fourth stanza, "The promise / Of moonrise will dawn," with hope, and in the short concluding stanza "Will dominate the sky, the world, the heart, / In white forgiveness" (541).[5]

In the middle pair of Section II, "Why You Climbed Up" and "Literal Dream," the pattern of descent and resurrection is reversed, as the first selection rises toward a vision of self-definition while the second descends into a literary nightmare. These paired poems also ring some interesting changes on the geographical tensions between West and East in Sections I and II. "Why You Climbed Up" recreates mountain ascent, but from the persona's relation to his setting this one seems to be in Vermont. Yet it might as well be a western ridge the persona climbs, compelled as he is to leave behind "All things, great and small, you call / The past, all things, great and small, you call / The Self," much as he will do again in death (542). In the "sweat and pant" of this warm afternoon, the persona recalls how years before "In the moonlit Pacific you swam west" until the life force drew him back to shore (542). Atop this height at last, he sees "The sun blaze down on the next and higher horizon," altitudes he is still not ready to ascend (542). As the final, single-lined stanza reveals, "Then all begins again. And you are you," in the moment of his return to self and life (542).

"Literal Dream" turns out to be a literary dream as well, for Warren's persona dreams himself within a gruesome scene from Thomas Hardy's *Tess of the d'Urbervilles*. The poem's extended subtitle, "(*Twenty Years after Reading* Tess *and / Without Ever Having Seen Movie),*" both sets the scene chronologically after the 1979 filmic adaptation and tries to explain psychologically the strange circumstances of his dream logic (542). The scene in question takes place in chapter 56 after the fallen Tess has stabbed her seducer to death, and his spilling blood seeps through the ceiling of the room below to reveal the crime to their landlady. Warren's narrative is clearly intertextual with Hardy's novel, but more important is his poetic gloss on the dream scene that seems to represent his own anxieties at the imagery of debility, death, and dissolution. The revelation he knows in his nightmare, "Was in no book, nor ever had been, nor / Such terror" (543).[6] As observed above, Warren is more often associated with Hardy's poetry than with his fiction, but in "Literal Dream" the American poet seems to have drawn similar themes and meanings from his reading of his English forebear's *Tess.*

"After the Dinner Party" and "Doubleness in Time" form the closest and the most successful of the three pairs of poems in the body of Section II. They better balance age-work and life review in their autobiographical references and psychological insights, much as in Warren's earlier volume *Now and Then.* In fact, that title phrase is referenced in both poems. The opening line of "After the Dinner Party" reads "You two sit at the table late, each, now and then," thinking of their recent dinner guests and musing on their friends from the past who have departed forever in death (544). The Warrens were celebrated hosts for frequent dinner parties at the Connecticut house, and their guest lists were like an artistic and academic guide to their times (Blotner 302–3). Warren's emphasis is not on those brilliant evenings "then," however, as much as on the silence and darkness that follows "now." His dominant images are of winter night encroaching on a fire dying into cold ashes. Taking the other's hand to mount old stairs that "Will creak with your grave and synchronized tread as each mounts / To a briefness of light, then true weight of darkness," the couple will clasp hands once more as they sink into sleep (544). "After the Dinner Party" employs a hybrid poetic form that also supports its parallel use of past and present—seven ABAB quatrains complicated by extended lines of multisyllabic diction in irregular rhythms.

Warren's reconsideration of his mother's death as he nears his own in "Doubleness in Time" returns to his more common late style marked by irregular stanzas with short unrhymed lines of monosyllabic diction in repetitive rhythms. As in "After the Dinner Party," his opening lines reference *Now and Then.*

> Doubleness coils in Time like
> The bull-snake in fall's yet-leafed growth. *Then*
> Uncoils like *Now. Now*
> Like *Then.* (544)

Here, Warren returns to autumn 1931 in another attempt to come to terms with his past and his future with a poem of his present. Although Ruth Warren's death was "then" in time, "the years, how many? / Fifty," it is also "now" in Time, for "at last it truly / Happens" so that her aging son fully understands (544). His mother's abstract glance toward "Infinity" as she expires still remains beyond his comprehension (545). More clearly remembered and understood are the glimpses of her aging husband and her three children, now young adults themselves, lost in their individual grief (545). At the moment of Ruth's passing, Robert Franklin Warren leans to kiss her cold lips while "Hand touches hand," much as in "After the Dinner Party," for "I am seeing that *Now*" (545). Later, the stunned father sits outside the hospital room, "as though an antique statue / Exhumed after centuries," and under his son's speculative gaze the old man's "eyes show nothing" (546). As Warren concludes, "It is not *Then.* / It is *Now.* For it / Has taken a long time for Truth to become true" (546).

The "Snowfall" in Warren's concluding selection of Section II is likely a classic "Nor'easter," as from "far north in Vermont" sweeping "Southward, two states, it strikes all the miles to the Sound" (547). The poem's aging persona recognizes the arrival of the inaugural snowstorm as an annual event that marks a passage of his life: "You do not remember what year was the first, / For many a year has passed" (548). This rite of winter is rife with dark images of annihilation that bracket the persona's memories of more exultant seasons of the year and of his life. In the opening stanza, "The whiteness of silence . . . / . . . comes / To blot the last dying crimson that outlines the slope" near his home (547). Near the conclusion, he imagines the storm reaching the nearby sound where "snowflakes / Die on the bay-swirl of small whitecaps" (547).

This suggestion of an ultimate dissolution in "Snowfall" prompts the persona to review the past, neatly paralleling the passing of the year and of his life. Spring announces "Earth's old immortality" in sightings of green shoots, returning songbirds, and the "new breasts" of a barely remembered girlfriend (547). Youthful sexual stirrings give way to the full-blown romance of summer as he remembers "The hand you held in late shadow of beeches" (547). Summer ends with an autumnal "'good-bye' on the station platform," in a fall "like a snake in weed-tangle" that slips quickly away from harvest to hibernation, when "The bear / Will soon sleep with no dream" (547). In the penultimate stanza of "Snowfall," the storm returns to "tramp out last embers of day," leaving Warren in the concluding couplet to "Stand in the darkness of whiteness / Which is the perfection of

Being" (548). This sublime balance of dark and white imagery, again recalling Robert Frost's late poetry, captures perfectly the natural blankness of nonbeing as well as the psychological transcendence resulting from life review and age-work.

4

Section III of *Altitudes and Extensions* consists of a single long poem in fifteen numbered parts under the overall title of "New Dawn," a narrative sequence that proves a historical reconsideration of the atomic attack that concluded the Second World War. "New Dawn" is dedicated to John Hersey, who commissioned the piece to serve as a preface to a new deluxe edition of *Hiroshima* (Blotner 472). In every way, Warren does a workmanlike job in response to his old friend's request. His account does not simply transmute Hersey's classic reportage, as Warren focuses on the American airmen above rather than on the Hiroshima residents below on that fateful morning. Warren's vision is both intensely realistic and subtly ironic, allowing his patient accumulation of minute factual details about the *Enola Gay* to counterpoint the moral enormity of its mission. "New Dawn" can be connected with *Chief Joseph*, as I have indicated above, in its revision of America's national myths of guilt and innocence. Although it does show the poet's changing perspectives, "New Dawn" provides little insight into age because Warren's point of view is so objective as to eliminate his persona's history from the poem. Despite its literal altitudes, we may wonder if "New Dawn" really belongs in this collection unified by themes closely related to Warren's age-work, life review, and search for transcendence. Because "New Dawn" was written for much different purposes, I believe it somewhat disturbs the order and effect of *Altitudes and Extensions*, though not in any way that seriously mars the collection's overall success.[7]

Warren does locate "New Dawn" in *Altitudes and Extensions* with some care, however. The poem's title image posits the sunburst of the nuclear blast as a false dawn both for Hiroshima and for humanity in the second half of his own life. The dusk of "Snowfall," the concluding selection of Section II, brackets "New Dawn" in tandem with the three poems of Section IV, all of which consider the frailty of human love in the fading light of evening. These three dusks in "The Distance Between: Picnic of Old Friends,"

"True Love," and "Last Walk of Season" in turn recall "Three Darknesses," the introductory selection of Section I and of the volume. If "New Dawn" had not been included in this collection, then those three short pieces well might have been distributed among the volume's remaining sections. The three crepuscular settings of Section IV seem located in Warren's eastern settings as they move among the stages of his life and loves, but his arrangement here seems based on different physical expressions of human emotion rather than on a geographical or chronological order.

Despite its title, "The Distance Between: Picnic of Old Friends" proves the most sexually intimate in its sudden rush to "seizure, penetration," though the psychological distance between these two old friends widens when dark descends after the picnic (557). The couple in question may have been more than just friends in the past, and a list of the others left behind at a picnic in the woods, "friends, husband, wife, / and small children," suggests they both are middle-aged and married, though not to each other (557). As they "wandered" away from these others, "in purposelessness . . . more aimless and aimless," they are caught up in "the shadowy / Uncoil of Time" (557). Outside their human commitments made over time, they consummate whatever relationship exists between them with "No resistance" (557). After this literal and figurative fall into "the rich, sap-bleeding, wild tangle of fern," they find "the world all strange, infinite / The distance between them," like Adam and Eve on the darkening path out from Eden (557). Nothing in the poem fixes its geographical or chronological setting, so the text reveals no autobiographical connection, even if the ages of the adulterous couple suggest the period of Warren's midlife marital crisis.[8]

The boy at the start of "True Love," the middle poem in Section IV, does seem a double for the young Warren: "I was ten, skinny, red-headed, // Freckled" (558). This identification locates the narrative near Guthrie in the years directly before World War I, and it realistically connects the loss of the boy's ironically named "true love" with the failure of her family's agricultural fortunes. She is like a local princess, set apart from the common folks of the little town not just by her personal "Beauty," but by her family's wealth (558). They display all the symbols of success, a "big black Buick" and a "big white farmhouse," though the father is "a drunkard" and the mother "a good Christian woman" and they spoil their children (558). The "grown brothers" become "slick-faced" idlers who wear the "shiny boots" of horsemen, and when the daughter is married early "it was so fashionable" that the boy is moved to wonder (558). Then their family fortunes collapse; "The mortgage was foreclosed. That last word was whispered" (558). The first is the one that should have been whispered, for "mortgage" derives from the Latin words for "death" and "pledge," and Warren's persona confesses that at ten, "I did not know what a mortgage was," any more than he knew then "if she would cry when something was done to her" on her wedding night (558).

Warren's postlapsarian consciousness of the joys and limits to be discovered in a truly mature love is neatly encapsulated in the last selection of Section IV, "Last Walk of Season." The final poem, once more, is the only sublime effort in this section's small gathering, and it proves intertextual not just with the two other selections here, but with both "Far West Once," which ends Section I, and with "Myth of Mountain Sunrise," the single selection of the volume's concluding Section IX. As in "The Distance Between: Picnic of Old Friends," a silent couple wanders a path through the woods at dusk; this time they are even older lovers, and their track is an abandoned logging road. The finality of age-work reverberates from the first lines, "For the last time . . . / we climb, / In the westward hour up the mountain trail / To see the last light" (559). Not only is it the end of day, but "A few high leaves / Of birch have gone golden" as the first frosts announce the fall—and "the blank sun-blaze of snow" that will inexorably follow (559). Their goal is "the mountain's cup," a "moraine-dammed" glacial lake "flame-huddled in mist" at sunset, where they drink what "happiness" may be found in nature; then, as in "After the Dinner Party," "a hand finds, on stone, a hand" (559). The final two-line stanza then connects animate with inanimate nature: "They are in contact. Past lake, over mountain, last light / Probes for contact with the soft-shadowed land" (559).

5

As I indicated at the outset of this chapter, Sections V and VI of *Altitudes and Extensions* replicate the overall division of *Now and Then* in two parts Warren gathered there under the rubrics of "Nostalgic" and "Speculative." All the critics recognize that Section V groups four obviously autobiographical selections, but they do not discern a contrasting philosophical gathering in Section VI. Most important for my study, this pairing of themes also suggests the theoretical concepts of life review and age-work. My discussion of *Now and Then* in chapter 3 also recognizes that these distinctions never become absolute—whether in regard to "Nostalgic" and "Speculative" themes or to the implied connections of what was then and what is now. Again in *Altitudes and Extensions,* the overall order is essentially chronological within Section V, while the organization of Section VI is geographical and topical. Warren's arrangement thus recalls the tensions of West and East and of South and North seen in Sections I and II; in turn, his ordering also prefigures my analysis of Sections VII and VIII in terms of "Space" and "Time," concepts I used with *Rumor Verified.*

Much like the "Nostalgic" section of *Now and Then,* Section V proceeds in the order of time here, as four aging personae recollect events from early childhood and youth through adulthood and age. Its four poems also divide themselves into two pairs by their subject matters, however; the first and third, "Old-Time Childhood in Kentucky" and "Re-interment: Recollection of a Grandfather," are focused by the patriarchal figure of Gabriel Thomas Penn, while the second and fourth, "Covered Bridge" and "Last Meeting," are connected by Warren's youthful escape from and tentative return to Guthrie. As we discovered earlier, Warren's maternal grandfather was an important mentor, especially during the years when the growing boy spent summers at his nearby tobacco farm, and the old man appeared in the varied guises of several characters in the earlier fiction and as versions of himself in the later poetry. *Being Here* was dedicated "*To Gabriel Thomas Penn (1836–1920)*" in 1980, and that grandfather manifests himself within that volume as the monumental patriarch of "When Life Begins" and "Safe in Shade," both of which are included once more in the contents of the 1985 *Selected Poems* (379). Grandpa Penn's importance to Warren's poetic imagination only increased as the poet became a grandfather himself, and he could view the continuities of family relationships and human knowledge from the opposite perspective of the youth and age continuum—now he was as old as his grandfather had been then.

"Old-Time Childhood in Kentucky" and "Re-interment: Recollection of a Grandfather" seem less archetypal and abstracted, more richly detailed and humanly complex, than his two earlier poems about his mother's father in *Being Here.* In comparison with each other, the two new poems reveal an arresting difference in that the first points back further into the past, while the second looks forward as far as it can into an ultimately unknowable future. The very title of "Old-Time Childhood in Kentucky" announces its nostalgic point of view, and the first two of Warren's five stanzas in varied nine-line patterns reminds us that his childhood was not all that far removed from Audubon's Kentucky frontier a century earlier. Like Warren's artist hero, the persona might see, "Canebrakes with / Track beaten down by bear paw," or "The great trout, / Motionless, poised in the shadow" (560). In stanza 2, handling the cultural relics of those violent times past, "I drew out a saber, touched an old bayonet" (560). Grandfather Penn appears in the third stanza, guiding the boy back over the years in colloquies on the battles of the Civil War, the strategies of Napoleon, and the history of ancient Egypt. After their mutual discovery in a "cave mouth . . . [of] . . . crinoid stems, / And in limestone skeletons of the fishy form of some creature" eons old, the boy persona realizes the true immensity of time revealed by the evolutionary evidence of these fossils (560). He then asks, "Grandpa, / . . . what do you do, things being like this?" (560). The old man states his stoic philosophy of life that seems to stem from these Darwinian premises and leaves his young grandson "waiting to discover / What I would be, might be, after ages—how many?—had rolled over" (561).

"Re-interment: Recollection of a Grandfather" reconsiders much of the same subject matter as "Old-Time Childhood in Kentucky," but in this poem Warren's persona remains an aged self in the act of recollection. Point of view is further complicated by the central image of reinterment, which is used here in a figurative rather than a literal sense. Warren's rather grotesque metaphor compares the vestige of his grandfather still alive deep in his memory with the old man's long-buried body trying to escape his grave. The concept proves almost metaphysical as the poem opens with an image of the dead man's first existence in his mother's womb, "a hundred and sixty-odd years ago" (562). Now the old man lives "locked in my head / . . . in my skull," manifested only in the persona's haunting dreams or in his own image aging in the mirror, "as I watch hair grow thin and pate gleam" (562). The last of five irregularly rhyming stanzas represents many of the same memories as "Old-Time Childhood in Kentucky"—his grandfather's "old-fashioned lingo [,] . . . at dinner the ritual grace, And . . . the use of a word like *honor*" (562). Yet "Some night, not far off, I'll sleep with no such recollection," as he too will be dead (562). Thus, the old man will be reinterred with the persona, who is the last person "in that after-while, / To love him—or recognize his kind" (563).[9]

"Covered Bridge" and "Last Meeting" also relate in their nostalgia for another time and place, as these two other selections in Section V are concerned both with Warren's youthful desire to leave home and his adult recognition that, like Thomas Wolfe, he can't go home again. In its age-work, however, Warren's imagination enables him to review the places and the people who had formed his life, "the shelf / Of memory in a sequence that I call Myself," as he calls it in "Covered Bridge" (561). That span over the Red River of Tennessee south of Guthrie that Warren describes as "Long, long ago, some miles away" is now preserved in Port Royal State Park; in Warren's youth, it still was a working bridge and one way to get to Nashville (561). Then, Warren was more concerned with its imaginative elements, of course, its tunnel-like dark that he would see by day and its haunting echo he would hear by night. Now, he tries to "understand / What pike, highway, or path has led you from land to land, // From year to year" in this brief life review (561).

The title of the final selection of Section V, "Last Meeting," echoes the overall themes of finality and age-work in *Altitudes and Extensions.* On a visit home at midlife, "some forty years back," Warren meets for the last time his black baby nurse on a summer Saturday night in Guthrie (563). At first glance, each has difficulty recognizing the other. Geraldine Carr had been a lively young woman about the same age as Ruth Warren forty years before (Blotner 9). The aging persona perceives a "shrunken old woman / With bleary eyes and yellow-gray skin, / And walking now with the help of a stick" (563). When he removes his hat, she comments that he is aging too; his graying, thinning hair is "Not fahr-red, like it used to be" (563). This wise old woman, while realizing that this once "little tadpole" is "'Now big and gone / Out in the wide world,'" commands him "—'but 'member me'" (563). During the intervening years, "Seely," as he called her, dies, and the aging "Ro-Penn," as she called him, "tried to find her grave, and failed" on a later trip to Guthrie. Although his final stanza of just two lines following twelve quatrains suggests somewhat doubtfully that he will return home again to pay proper respect by bringing flowers to her grave, "It's nigh half a lifetime I haven't managed, / But there must be enough time left for that" (563).

6

Warren's sixth section is the longest in *Altitudes and Extensions* with its thirteen selections, that is, if like most other critics we count the two parts of the short sequence "Seasons" as separate poems under their individual titles, I, "Downwardness," and II, "Interlude of Summer." Recalling the "Speculative" pieces in *Now and Then,* these thirteen are more concise, abstract, and philosophical than the nostalgic poems preceding them. Although nostalgia reappears occasionally in Section VI, it becomes more universalized, and it is judged more objectively. Warren's overall organization of these selections is looser, again like the "Speculative" section of the earlier volume. For the most part, these poems are ordered in topical pairings of subject matter or by tonal echoes of poetic form, as seven selections counting both parts of "Seasons" employ regular ABAB quatrains. As in the earlier sections, the first and last selections, "Muted Music" and "Winter Wheat: Oklahoma," become the most important to the section's overall themes and meanings.

Warren used two working titles during the evolution of "Muted Music," the more nostalgic "Sunday Afternoon in Summer in Old Barn" and the more speculative "The Sound Truth Makes" (Burt 787). The final title phrase appears twice within the text itself, referring first to the remembered "cruising hum / Of a single fly" in an old barn on a quiet afternoon long past and later to "the only sound that truth can make" in his memory of that lost moment (565). Such "muted music" proves most apt in regard to both subject and sound, as it images the barely perceived notes of meaning from the natural world in a lyrical murmur of alliteration and assonance. Indeed, vowel sounds predominate in the poem to the point of becoming a ululating emanation of nature perceived yet not fully understood in the past: for some examples, "In a cunningly wrought and mathematical // Box of shade," "That sultry hum from the lone bumbler, cruising high / In shadow," and "the song the moth sings, the babble / Of falling snowflakes (in language / No school has taught you)" (565). The persona's speculative task is to discern "*Which* was *what, what, which*" in the compass of his nostalgia (565). As age-work and life review, his final task is "To hear at last, at last, what you have strained for / All the long years" in the "muted music" of the universe (565).

Questions of selfhood and identity are considered in this section of philosophical pieces, most often by way of remembered revelations apprehended in the mysterious language figured in the motions of time and space, especially in the seasonal passages of life and of death. "The Whole Question" suggested in the title of Warren's next selection is the conundrum of human reality. "This / Getting born business is not as simple as it seemed," the first quatrain stanza tells us in extended lines and with exaggerated rhymes (566). In the next stanza, the initial breath of birth thrusts us "into what Paul called the body of this death" (566). This Pauline allusion reads in full, "Oh wretched man that I am! Who shall deliver me from the body of this death?" in the King James Version (*Romans* 7:24). The five quatrains that outline Warren's answer to "The Whole Question" also trace the course of existence from ignorant infancy to inadequate age. "Perhaps / It is only a matter of language that traps you," an inability to learn "Words . . . that make the Truth come true" (566).

Those images of sound echo the speculations about language in "Muted Music" once again in "The Whole Question," but they also foreshadow the visual images of the faintly nostalgic "Old Photograph of the Future" that follows and completes the first pairing in Section VI. Through the poem's five ABAB quatrains, Warren's persona contemplates a fading photograph in a family album, a tableau of himself as an infant posed with his proud parents. The center of this picture is "an infantile face" much like the one whose "face got twisted" to a smile in "The Whole Question" (566). The photographic details demonstrate the era of this family portrait: the infant "swathed in a sort of white dress" that matches his mother's, while his father stands apart "In black coat, derby at breast" (566, 567). After "around seventy-five" annual passages of the seasons, "They lie side by side in whatever love survives" after death, "and that child, years later, stands there" by the family plot in the local cemetery, "While old landscapes blur" with tears as "he in guilt grieves / Over nameless promises unkept, in undefinable despair" (567). Once again, Warren's persona has not learned how to decipher the world's language despite his lifelong effort.

Another pair of poems in quatrains follows, and both "Why Boy Came to Lonely Place" and "Platonic Lassitude" play on similar patterns of nostalgia and speculation, not just from the preceding pieces but from many others in earlier sections and collections. In the first of the two, a thirteen-year-old persona wanders in a lonely landscape of "Limestone and cedar" recalling Warren's autobiographical descriptions of Kentucky and Tennessee in volumes as far back as *Promises.* Only five years before, *Being Here* presented a notable example of similar images and ideas in "Speleology," where the twelve-year-old persona pondered his individual existence while experiencing a limestone cavern in absolute darkness. That earlier seeker thinks, "*This is me.* Thought: *Me—who am I?*" (382), while this later one says his name aloud, moves his fingers over his face, and wonders what he is and how long he will exist. Like "Speleology," "Why Boy Came to Lonely Place" concludes with a stanza of a single extended line in contrast to the regular lines and stanzas preceding it: "But what is that? To find out you come to this lonely place" (567).

A sort of naturalistic Platonism provides a common thread in another brace of speculative poems readily connected from *Being Here* and *Altitudes and Extensions,* "Platonic Drowse" and "Platonic Lassitude." Both pieces present moments seemingly perceived outside of time that arrest all natural motion and cause their poetic personae to question the very nature of their own reality in both existential and speculative terms, through "the world's ontological collapse" on a summer afternoon (568). From its Greek roots, ontology denotes the philosophical study of being, so that both poems really frame the same questions that the younger personae ask themselves in "Speleology" and "Why Boy Came to Lonely Place." These two Platonic poems differ, however, in their narrative angles on the development of the individual self. In the first, the aged poet seemingly recalls a youthful experience lost in his past, one that he then found mournful "in unaimed pubescent / Grief," though it proves more tolerable now many decades later "In Platonic joy for the world" (390, 391). "Platonic Lassitude" comes closer to the present, as the persona now masters his ontological despair in order to know "a new joy, that unlike the old, cannot end" (568). Yet end it might when a "crow calls from the black cliff forgotten," telling the timeless truth "That nothing defines itself in joy or sorrow" (568).

In Warren's two-part sequence "Seasons," Part I, "Downwardness," begins in early spring, while Part II, Interlude of Summer," ends in late summer, presenting an even more obvious pair in something like a diptych. Warren pauses the passage of the year at its pivotal moments of immanence, thus suggesting both birth and death. This delicate balance of natural and human change is maintained by the subtle misdirection of Warren's seasonal imagery. Here the poet reverses the natural progress of the seasons, where nature springs up with the vernal equinox and falls back at the autumnal equinox. In Warren's "Seasons" sequence, early spring sinks downward in his first panel, while late summer blazes upward in his second. Part I is entitled "Downwardness" quite appropriately, as the word reappears twice within its six quatrains—once as the spring melt's initial "lust for downwardness" and once again as the thaw's "desperate downwardness" in a world where "gravity is the only god" (569). Warren's imagery traces this "Downstream" descent of "snow-waters, ice-waters, earth-waters" from "the vast mountain" to "the last icicle / Drip, drop by drop" in "a sacred cycle" (569). At the opposite end of this seasonal round, Part II depicts the "Interlude of Summer" in images of crimson sunrise projected onward to the "climactic melodrama" and "majestic pyre" of a purple sunset (569). Everything, from "the children" to "garden and grape-arbor" continues to grow upward long past the summer solstice (570). Although death encroaches when "An old friend dies this summer," the persona appreciates that his "own health is good," and he even anticipates autumn when the "New England foliage" will conclude the turning of the year with transcendent beauty. Warren ends the poem's six quatrains with a stanza of one line, speculating, "After all, aesthetics is a branch of philosophy," perhaps as useful as ontology for understanding the world (570).

The pair of poems that follows the two parts of "Seasons" also recalls several pieces that have preceded it in this section and even earlier. Most notably, "The Place" echoes "Why Boy Came to Lonely Place" in both title and image, while "First Moment of Autumn Recognized" reconsiders the theme and meaning found in "Interlude of Summer." The setting of "The Place" proves as isolating as that described in "Why Boy Came to Lonely Place," though the reader senses a geographical shift from the upper South to New England reflected in the maturation of Warren's persona from lad of thirteen to man of rapidly advancing years. If anything, this longer poem of noticeably irregular lines and stanzas presents a place even more solitary, especially at this late afternoon's "hour of the unbounded loneliness" (570). Yet the two pieces view "the self's uncertainty" in regard to the past and the future in their progression from life review to age-work. Here, nature provides more transcendence, as "From shelving cliff-darkness, green arch and nave / Skyward aspire, translucently to heights" (570). Although the persona remembers dark nights and black lies from his past life, his future direction here is "Upward," where "The eye probes infinite distance, infinite / Light" (570). Appropriately for *Altitudes and Extensions,* Warren ends the poem with starlight, knowing that "you are not the first / To come to such a place seeking the most difficult knowledge" (571).

"First Moment of Autumn Recognized" is another of Warren's poems of natural and transcendent immanence suggested by the annual progression of the seasons. If a similar instance of equinoctial balance was anticipated in Part II, "Interlude of Summer," that poem's six quatrains glanced back to the declining season for the most part, while this one's nineteen irregular lines look forward steadily into an uncertain future. The "glitter of afternoon . . . [is] more champagne than ever / Summer" and proves as "delicious / On tongue of spirit, joyful in eye-beam," but "Moment means time" and "the leaf, gold, of birch, / Of beech" is only "vegetable matter mortal" (571). In this autumnal "Perfection of crystal" that may be remembered from Kentucky or experienced in Vermont, the persona stands alone, "being perfected / At last," though "in the instant itself which is unbreathing," as he experiences a prefiguration of death (571). In a second and final stanza of two short lines that contrast with seventeen longer ones in the initial stanza, Warren concludes, "Can you feel breath brush your damp / Lips? How can you know?" (571).

Both the closing interlude of summer and the opening moment of autumn recognized in earlier poems could have their proper places in the "Paradigm of Seasons" presented in the title of Warren's next selection. The poet seems to be using "paradigm" here in its primary, grammatical sense, as the set of inflectional forms that present the varied aspects of a word for study. In his first line, Warren images this annual cycle of the seasons as "a snake that swallows its tail" (571). His reference here is to the ouroborus, the archetypal symbol of continuity, infinity, and completion that Jung adapted from alchemy to represent the integration of the self and the shadow, or life and death, in the process of psychological individuation. As developed above, such speculation concerning transcendence became the theoretical basis of Erikson's age-work and Butler's life review. In "Paradigm of Seasons," the first of two long, irregular stanzas of extended lines traces the regular succession of the four seasons. It starts at the end of summer when fall comes, "north-bred," conveying "red leaf, gold leaf, then winter's choked road" until "Spring / Brings hope," and "Summer dreams of glut" in sensual imagery (571, 572). In the other long stanza, autumn again declares itself in "The sight of New England foliage in splendor" and the sound of "the report / Of the authoritative rifle" (572). A brief conclusion brings Warren back to winter, which is heard here as "The painful bellows of the lungs of an aging man / Who follows, with a burden of supplies upon his back, / A snow-choked trail," recalling the earlier "Passers-By on Snowy Night" (572).

Warren's next selection in Section VI, "If Snakes Were Blue," also suggests the ouroborus, though here it is not the diurnal circle of the year but the hourly cycle of the day that symbolizes the continuity of human life. The poem's title likewise becomes the conditional first clause of its opening line, "If snakes were blue," that then is answered in the initial line of the next unrhymed quatrain, "It was the kind of day that takes forever" (572). Like "The First Moment of Autumn Recognized" in an earlier selection within this section, the sky is like "crystal liquid pure enough to drink" (572). In such "luxurious ease," there exists "no distinction now between / Light and shadow," or between day and night, "As light diminished and the first star shone" (572). When dark falls, the last song of a thrush "could not be // Less than a blessing," somewhat like "the kind of promise / We give ourselves in childhood when first dawn / Makes curtains go gold" and "all night's dreams . . . / . . . guaranteed our happiness forever" (573). "True," Warren tells us in his final quatrain, "few fulfillments" are found within the cycle of life between youth and age, yet he concludes, "but look! In the distance lift peaks / Of glittering white" (573). Once again, images of transcendence appropriate to a volume of autobiography and age-work titled *Altitudes and Extensions* abound even in Warren's section of speculative poems.

In the last two selections of Section VI, "Little Girl Wakes Early" and "Winter Wheat: Oklahoma," Warren moves away from such poetic speculations toward narrative poetry about others. The little girl who wakes early in the first poem of this final pairing could be suggested by the Warren's now-grown daughter, here imagined years later when her "mother's long dead" much as in "Old Dog Dead" from Section II (573). Whether the young girl in this poem is based on Rosanna Warren or not, she seems to embody childhood intimations of mortality that contrast with the youthful intuitions of transcendence earlier discovered in "If Snakes Were Blue." "Little Girl Wakes Early" also reiterates the quatrain format of the preceding poem, but here the extended lines of these five stanzas rhyme in a regular ABAB pattern that suggests a lyrical inevitability to this little girl's early sorrows. Waking before her family, she imagines them all lifeless, "behind shut doors no breath perhaps drew, no heart beat" (573). Running out to reaffirm life in the "dew wet" dawn, she is afraid to call out for her "dearest friend" next door, lest "there was no breath there / For answer" (573). "Tears start," ones not to be assuaged even by her wakened mother. Now long after her mother's death, she has "learned that when loneliness takes you / There's nobody ever to explain to—though you try again and again" (573).

"Winter Wheat: Oklahoma" proves a parallel story in six stanzas of five unrhymed lines; the narrative centers on the created character of an aging farmer who suffers the same existential loneliness after the death of his wife as the little girl felt in the preceding piece. This poem also recalls "Immortality over the Dakotas" from Section I, though the angles of the paired protagonists' relations to mortality are reversed; the first farmer is dying and cannot tell his wife, while this one cannot accept the death of his life mate. After planting winter wheat, "He hates to go home," as every detail of his place on the prairie—"lawn-patch, two maples," and a little house with "No smoke in the chimney, / These nights"—reminds him of his loss (574). "He sits alone," doubting a God who would let "A man's honest sweat just go for nothing," as Warren concludes in the last stanza of a single line (574). The only hopeful aspect of this final selection in Section VI is the winter wheat itself; his sowing in fall and reaping in summer shows the Oklahoma farmer's implicit faith in an ultimate transcendence of the seasonal cycle, despite his doubt about a seemingly indifferent or at least careless God.

7

If Sections V and VI of *Altitudes and Extensions* can be considered in the terms Warren used for the two parts of *Now and Then*, "Nostalgic" and "Speculative," then Sections VII and VIII can be read under rubrics I employed earlier to discuss *Rumor Verified,* "Space" and "Time." As if to countenance such a reading, the two pieces Warren pairs to introduce the seven speculations of Section VIII each juxtaposes these abstractions, as "Space . . . // . . . And Time" in "Milton: A Sonnet" and as "Time and Space" in "Whatever You Are Now" (579). Section VII consists of four poems, all of moderate size and scope, and their juggling of past, present, and future is less abstract and more nostalgic than in the seven that follow. Warren's arrangement of his selections in Section VII seems less complicated as well. The first pair, "Youthful Picnic Long Ago: Sad Ballad on Box" and "History During Nocturnal Snowfall," share themes of time and love, and the second pair, "Whistle of the 3 A.M." and "Last Night Train," are connected by their images of railroads. Comparing these two pairs of poems reveals another common organizing pattern. Although the persona in all four selections exists in the present, the first poem of each pair looks backward into a shadowy past while the second peers forward into an indistinct future.

"Youthful Picnic Long Ago: Sad Ballad on Box" and "History During Nocturnal Snowfall" demonstrate just such a corresponding arrangement of past, present, and future. In this pairing, both selections reveal the complex relations of time and love, but by way of remembrance in the first poem and of experience in the second. In "Youthful Picnic Long Ago: Sad Ballad on Box," Warren's title and opening line, "In Tennessee once the campfire glowed," establish the events recalled as long ago and far away (575). As the "box" referenced is archaic southern vernacular for a guitar, Warren seems to underline the nostalgic coloring of these recollections. Then, a group of young people, "Faces // In grave bemusement," listened as a dark-haired beauty played an old ballad with "fingers white in their delicate dance / On the strings of the box" (575). The tension here is between youthful "melancholy that swelled each heart, and timed / The pulse in wrist" and what "Time unveiled" later in age, "A truth far past the pain declared" by the singer (575). Although the persona was infatuated then, he cannot even recall her name now. In ironic contrast to the looser lines and stanzas of the nostalgic memory piece, "History During Nocturnal Snowfall" employs the ABAB stanzas typical of folk ballads to present Warren's persona realizing the history of mature love in a "buried narrative . . . / . . . of chance? Or miracle?" (576). In winter, an aging couple sleep like hibernating creatures in a "burrow" dug by "clawing through blindness of joy and sorrow," not imagined in their youth (576). As the poem concludes: "Could it matter less as whiteness and darkness blending fall / And my finger touches a pulse to intuit its truth?" (576).

Similar organizational patterns are also evident in the paired images of the twin railroad poems. In "Whistle of the 3 A.M.," an aged persona awakened late at night, perhaps by the sound of a passing airliner, recalls from his youth the nocturnal whistle of the nightly express racing past. As a boy, he woke to that melancholy sound and rose to see the "magisterial" sweep of the engine's headlight expose his humble hometown (576). Then, he could imagine being whirled across the country in his own "dark cubicle," peering disdainfully from the window of a Pullman berth at "some straggle of town" much like Guthrie (576). Although these images of that place as a "pale ghost, unloved, unkempt" hearken back to Thomas Wolfe and William Faulkner, Warren is quick to move beyond mere nostalgia; he contemplates the complications of his life in the present and in the foreshadowing of the future, for "Times change, man changes" (576. 577). His vision incorporates the silent altitudes of "thirty-five thousand / Feet," "the raging sand / Of the sandblast of History" on earth, and finally the graveyard where none sleeping below the surface now "wonder why // The schedule's gone dead of the 3 A.M." (577).[10]

The older persona of "Last Night Train" rides the final commuter local of the night from New York City to the Connecticut suburbs, but the description of the trip recollects Warren's southern train poems where the iron logic of the railroad represents a naturalistic determinism. Most interesting here is the realistic detail of the dilapidated railroad bed of the Northeast railroad corridor that Warren uses to symbolize the ordering of the twentieth century by the nineteenth, not just in terms of physical infrastructure but of psychological legacies: "In that slick and new-fangled coach we go slam-banging / On rackety ruin of a roadbed, past caterpillar- / Green flash of last light on deserted platforms" (577). The night train too is almost deserted; only the persona and one other sleeping passenger remain, a "black, female, middle-aged" yet still vital and even regal in "A purple dress. Straps of white sandals / Are loosened" (577). Watching her sleep, he wonders if he could "Have walked so far" as she has (577). At his stop, the sound of a "last cricket" makes him feel the "quickly suppressed / Nostalgia of /A country lane, late night, late autumn—and there / Alone, again I stand, part of all" (577). Above him, "The complex of stars is steady in its operation," while the odor of "salt sedge" drifting from Long Island Sound makes him "think of swimming, naked and seaward" into the night, as he will in death (577). Looking up the tracks at the train's lights fading into the dark, Warren's persona feels "Like blessing" that sleeping other who inspires him to examine the reality of his past and anticipate the possibility of his future (578).

By contrast with the four somewhat doleful considerations of time gathered in Section VII, Section VIII presents seven poems concerned, for the most part, with spatial images probing the possibilities of transcendence in their prefiguration of the sublime single selection in the concluding Section IX, "Myth of Mountain Sunrise." As indicated above, the opening brace of poems in Section VIII, "Milton: A Sonnet" and "Whatever You Now Are," are paired by their corresponding considerations of Time and Space as capitalized abstractions. In keeping with the subjects and themes of this volume, Warren's sonnet on Milton ponders that precursor poet in his age and blindness. One indication of Warren's purpose here is the traditional form of his homage within the compass of an English sonnet not much different from one of Milton's, save for somewhat freer rhythms and extended lines. This sonnet proves one of Warren's best, particularly in its predication of a complicated thematic concept in a single complex sentence. Although the poem begins with Milton remembering his past, the blind man recalls how "Late carmine had bathed the horizon with its wide kindness" (579). In his fusion of prayer and poetry as age-work, the blind poet "Knew burgeoning Space in which old space hummed like a fly" and "Time" as a nobler dimension of that self" (579). In his new consciousness, "past and future are intrinsicate / To form a present" blessed by images of transcendence (579). The most significant is "a gleaming fish" that leaps into sunlight, dives back into dark depths, and trails a "pavane of bubbles like pearls," before emerging in the concluding couplet "to slash/ Upward, and upward again, and, in joy, flash" (579). Warren's allusions to traditional Christian images are blended skillfully with his natural symbols in this sublime evocation of the transcendent possibilities inherent in the poetic vision of age, whether Milton's or his own.

"Whatever You Now Are" proves a similar, if more philosophical consideration of the "region past categories of Time and Space," employing traditional form and imagery much as in "Milton: A Sonnet" (579). Warren's second poem in Section VIII is divided into three ABABCC stanzas of regular if elongated lines, while his images derive both from the visions of dream and the perceptions of consciousness. The poetic persona begins by trying to differentiate between "What is the dream and who the dreamer?" (579). For in sleep, "the stream beneath your window . . . / . . . and the Self [are] conjunct all night long," so that the muted music of its "murmurous flow" begs the question of "How is the difference defined between singer and song?" (579). The persona then wonders if the self through space "flows from distance, to distance," as if one "With the tune of time" (579). In turn, "the dark stream" that forms "the pattern of your whole life's endeavor" becomes real beyond the Kantian "categories of Time and Space" (579). The persona also tells us that celestial "music drifts to your shadowy cave / Of consciousness," in a Platonic allusion reiterated in the concluding couplet. "But dawn breaks soon, and that self will have fled away. / Will a strange one yet inhabit the precinct of day?" (579).

"Wind and Gibbon" continues these patterns of cultural allusions and spatial images as discovered in the first paired poems in Section VIII, and it too forms a similar pairing with "Delusion?—No!" which follows it, by presenting a literary intertext that determines directions of theme and meaning for both. The neoclassical historian Edward Gibbon is known for his six-volume *The History of the Decline and Fall of the Roman Empire,* of course, and Warren's allusion to him conflates the chronological changes that become cultural history with the spatial movements of the wind in nature. Awakened by a nocturnal storm, the poetic persona announces "The wind / Is like a dream of History" (580). In contrast, Gibbon's magnum opus sits "on the shelf, volume by volume, solid as masonry," and of it the persona also pronounces "This is History" (580). The poem speculates that if "History is not truth," then "Truth is in the telling" (580). At dawn, "the wind has stopped," but the rising sun sends "a single / Beam, sky-arrowing, [that] strikes / The mountain to dazzlement," in another natural image that confirms the transcending power of narrative (580).[11]

"Delusion?—No!" continues this section's transcendent spatial imagery as its persona becomes the historian and poet of his life experience by transforming an ascent to the high altitudes atop a mountain into a metaphor of natural deliverance. Observing earth and sky while perched on the edge of the high crag, "In atmosphere almost too heavenly / Pure," he experiences a "divine osmosis" as "I entered in. / Was part of all" in this "Glorious light" (581). The persona then experiences mystical extensions and heights by way of a metamorphosis that once again recalls Warren's signature hawks. Is his imagined transformation a transcendent vision or just a silly fantasy? Two stanzas of single lines assure us not; the first repeats the title: "Delusion?—No! For Truth has many moments"; the second urges hope: "Open your eyes. Who knows? This may be one" (581).

The third pair of poems in Section VIII, "Question at Cliff-Thrust" and "It Is Not Dead," extends these spatial images and transcendent themes, though without the many allusions of the preceding pairs. In the direction of its movement through space, "Question at Cliff-Thrust" reverses "Delusion?—No." Rather than imaginatively ascending upward from a high crag, this persona descends downward from a sea cliff, at least in his imagination. Balanced on "the outthrust ledge," he discerns the darkening depths of the sea below in a waking trance, until a dropped stone suggests the possibility of his own plunge (581). Despite its "beckoning downwardness" suggestive of death and dissolution, the poem ends with another ascent, "the long climb toward lighter green, and light" to the surface where he watches "one gull that screams from east to west" across the sky in yet another spatial image of transcendence (582). The title of the companion piece, "It Is Not Dead," also opens that poem's first line, but the object designated by this initial pronoun is not revealed fully until the conclusion. It is conceived in "depth and darkness . . . // . . . To await what cataclysmic birth," then exposed to cosmic forces that shape it with "determination interminable" in glacial slowness, "until / Half in, half out of my brook it lies" (582, 583). Since the persona can now "lie on it, / "Brooding on our common destinies," it must be a great stone, a monolith marking his mortality, but with the final suggestion of the transcendent as both "will lie there under the stars" and "the immensity of the night sky" (583).

Warren's last selection of Section VIII follows these same patterns of spatial images and transcendent themes demonstrable in its six other poems, yet "Sunset" also forms an obvious pairing with the single selection that comprises the concluding Section IX, "Myth of Mountain Sunrise," a connection remarked by almost all of this volume's critics. This parallel placement deriving from the solar cycle of the day proves a wonderful way for Warren to end the volume in an archetypal pairing of sunset as a symbol of decline with sunrise as symbolic of renewal. At the conclusion of the penultimate section, "Sunset" considers a mountain twilight with a slight suggestion of transcendence beyond. The sunset that gives a title to the first poem of this pair seems more a preparation for dark, for it occupies only one of three stanzas. It flares spectacularly, if briefly, as the "Vulgar and flaming apocalypse of day," however, "Like fire in a lint-house" (583). Night then is equated with the biblical "dire hour," or "the time when you must speak / To your naked self—never / Before seen, nor known" (583).

The single selection of the final Section IX, "Myth of Mountain Sunrise" also begins at dark altitudes, "crags steel-ringing / To dream-hoofs nightlong," when these night mares reveal "proverbial / Words, stone-incised in language unknowable" (584). In the first of the poem's three regularly rhyming AABBCC stanzas of extended lines, the sound seems that of the mythlike "wisdom-song against disaster of granite and all / Moonless non-redemption on the left hand of dawn" (584). It is as if the mountain awakens itself in the second stanza as "curdling agony of interred dark strives dayward" from earth, through tree, at last to leaf (584). Then "Leaf cries: 'I feel my deepest filament in dark rejoice'" (584). The third stanza's classical imagery evokes the "Pompeian glory" of sunrise in the myth of the dryads, the tree nymphs from Ovid's multiform *Metamorphoses* (584). Warren's invocation of these sacred mysteries of regeneration begins in material nature with, "a girl-shape, birch-white sapling, rising now," but is soon invested with human nature as well, "head back-flung, eyes closed in first beam, / While hair . . . / Spreads end-thin, to define fruit-swell of haunches" (584). Warren's predominant images and symbols are achieved in the pair of simple statements that the poem's extended final line comprises, "The sun blazes over the peak. That will be the old tale told" (584).

Separate in Section IX, "Myth of Mountain Sunrise" then becomes both an epilogue and a coda to the eight preceding sections of *Altitudes and Extensions* in its sublime realization of the transcendent myth of eternal return as the completion of the natural cycle that began with the opening selection, "Three Darknesses." The poet's later concerns thus are evidenced by the directions of Warren's shaping imagination in the organization of the collection and of its constituent parts. It also becomes important to note that during the four years after *Rumor Verified* Warren published fourteen pieces that were not included in the new gathering of the 1985 *Selected Poems.* Most of these omitted works were not concerned with the poet's later themes, and none of the few that are rises to the level of the poems included.[12] At the end of his eighth decade, Warren clearly intended his final volume as his last grand statement of the themes that preoccupied his poetic productions after *Audubon*—the pervasive life review and age-work that marks the sublime and transcendent efforts suggested in the title of his last published volume of poetry, *Altitudes and Extensions.*

Epilogue

Autobiography, Aging, and Warren's Poetry in a New Century

And now you must have known
The joy stars know as, soundless, they slip,
Degree by precise degree, without care or cark,
Each to its place in the great Chart of Being, careless of light or dark.

—"John's Birches"

1

Although Warren would live more than four years beyond the appearance of *Altitudes and Extensions* in *New and Selected Poems: 1923–1985*, his steadily declining health put an end to his poetic age-work at the last. His prostate cancer metastasized in the summer of 1985, and the "excision of the testes" his doctors routinely prescribed did little to stop its spread (Blotner 482–83). As always, Warren summoned his characteristic stoicism and made the best of his final years despite his privation and pain, but his poetic energies now were depleted by what he only could describe to friends as a "deliquescence" to (Blotner 487). Warren's concern for his own poetic legacy did lead him to consider the preparation of a selected poems in another arrangement and a complete collected poems, though neither project came to fulfillment (Burt 629–31). Greater recognition of Warren's importance as a poet continued to come during his last years. He received the Gold Medal for Poetry from the American Academy and Institute of Arts and Letters in 1985, and the next year he accepted the inaugural appointment as the Poet Laureate Consultant in Poetry from the Library of Congress (Blotner 485). Publicity about the laureateship demonstrated that Warren was the contemporary "Dean of American Letters" (Blotner 486).

The irony of these late honors surely was not lost on Warren—he had achieved his highest poetic recognition when he was no longer able to create new poems (Blotner 486). He seems to have written poetry only sporadically after his last volume appeared. For many years, Warren had exchanged new poems with his daughter Rosanna, now an established poet in her own right, but his contributions to their poetic dialogue grew ever less frequent during his last years. In his answer to Rosanna's concerned inquiry about his latest poetic efforts, Warren responded grimly, "They are shit" (Blotner 481). Warren published but two more poems after *Altitudes and Extensions:* the negative and negligible "The Loose Shutter" and the nostalgic and substantial "John's Birches."[1]

Originally entitled "Recollection," "John's Birches" balances a dusky lane lined by birches changing from white to black in the decline of a day in the present with a day and a lane much the same from his boyhood (808). The poem is also notable for its themes of age-work and autobiography realized in irregular lines forming a complex rhyme scheme. The final stanza begins, "If boyhood is lonely enough, the moss-bearded stone / Communicates wisdom," perhaps recalling Robert Frost's "Birches" (1915) in natural imagery drawn from a lonely childhood (624). Thus, Warren's final published poem takes us back to where we began our study of the later poetry: in the last section of *Audubon,* where the aging poet traced his evolving selfhood back to a moment when "Long ago, in Kentucky, I, a boy, stood / By a dirt road, in first dark," at the beginning of his life narrative in "a story of great distances, and starlight" (266, 267).

Warren did publish several prose works in his final years, however. The most important of them included new editions of older work, *A Robert Penn Warren Reader* in 1987 and *New and Selected Essays* in 1989, as well as *Portrait of a Father* in 1988, a new effort of life review and age-work. His memoir of Robert Franklin Warren appeared first in 1987 as a long essay in the *Southern Review,* and then it was revised and reprinted as a book that also included his first piece about his father's death and life, "Mortmain," from his 1960 collection *You, Emperors, and Others.* The poem is discussed above in my "Prologue," and Warren made only incidental changes for its new publication. His revised essay proves interesting not just as a gloss on one of his most powerful poems, but for its additional biographical information and for its extension in prose of the same concerns that had determined his later poetry. *Portrait of a Father* concludes with the deathbed scene that opens "Mortmain," with his father dying from the same cancer that would take his own life only a year after this remembrance was published. The last words in Warren's essay are not his own but his father's, who reflected at eighty-five, "I have lived a very happy life" (*Portrait* 80).

Warren may have been letting his father speak for him as well while he endured the end of his own life at the age of eighty-four. A final happiness for him was the birth of his first grandson, his son Gabriel's son, less than a month before his death (Blotner 499). His biographer's account of Warren's final days are a testament of personal courage and concern for others that provides the capstone, not just to a productive existence, but for a decline and death marked, if not by transcendence, then a dignity and grace that seem at least partially the products of his age-work and life review. In the early hours of September 15, 1989, Warren died at the summer home in Vermont. On October 8, after a brief memorial of reminiscences and readings, his ashes were interred in the old church graveyard in nearby Stratton (Blotner 500). Those readings included the poet's own "Grackles, Goodbye!" from *Being Here,* a poem in which Warren associates his mother's death and funeral with the annual migrations of these raucous flocks. Warren's concluding lines on their autumnal reappearance, "Confirming the year's turn and the fact that only, only, / In the name of Death do we learn the true name of Love," must have seemed as moving for his family and friends then as they might for his readers and critics now (391). I read the passage in this way, or as a final evocation of Warren's age-work, life review, and transcendence as realized in a sublime instance of his later poetry.[2]

2

In the two decades since his death, Warren's literary legacy has undergone considerable reconfiguration. His death elicited both a great quantity and quality of obituaries, reminiscences, and critical reconsiderations that reconfirmed Warren as a major figure of American literature in the twentieth century. Most of these commentators thought Warren would be remembered best for the works that won his three Pulitzer Prizes: *All the King's Men, Promises,* and *Now and Then,* with the last volume as representative of his overall poetic achievement during the two decades that separated his two prizes for poetry. Warren's three Pulitzers do seem to mark the three major stages of his career—his maturity, during which his best efforts were as a fictionist; his midlife, during which he became more the "man of letters"; and his age, during which he emerged as a major poet. Recent Warren scholarship has corroborated my focus on his later poetry in *After Audubon,* especially by the publication of the authorized biography and the collected poems in 1997 and 1998, respectively. As I have indicated, this reassessment of the achievements represented in his canon continues to become more readily accepted, especially since the Warren centennial in 2005, which elicited another round of increasingly positive critical reevaluations.[3]

Although it is impossible to predict the future directions of Warren studies with absolute certainty, I believe that the literary excellence of his legacies in fiction, criticism, and poetry ensures him the place in the American canon for the twenty-first century that he earned during much of the twentieth. After all, who could prove a better literary mentor for rapidly graying American generations than an author who began his best work at retirement age? Warren's productive life proves as exemplary as his extensive work, and both coalesce significantly in his later poetry, particularly in his later poems ordered by autobiography and the work of aging that consistently rise to transcendence and the sublime. In the closing lines of *Audubon*—"Tell me a story. . . . Make it a story of great distances, and starlight. . . . Tell me a story of deep delight"—Robert Penn Warren invokes his autobiographical epic, a narrative that surely remains just such a source of ever deeper delights for all of his readers (267).[4]

Notes to Text

Prologue

1. Unless otherwise indicated within my parenthetical citation, all page numbers given for Warren's works are from John Burt's definitive edition of the *Collected Poems* (1998), though I have differentiated my citations of Harold Bloom's "Foreword" to and John Burt's editorial "Notes" from the volume by the use of their names. The collection proves an exemplary effort of recent scholarship that helped shape my own reading of Warren's poetic canon, and especially of its later phase. Moreover, my analysis of Warren's later poetry is textually dependent on Burt's edition, and having it close at hand will make reading this study much easier and more enlightening.

2. My major source for the writer's life in relation to his work is Joseph Blotner's authorized volume, *Robert Penn Warren: A Biography* (1997), an excellent example of literary life writing Although Blotner's reading of Warren's career also has influenced my reading of his canon, I have developed a somewhat different interpretation of the later life and work. I do cite Blotner often, however, to document factual information most conveniently available in his substantial biography. A reader of Warren's works, including his later poetry, could have no better introduction than Blotner's fine book. As with the collected poems, I recommend consulting it in conjunction with my study.

3. *All the King's Men* was reputed to have sold to Columbia Pictures for $200,000, and it eventually would become an Academy Award Best Picture directed by Robert Rossen in 1949 (Blotner 239).The endurance of Warren's Willie Stark as an icon in American popular culture was confirmed by Sidney Lumet's live television production of the novel on the popular Kraft Theater in 1958. Between these recreations of *All the King's Men, Band of Angels* was adapted for the screen in 1957 by Raoul Walsh, a presentation that earned Warren another $200,000 (Blotner 302).

Chapter 1

1. *American Literature: The Makers and the Making,* the anthology he edited with Cleanth Brooks and R. W. B. Lewis and published in 1973, remains an interesting, if somewhat neglected, work in Warren's canon. Not only was it a groundbreaking critical textbook, as the first of the cultural gatherings of American literature, but Warren's

contributions for it were often the beginnings of more extended critical and creative reconsiderations of his forebears in American letters—in particular, Whittier, Dreiser, and Audubon.

2. Although poetic sequences are a feature of Warren's poetry from his earliest efforts forward, the sequencing of his collections does not seem an important issue until the start of his middle period with *Promises,* at least in my view. I believe Warren continued to probe the possibilities of sequential forms in *You, Emperors, and Others, Tale of Time, Incarnations,* and *Audubon.* His most ambitious effort is essayed in *Or Else,* but he moved to less complicated forms in the five later collections—as I will develop in my succeeding chapters. The greater complexity of *Or Else* again suggests that my study is best understood with a copy of the text, or at least of its table of contents, close by.

3. Randolph Paul Runyon's chapter on *Or Else* in *Ghostly Parallels* proves the closest, most careful, and most extensive reading of Warren's collection; his readings of individual poems often influence my own, even though I develop very different thematic emphases in terms of age-work and life review, sublimity and transcendence. Runyon's insistence on the intertextual continuity of each individual poem in Warren's collections sometimes becomes problematic, however. With *Or Else,* Runyon's predication of continuities proves especially tricky because of its textual web of previously collected, previously published, and previously unpublished poems in counterpointed sequences identified with Roman and Arabic numerals (143–44, 216 n. 2).

4. The Freudian connection between emasculation, both literal and figurative, and death often surfaces in Warren's later fiction and poetry, as we will see later. Uncannily in psychological terms, it reappears in his personal experience directly before his death; see my "Epilogue" below.

5. James Justus makes the same point in several convincing essays beginning with "Warren's Later Poetry: Unverified Rumors of Wisdom," *Mississippi Quarterly* 37 (1984): 161–71.

6. As we would anticipate from his fascination with dreams, Warren had a lively interest in trance states, including hypnosis. In particular, he seems to connect poetry with trance, even in his own creative process. In an interview with *U.S. News & World Report* after receiving the laureateship, Warren seems to believe that his early morning swimming induced a kind of trance state: "I get many ideas while on long swims. I sort of half-dream. It's a numbing, bemusing experience. And a thousand ideas drift in the head. There's rhythm and blankness, and you feel detached from yourself. It opens the head to suggestion" (73). Age regression is a psychoanalytic technique, often employing hypnosis, and Warren's poetic recollections of his youth operate like this for his life review.

7. Warren opens his critical study *Homage to Theodore Dreiser* with the observation that "the career of Theodore Dreiser raises in a particularly poignant form the question of the relation of life and art," much like the one he was negotiating in his own age-work (*Homage* 9). Warren's reader also learns that Dreiser complicated his

particular answer to that universal question by way of his voluminous autobiographical works, "writings . . . scarcely distinguishable from his fiction" (*Homage* 9). Warren could now accept the close relation between art and life in fiction that he could not in the earlier part of his critical career, particularly in terms of his southern colleague Thomas Wolfe. For a more extensive discussion of these connections between the two southern fictionists, see Patricia L. Bradley, "Robert Penn Warren, Thomas Wolfe, and the Problem of Autobiography," in *South Carolina Review* 38 (2006): 136–45.

Chapter 2

1. Well into her sixties by then, Eleanor Clark was engaged with her own age-work as she wrote a study of her visual infirmity and its impact on her and her family in several essays eventually collected as *Eyes, Etc.: A Memoir* (1977).

2. In the December 1976 issue of *Esquire,* Warren published "Bicentennial," a poem that comprises thirty-five stanzas that reiterate the central themes of *Democracy and Poetry.* The poem's narrative crosscuts the selfish lives and empty deaths of several Americans over the July 4th weekend of the bicentennial year. This chronological setting allows Warren to ironically contrast the American dreams of the past with the national nightmares of the present. Unfortunately, most of the Americans Warren presents here prove to be national types more than well-realized individuals. Warren rightly excluded "Bicentennial" from his poetry collections, and its topical nature leads me to omit further discussion of it here.

3. For a different and interesting reading of the novel from the perspective of age, see Linda A. Westervelt, "Robert Penn Warren's *A Place to Come To:* An *Altersroman* Inspired by Dante," *Genre* 34 (2001): 101–24.

4. In my biographical reading of the poem's somewhat hazy narrative, unlike those of most critics, the anonymous dancer at the party is a different woman than the persona's later sex partner; the persona flirts with the party goer to goad his lover, whom I identify as Warren's first wife, Cinina.

5. This earlier poem was never published, and it is not clear if Warren ever circulated it for publication. The sonnet is reproduced conveniently by John Burt in his edition of Warren's *Collected Poetry* (813).

6. This is not to say, however, that the poem can be read apart from the racial issues it quite obviously raises. In his later poetry, Warren is clearly still trying to come to terms with the complex legacy of race in both cultural and personal terms. However, questions about the poem's racial politics seem to focus on the use of "nigger," a term which has become ever more contested in the thirty years since the first publication of Warren's poem. In 1990, Cleanth Brooks told me in conversation that after his initial reading of the poem in a draft, he had advised Warren not to use the problematic phrasing, but the poet insisted that both the historical and philosophical situation of the poem required it. Recent readings also protest the authenticity of the persona's putative reconciliation with his black "brother," a resolution that in recent years has

come to be questioned also. I hope my reading in this chapter supports Warren's honesty and sincerity by contextualizing his poem within his age-work and life review. For a fuller discussion of race in regard to Warren's prose, see my article "Warren's Faulkner," *Mississippi Quarterly* 60 (2007): 351–67. John Burt makes a thoughtful argument for accepting Warren's genuine use of poetic conventions in his later poetry; see his fine article "Warren Reflects on the Discontinuities of His Poetic Career," *Style* 36 (2002): 292–307. The most extensive discussion of racial complications in Warren is Anthony Szczesiul's *Racial Politics and Robert Penn Warren's Poetry* (Tallahassee: University of Florida Press, 2002), in which "Old Nigger" is given a provocative, if different, reading from the one it receives in my studies.

Chapter 3

1. Warren considered a third part for *Now and Then* consisting of a single long poem in "thirty sections," probably the uncollected "Bicentennial" referenced in note 2 of my previous chapter (*Talking* 297). He finally excluded it and three other pieces published between 1976 and 1978—"A Few Axioms for a Young Man," "Somewhere," and "Praise." Although the three shorter poems seem as successful in their achievements as several he did include, they do not really fit under the rubrics of "Nostalgic" and "Speculative," while "Bicentennial" is an interesting text that does not quite rise to the level of Warren's best work. All four of these works are included in *Collected Poems,* however (587–602).

2. If Warren's title provides a good indication of his authorial intentions in regard to both structure and theme in *Now and Then,* his epigraph, ". . . Let the inhabitants of the rock sing . . . *Isaiah 42:11*" proves more problematic (337). As Warren's biographer observes about the epigraph, "Like the poems' occasional references to God, this is no undergirding theme" (Blotner 441). In its biblical context, however, the passage perhaps suggests the sense of a spiritual transcendence beyond earthly travail occasionally celebrated in *Now and Then,* particularly in "Heart of Autumn."

3. The etymology of "nostalgia" derives from Greek roots for return, home, and pain to form a neologism that originally meant something more like the German *Sehnsucht,* an exaggerated longing for home on the part of the expatriate which was once considered an actual psychological condition amenable to diagnosis and cure. Romantic literature added chronological nostalgia to a longing for the home place, especially in regard to the lost innocence of youth. Contemporary cultural theory has reconstituted nostalgia in the present age of individual and national displacements and diasporas.

4. Although "American Portrait: Old Style" implies a late reunion between the two friends that the critics seem to accept on face value, it is less than clear from Warren's biography when it would have taken place. Because Warren obviously invents much of his narrative, it well may be that this meeting is only imagined. If so, it is also worth noting that the poem never really deals with Greenfield's mature years after his return

to Guthrie, when he evidently lived a life exemplary enough to have the local Little League ballpark named in his honor.

5. For more on "Goodwood Comes Back" and the symbolism of American dreams and nightmares as imaged by baseball during the decades between the world wars, see my *Robert Penn Warren: A Study of the Short Fiction,* 34–40.

6. See Floyd C. Watkins's *Then & Now: The Personal Past in the Poetry of Robert Penn Warren,* 161. Watkins's book and Will Fridy's article "The Author and the Ballplayer: An Imprint of Memory in the Writings of Robert Penn Warren," in *Mississippi Quarterly* 44 (1991): 159–66, provide the most detailed readings of the relationships between Kent Greenfield and his literary incarnations in Warren's works. These sources must be considered cautiously, however, as both critics rely on interviews of Warren, Greenfield, and other elders from Guthrie that were conducted long past the events recalled, and both scholars tend to read the author's biography backward from his literary texts, which are often imagined.

7. Patricia Bradley reminded me that Warren also uses a similar trench in the opening pages of *Band of Angels* (1955) to image the sunken grave of Amantha Starr's mother; his only female narrator played there with her dolls and often lay back to view the heavens in a vain attempt to find her place in the world.

8. Randolph Paul Runyon presents an interesting connection among the several "women intimately associated with death" who haunt the poems of the "Nostalgic" section (*Braided Dream* 180). In my view, each of these women functions as a memento mori, whether if remembered from youth or if encountered in age; thus life review again becomes a necessary part of the process of age-work in preparation for possible transcendence.

9. In another triangulation with Warren and Bloom, Dave Smith uses the pivotal line "Some dreams come true, some no" from the penultimate section 9 of "Red-Tail Hawk and Pyre of Youth" as the epigraph for his "Two Dreams" (1997), an anxious poem about the influence of Warren as personal and poetic mentor (350). Smith's epigraph proves an apt introduction not just to dream as subject in this poem but to dream as metaphor in his other work, as well as in Warren's hawk poems and his later canon. In these two intertextual poems, both of these autobiographical personae must come to terms with their lost dreams of youth, including visions of personal transcendence and poetic immortality, through archetypal quest rituals that function much like dream visions. In "Red-Tail Hawk and Pyre of Youth," Warren tells his own dreamlike hunting tale and then contemplates his mortality as he burns the lifeless effigy of his now tattered hawk, which like the poet himself has lost an eye. In "Two Dreams," Smith sees himself reflected in the glass eye of his aging literary mentor and recalls a youthful hunting story of his own, a failed hunt at that, also seemingly more dream than reality. Interestingly enough, Smith dedicates "Two Dreams" to David Bottoms, another contemporary southern poet whose work owes a good deal to Warren's earlier example.

10. In an insightful study, Anthony E. Szczesiul makes a convincing case for read-

ing "Red-Tail Hawk and Pyre of Youth," as well as "One-Mule Cart," in terms of Warren's evolving poetic manner. See "The Immolation of Influence: Aesthetic Conflict in Robert Penn Warren's Poetry," *Mississippi Quarterly* 52 (1998): 47–72.

Chapter 4

1. If most of his critics agree with Warren about the superiority of his 1979 revision of *Brother to Dragons* to the original 1953 work, not all do so. For example, see the contesting essays in James A. Grimshaw Jr., *Robert Penn Warren's "Brother to Dragons: A New Version"* (Baton Rouge: Louisiana State University Press, 1983). Personally speaking, I enjoy Warren's revised text more as "pure" poetry, but in it I miss the "impure" intellectual and historical impact of the original.

2. Randolph Paul Runyon extends Peter Stitt's earlier remarks on womb imagery in "Speleology" by connecting the stream's seeming lullaby to the mother's song that lulls the boy to sleep in "October Picnic Long Ago" (*Braided Dream* 129–30).

3. Although the poem's "white trash" couple, Zack and Mag, are based on actual denizens of Guthrie, Kentucky, the real people evidently died much later and less dramatically in real life than in this fictive recollection of them (Warren, *Jefferson Davis* 11–14, 108–10). Because this selection proves more creative writing than autobiographical recollection, it merits less attention in my study of life review compelled by agework. As "Recollection in Upper Ontario, from Long Before" is one of the longest and most arresting poems in *Being Here,* however, I consider its technological symbols at more length in the chapter on Warren's poetry in my study of railroads in Southern literature, *Dixie Limited,* especially 107–9.

4. Warren dedicated his railroad "recollection" to contemporary poet Richard Eberhart, a longtime friend, and one intriguing response to its puzzling ambivalence is found in a piece by another friend and poet, William Meredith. "Not Both" appears in Meredith's collection *The Cheer* (1980), printed on a single page opposite to a page-long quotation from Warren's poem. This extended epigraph is actually seven lines longer than Meredith's poem, and it contains all of the central nightmare up to the point of Mag's death. Applying Meredith's formulations to Warren's narrative forces the reader to contemplate once again the ambivalence at the heart of this terrible event.

5. Interestingly enough, the couple who left their baby daughter with the wife's maternal grandmother to pursue their literary careers in New York City were Caroline Gordon and Allen Tate, Warren's lifelong friends and literary colleagues (Blotner 553 n. 17).

6. "Grackles, Goodbye" is not Warren's only use of these common birds as regional images and universal symbols. Opening the ninth chapter of his first published novel, *Night Rider* (1939), Warren spends three long paragraphs describing how the seasonal passages of their flocks affect his very faintly autobiographical protagonist, Perce Munn. Several images are common to the descriptions in prose and poetry, and

one wonders if Warren was recalling his earlier writing as seen in the novel's treatment of these creatures' "victorious indifference" and Munn's "over-mastering loneliness" (*Night Rider* 207–8).

7. "Deep—Deeper Down" obviously recalls "Rattlesnake Country," the poem derived from Warren's period of legal residency for divorce in Nevada that was discussed earlier in connection with *Or Else;* in reversed chronological order, the poems bracket the failure of his first marriage with two narratives about killing snakes in seeming rites of sexual passage. Again, the psychological implications of both poems prove interesting for Warren's age-work and life review, as well as for his contemplation of transcendence within both symbolic landscapes.

8. My overall assessment of Tate in another study seems useful here for affirming the accuracy of Warren's poetic summation: "Tate's restless, powerful, and ruthlessly honest intellect created his poetic canon, one best appreciated as quest for moral and spiritual certainty in a life of cultural and personal insecurity." See "Allen Tate: Classical Matters, Seasons of the Soul, and Recovered Memories" in *A Backward Glance,* my study of the classical tradition and the Southern Renascence (41–42).

9. The tramp is an important figure not only in Warren's poetry, as we have seen, but in his fiction as well; perhaps his most significant appearance is in Warren's finest short story, "Blackberry Winter" (1946). For another reading of "Ballad of Your Puzzlement" that corroborates mine while developing a differing emphasis, see Patricia L. Bradley, *Robert Penn Warren's Circus Aesthetic and the Southern Renaissance* (Knoxville: University of Tennessee Press, 2004), 11–12.

Chapter 5

1. *Rumor Verified* actually was Warren's third choice for the title of his newest col lection. His biographer tells us that the working title was *Life Is a Fable* (Blotner 533). In *Collected Poems,* John Burt's "Notes" reveal that Warren also considered another title appropriated from one of the volume's selections, "Have You Ever Eaten Stars" (759). We also noted earlier that the chronological range in Warren's subtitle overlaps that of his preceding volume, *Being Here: Poems 1977–1980,* again indicating that his collections are shaped as much more than simple gatherings of his poems written over a certain span of time.

2. Given the fatal outcome of his father's prostate cancer, it seems puzzling that Warren did not elect a more aggressive course of treatment for his own, even considering then current medical practice, which was not assertive about treating such conditions in patients of advanced years. In recounting Warren's final illness, his biographer seems to imply medical miscommunication regarding the gravity of the writer's prognosis at this stage of his life (Blotner 474).

3. One notable exception was a dismissive review by Donald Hall that appeared in the *New York Times Book Review* on November 8, 1981. Although Hall does point out

several weaknesses in a few of the selections, he seems determined to ignore the overall strengths of *Rumor Verified.* Blotner notes that this unwarranted negativity may be "continuing fallout from the Paleface-Redskin controversy" that had determined much of the politics of contemporary American poetry (463).

4. In *The Braided Dream,* Randolph Paul Runyon presents a convincing analysis of the epigraph from Dante and the overall contents of *Rumor Verified* (90–94).

5. For an extended discussion of the West in Warren's canon, see my essay "Robert Penn Warren's West," *Southern Literary Journal* 26 (1993): 54–63.

6. Warren must have been aware of his title's intertextuality with Rudyard Kipling's well-known "If," first published in 1895 when its creator was but thirty, which begins each of its quatrains with the conditional preposition of its title. "If" Kipling's auditor can fulfill all of the various conditions, then, as the poem famously concludes, "you'll be a Man, my son." Warren's conditionals and conclusions prove ironically different as he surmises that those "who had long thought / Courage enough to live by," like the masculinist personae of Kipling's poem, may be in need of a finer kind of consciousness for real maturity (474).

7. For James A. Grimshaw Jr., the green vine in "Dead Horse in Field" recalls the long first paragraph of *All the King's Men,* which ends with a love vine growing around the skull and bones on a death marker (176). In my view, that symbolic passage also relates back to the novel's epigraph from Dante's *Commedia: "Mentre che la speranza ha fior del verde"* (*Purgatorio* III, 135), or "While hope has any flower of green" in my own rough translation. Thus it seems this natural imagery of death and resurrection in nature has a long history in Warren's overall canon, ranging from his midcareer fiction to his mature poetry.

8. In "A Hardy American," his chapter on Warren in *American Ambitions,* Monroe K. Spears connects "Immanence" and "The Corner of the Eye," as well as "Convergences" and "Afterward," with Thomas Hardy's Immanent Will (98–99).

9. Warren's phrasing makes one wonder if his cold shock of experience echoes Joseph Conrad's "destructive element," imaged in the depthless sea of life as formulated by his character Stein to frame advice to his narrator Marlowe on "how to be" in the cold world of experience that destroys the title character of *Lord Jim.* As the wise elder Stein phrases it in English, his second language as well as his creator's: "The way is to the destructive element submit yourself and with the exertions of your hands and feet in the water make the deep, deep sea keep you up." Conrad and his best-known novel are regarded highly by most writers and critics, of course, and Warren wrote a definitive essay on *Nostromo* published by the *Sewanee Review* in 1951.

10. Although Warren is clearly alluding to the conclusion of Dante's *Inferno,* it may be that he also is suggesting Plato's allegory of the cave from book 7 of *The Republic.* Remember that Plato's prisoners are chained in the cave so that they can see only the shadows on its walls rather than the true light of the heavenly sun. Thus, their liberation allegorically represents a transition from "impure" reality to the "pure" realm of

the ideal. The passage interested Warren, and he used it as the epigraph of his earlier novel *The Cave;* Plato is referenced in several of Warren's later poems, as we have seen earlier and will again.

Chapter 6

1. Warren's dedication of *Altitudes and Extensions* "To our granddaughter, Katherine Penn Scully" reinforces the sense of transcendence suggested in his title and in his epigraph adapted from Saint Augustine, "Will ye not now after that life is descended down to you, will not you ascend up to it and live?" (527).

2. Interesting critical formulations of some possible parallels among Warren's three longer narratives include those by Calvin Bedient, who makes autobiographical connections among all three efforts (87); William Bedford Clark, who sees all three as "frontier poems" (130); and Jonathan S. Cullick, who relates history, biography, and autobiography in all three works (169). The most extensive consideration of the relations among the "three great long poems" is found in Hugh Ruppersburg's *Robert Penn Warren and the American Imagination* (2). Although *Chief Joseph* is regarded well by Warren scholars, some early reviews in popular publications and some later analyses in Native American studies have proven skeptical of the poem's ultimate achievement (Cullick 170).

3. Although Warren indicated that his interest in Chief Joseph dated to the early 1930s, there is no evidence that he began writing about him until he had the time afforded by the MacArthur "genius" grant in 1981, well after the centennial observances of the Nez Perce War in the late 1970s (Blotner 461).

4. In *The Braided Dream,* Randolph Paul Runyon discusses Warren's use of "detritus" in several successive poems to an interesting effect. He is less convincing in connecting Warren's "Old Dog Dead" with Walt Whitman's "On the Beach at Night" by way of their common observations of the planet Jupiter (36–40). I believe "Old Dog Dead" connects more immediately with "English Cocker: Old and Blind" from *Rumor Verified,* as both pieces seemingly concern the same pet canine.

5. In a reminiscent essay written for his centennial in 2005, Rosanna Warren uses "Hope" as an example of her father's transformation of the Vermont setting into "an inner landscape" and of "private mood to some larger acceptance" (234).

6. Randolph Paul Runyon's Freudian reading of "Literal Dream" and its relation to other selections in this section also proves ingenious (*Braided Dream* 40–48). Runyon does not compare closely the scenes in the novel and dream, however, nor does any other critic as far as I know. Such comparison shows Warren revising Hardy in several respects—either in his literal dream work, if this is actually the source of the poem, or in his revision of the literary scene, if it is his more direct source in the composition of the poem.

7. Randolph Paul Runyon provides a provocative reading of "New Dawn" in psy-

chosexual terms (*Braided Dream* 49–57). Another extended discussion of the poem is presented in Bill King's "Tragedy in the Technetronic Age: Robert Penn Warren's 'New Dawn,'" *Mississippi Quarterly* 50 (1996–97): 85–100.

8. In a letter to Randolph Paul Runyon, Warren recalls that "'Picnic' was written well before the other poem ["New Dawn"], probably years" (*Braided Dream* 55). Warren excised a graphic depiction of the adulterous coupling to good effect.

> At division no moan, no gasp at heave: nor at breast torn bare.
> Only when, hair seized, the white throat was drawn back for
> A last swollen thrust. Then stillness of death. (Burt 796)

Again, Pat Bradley has pointed out to me how this picnic seems a perverse retelling of the innocent one in "October Picnic Long Ago" from *Being Here*.

9. As far as I can discover, Gabriel Thomas Penn's body never was reinterred. Warren may have derived the image from the 1893 reinterment of Jefferson Davis in Richmond, a fact he recreates in his account of the Confederate president, *Jefferson Davis Gets His Citizenship Back* (1980). Warren's work on Davis opens with a recollection of his own grandfather, while its analysis of its subject's character insists on his overarching sense of "honor" (1, 68).

10. In his notes, John Burt mentions that in the early proofs for his new collection Warren had placed a previously unpublished poem, "With or Without Compass," between the two railroad selections (801). Although that poem also refers several times to "tracks," they seem more like "footprints in the sands of time" than the rails that pair "Whistle of the 3 A.M." and "Last Night Train."

11. In my own view, "Wind and Gibbon" is encumbered by the weight of the extravagant pun Warren unfolds in the seven lines of the second stanza. His awakened persona reads Gibbon rather than the morning paper, which he knows "Will gabble like paranoia, chitter in a strange tongue like / A capuchin, the organ-grinder's monkey" (580). Warren's clever imagery reminds us that a "gibbon" is also a small ape, but his pun on the anthropomorphic names of both primates seems more distracting then telling—even with the further illustration of Gibbon's "hot lava" of "incandescent irony" engulfing Rome within the eleven lines of stanza 3 (580).

12. *Altitudes and Extensions* is the longest of the later collections, even without these additional examples; indeed, Warren might well have edited it even more closely, as suggested above. Interestingly enough, several of the omitted poems concern love affairs remembered or imagined, including "You Sort Old Letters," "Aging Painter Sits Where the Great Tower Heaves down Midnight," "Goodbye," "Instant on a Crowded Street," and "Old Love." Although they all can serve as a comparative gloss on several pieces in *Altitudes and Extensions* and earlier collections, they also exhibit the sometimes self-indulgent and occasionally prurient attitudes discovered in *A Place to Come To*. A few others among the remaining poems also are not up to Warren's unusually high poetic standards—"Commuter's Entry in a Connecticut Diary," "Was It One of the Long Hunters of Kentucky Who Discovered Boone at Sunset," "Remark for Histori-

ans," "Problem of Autobiography Vague Recollection or Dream" and "Upwardness,"for example. "Institute of the Impossible" is a strange experimental piece that seems to be a successfully surrealistic take on the later themes set in a home for the aged, but the piece proves so different from Warren's more typical efforts that it would have disturbed the tone of this last collection. The nature poems "Winter Dreams," "Breaking the Code," and "Uncertain Season in High Country" seem to me as successful as several selections in *Altitudes and Extensions,* though they are not sufficiently different from them to demand inclusion of them in Warren's collection or consideration of them in my study. Again, John Burt includes all of these omitted poems in the *Collected Poems* (604–22).

Epilogue

1. Warren did leave a number of additional poems and fragments of poems among his unpublished papers now housed in the Beineke Library at Yale. I have examined these pieces, and they do extend the matters, forms, and themes of the later poetry. Although they support my reading of the later work, I have decided not to consider them in my study because Warren evidently did not believe them shaped to the point of publication nor do I. My decision in this regard also was influenced by John Burt's example in his editing of the *Collected Poems* (626).

2. A moving evocation of her father's death is provided by Rosanna Warren's elegy "His Long Home," the second selection of the elegiac fourth section of her second poetry collection: *Stained Glass* (New York: Norton, 1993), 50–52.

3. Warren's work also forms an important part of our popular culture in our new century, as evidenced by the artistically excellent, if critically and popularly unsuccessful film adaptation of *All the King's Men* by Steven Zaillian in 2006.

4. I will conclude with a personal note echoing my "Preface." If my reading of Warren's later poems from the perspectives provided by my own retirement does not achieve the lofty standard he set in his age-work, I still can take some lesser personal satisfaction in my effort. For it has been the greatest pleasure of my academic career to enjoy an extended dialogue with the creative and critical legacies of Robert Penn Warren as displayed in both his life and work.

Works Cited

Bedient, Calvin. *In the Heart's Last Kingdom: Robert Penn Warren's Major Poetry.* Cambridge: Harvard University Press, 1984.

Bloom, Harold. *Agon: Towards a Theory of Revisionism.* New York: Oxford, 1982.

———. "Re: Arcturus Reference." E-mail to the author. November 3, 2006.

———. "Foreword." In *The Collected Poems of Robert Penn Warren,* ed. John Burt. Baton Rouge: Louisiana State University Press, 1998. xxiii–xxvi.

———. "Sunset Hawk: Warren's Poetry and Tradition." In *A Southern Renascence Man,* ed. Walter B. Edgar. Baton Rouge: Louisiana State University Press, 1984. 59–79.

Blotner, Joseph. *Robert Penn Warren: A Biography.* New York: Random House, 1997.

Brooks, Cleanth. "Episode and Anecdote in the Poetry of Robert Penn Warren." *Yale Review* 70 (1981): 551–67.

———. "Robert Frost." In *American Literature: The Makers and the Making,* ed. Cleanth Brooks, R. W. B. Lewis, and Robert Penn Warren. New York: St. Martins Press, 1973. 1856–66.

Burt, John. "Notes." *The Collected Poems of Robert Penn Warren.* Baton Rouge: Louisiana State University Press, 1998. 625–816.

Butler, Robert N. "Age, Death, and Life Review." In *Living with Grief: Loss in Later Life,* ed. Kenneth J. Doka. Washington, DC: Hospice Foundation. www.hospicefoundation.org/teleconference/2002/butler.asp.

———. "The Life Review: An Interpretation of Reminiscence in the Aged." *Psychiatry* 26 (1963): 65–73.

Clark, William Bedford. *The American Vision of Robert Penn Warren.* Lexington: University Press of Kentucky, 1991.

Cole, Robert. *Erik H. Erikson: The Growth of His Work.* Boston: Little, Brown, 1971.

Cullick, Jonathan S. *Making History: The Biographical Narratives of Robert Penn Warren.* Baton Rouge: Louisiana State University Press, 2000.

Erikson, Erik. *Dialogue with Erik Erikson.* Ed. Richard I. Evans. New York: Praeger, 1981.

———. *Dimensions of a New Identity.* New York: Norton, 1974.

———. *Identity and the Life Cycle.* New York: Norton, 1959, 1980.

———. With Joan M. Erikson. *The Life Cycle Completed.* New York: Norton, 1997.

Erikson, Joan M. "Gerotranscendence." In Erik Erikson, *The Life Cycle Completed.* New York: Norton, 1997. 123–29.

Frost, Robert. *The Poetry of Robert Frost: The Collected Poems, Complete and Unabridged.* Ed. Edward Connery Lathem. New York: Holt, 1969.

Grimshaw, James A., Jr. *Understanding Robert Penn Warren.* Columbia: University of South Carolina Press, 2001.

"Hospice." National Hospice and Palliative Care Organization. www.nhpco.org/hospice.

Justus, James H. *The Achievement of Robert Penn Warren.* Baton Rouge: Louisiana State University Press, 1981.

Millichap, Joseph. *A Backward Glance: The Southern Renascence, the Autobiographical Epic, and the Classical Legacy.* University of Tennessee Press, forthcoming 2009.

———. *Dixie Limited: Railroads, Culture, and the Southern Renaissance.* Lexington: University Press of Kentucky, 2002.

———. *Robert Penn Warren: A Study of the Short Fiction.* Twayne's Studies in Short Fiction, no. 39. New York: Macmillan, 1992.

Morrison, Valerie M. "The Tangled Hieroglyphics of Robert Penn Warren's Late Poetry." *rWp: An Annual of Robert Penn Warren Studies* 4 (2004): 123–41.

Parini, Jay. *Robert Frost: A Life.* New York: Holt, 1999.

Perkins, David. *A History of Modern Poetry, Volume II.* Cambridge: Harvard University Press, 1987.

Runyon, Randolph Paul. *The Braided Dream: Robert Penn Warren's Late Poetry.* Lexington: University Press of Kentucky, 1990.

———. *Ghostly Parallels: Robert Penn Warren and the Lyric Sequence.* Knoxville: University of Tennessee Press, 2006.

Ruppersburg, Hugh. *Robert Penn Warren and the American Imagination.* Athens: University of Georgia Press, 1990.

Smith, Dave. "Notes on a Form to Be Lived." In *Homage to Robert Penn Warren,* ed. Frank Graziano. Durango, CO: Logbridge-Rhodes, 1981. 33–55.

Spears, Monroe K. *American Ambitions: Selected Essays on Literary and Cultural Themes.* Baltimore: Johns Hopkins University Press, 1987.

Stitt, Peter. *The World's Hieroglyphic Beauty: Five American Poets.* Athens: University of Georgia Press, 1985.

Strandberg, Victor. "Robert Penn Warren: 1905–1989." In *American Poets, 1880–1945, Second Series,* ed. Peter Quatermain. Vol. 48 of *The Dictionary of Literary Biography.* Detroit: Gale, 1986. 425–44.

———. "Poet of Youth: Robert Penn Warren at Eighty." In *Times Glory: Original Essays on Robert Penn Warren,* ed. James A Grimshaw Jr. Conway: University of Central Arkansas Press, 1986). 91–106.

———. "Warren's Poetic Vision: A Reading of *Now and Then.*" *Southern Review* 16 (1980): 18–45.

Tornstam, Lars. *Gerotranscendence: A Developmental Theory of Positive Aging.* New York: Springer, 2005.

Warren, Robert Penn. *Brother to Dragons.* New York: Random House, 1953.

———. *The Collected Poems of Robert Penn Warren.* Ed. John Burt. Baton Rouge: Louisiana State University Press, 1998.

———. *Democracy and Poetry.* Cambridge: Harvard University Press, 1975.

———. *Homage to Theodore Dreiser.* New York: Random House, 1971.

———. *Jefferson Davis Gets His Citizenship Back.* Lexington: University Press of Kentucky, 1980.

———. *The Legacy of the Civil War: Meditations on the Centennial.* New York: Random House, 1961.

———. *Night Rider.* Nashville. J. S. Sanders, 1992.

———. "Notes on the Poetry of John Crowe Ransom at His Eightieth Birthday." *New and Selected Essays.* New York: Random House, 1989. 303–31.

———. *A Place to Come To.* New York: Random House, 1977.

———. *Portrait of a Father.* Lexington: University Press of Kentucky, 1988.

———. *Talking with Robert Penn Warren.* Ed. Floyd C. Watkins, John T. Hiers, and Mary Louise Weaks. Athens: University of Georgia Press, 1990.

———. "The Themes of Robert Frost." *New and Selected Essays.* New York: Random House, 1989. 285–302.

Warren, Rosanna. "Places: A Memoir." *Southern Review* 41 (2005): 233–42.

Watkins, Floyd C. *Then & Now: The Personal Past in the Poetry of Robert Penn Warren.* Lexington: University Press of Kentucky, 1982.

Index